T0399803

Planning Small and Mid-Sized Towns

Small and mid-sized suburban towns house two-thirds of the world's population and current modes of planning for these municipalities are facing challenges of both philosophy and form. Common approaches that have prevailed in past decades no longer sustain new demands and require innovative thinking. Rather than dismissing small and mid-sized towns as unattractive suburban sprawl, *Planning Small and Mid-Sized Towns* offers ideas and methods on how small isolated and edge towns can be designed and retooled into sustainable, affordable, and adaptable communities.

Coverage includes:

- the evolution of small towns;
- mobility and connectivity;
- neighborhood and sustainable dwelling design;
- town centers and urban renewal;
- economic sustainability and wealth generation, and more.

With numerous case studies from North America and Europe and over 150 color photographs, maps, and illustrations, *Planning Small and Mid-Sized Towns* is a valuable, practical resource for professional planners and urban designers, as well as students in these disciplines.

Avi Friedman, Ph.D., studied architecture and town planning in Italy, Israel, and Canada. In 1988 he founded the Affordable Homes Program at McGill University in Montreal, Canada. Over several decades he consulted many small towns on sustainable planning and urban renewal issues. He published extensively in academic and trade publications and has authored 14 books including *Sustainable Residential Development* (McGraw-Hill) and *Town and Terraced Housing: For Affordability and Sustainability* (Routledge). He is also a practicing architect and a planner and the recipient of many awards, including the Manning Innovation Award and the World Habitat Award. In 2000 he was selected by *Wallpaper* magazine as one of ten people from around the world "most likely to change the way we live."

Planning Small and Mid-Sized Towns

Designing and Retrofitting for Sustainability

Avi Friedman

Routledge
Taylor & Francis Group

NEW YORK AND LONDON

First published 2014
by Routledge
711 Third Avenue, New York, NY 10017

and by Routledge
2 Park Square, Milton Park, Abingdon, Oxon OX14 4RN

Routledge is an imprint of the Taylor & Francis Group, an informa business

British Library Cataloguing in Publication Data
A catalogue record for this book is available from the British Library

Library of Congress Cataloging-in-Publication Data
Friedman, Avi, 1952-
   Planning small and mid-sized towns : designing and retrofitting for sustainability /
   by Avi Friedman.
      pages cm
   Includes bibliographical references and index.
   1. Sustainable urban development. 2. Small cities—Planning. 3. City planning—
   Environmental aspects. 4. Sustainability. I. Title.
   HT241.F75 2014
   307.1′216—dc23   2013045935

ISBN: 978-0-415-53928-9 (hbk)
ISBN: 978-0-415-53930-2 (pbk)
ISBN: 978-0-203-10781-2 (ebk)

Typeset in Galliard by
Keystroke, Station Road, Codsall, Wolverhampton

Contents

Preface

As a child growing up in the small Israeli town of Petach Tikva, I envied those who lived in big cities. On my occasional trips to the nearby bustling city of Tel Aviv, I was mesmerized by the sights, sounds, and smells. The store window displays, the latest car models, and the crowded wide treed sidewalks left an impression.

Years later, I joined the ranks of big city dwellers. I studied and lived in what one would consider a big urban hub. While pursuing an architecture and town-planning career, I sought a yardstick, a model of sorts, for a well-planned city. I pondered what should the population size and land mass be to make for a vibrant and well-functioning place? How might these attributes affect human interaction? My thoughts kept drawing me back to the town where I spent my formative years. When reflecting on what set small places apart from other settlements, I intuitively could think of a single feature: scale. Towns, those with populations no greater than 50,000 people, are likely to have many of the urban components that one finds in larger hubs; yet, their small size guides their appearance, function, and social dynamics. It fosters the unique mix of both physical and human features that I was after when writing this book.

When I set up my own design practice, I was drawn to small towns once more. I was invited to consult some, and visit others. I was given an opportunity to view them through a different lens—that of a designer.

I developed sustainable master plans, urban renewal schemes, economic retooling strategies, and neighborhood designs, among others. Most of my work has centered in North America, yet my travels have taken me to other continents where I was able to examine firsthand planning strategies, urban makeup, and local cultures.

However, times have changed since I left my small town. Recent societal transformations are altering commonly accepted social, environmental, economic, and cultural philosophy and practice. Just as the Industrial Revolution led to the massive migration of people from farming communities to crowded cities, the dawn of the twenty first century marks a challenge to the vitality, prosperity, and to some extent the existence of small towns. It is appropriate to closely observe their core values and functioning principles and to offer strategies for planning new communities and retooling existing places.

A review of literature shows that much research has been devoted to large metropolitan areas. For a variety of reasons, issues occupying small towns have not captured the attention of scholars, even though they are home to more than half the population of some countries. Design aspects related to transportation, environment, economic performance, and urban renewal, to name a few, have not been studied extensively by social scientists in light of the contemporary changes.

As an urban planner and an architect, I have made these discrepancies front and center in my research. This book attempts to pay close attention to and understand the fabric and the functioning of small hubs. It also displays design principles and strategies that are the result of my own work. I reviewed societal trends and their manifestations to draw conclusions about shaping new places and renewing old ones.

When recalling social issues and making generalizations about urban aspects, it is hard to draw parallels between towns, even those of the same size, on the far ends of a geographic spectrum. Historic events, urban characteristics, or economic conditions, for example, that have shaped a Midwest North American town are markedly different from attributes that through accretion formed a small hillside Tuscan town or shaped a small community in rural China. Yet, one can nonetheless identify principles fundamental to how all places evolved and coped with contemporary challenges.

Urban environments are the agglomeration and the layering of their sub-components. The well-functioning of a city is the outcome of its transportation, economy, governance, and consideration of environmental issues, among others. By examining and overlapping these elements, one can appreciate the whole. In the book, I look at each element separately to gain an understanding of its importance and the principles of its working, while keeping in mind how it relates to the broader perspective.

The first chapter defines the book's perimeters, offers definitions, and draws the unique characteristics of small towns. In addition, societal shifts—demographic, environmental, and economic and their possible effects on small towns—are laid out. It then dwells on sustainability and its principles.

Chapter 2 examines the form and function of small towns and their effect on sustainability. It begins by offering an historical chronology of small towns' urban planning, and then looks into forms of settlements, the effect of form on functional patterns, and sustainability. A case study that recalls the retooling of a town's master plan concludes the chapter.

In Chapter 3 I review environmental aspects of small towns and outline a number of strategies that can further improve their performance. It begins by drawing a link between a place's area and its sustainability, lists practices for managing land, conserving energy, saving, harvesting, and recycling water, and describes the design of a green neighborhood in a small town.

Chapter 4 looks at mobility and connectivity systems. The chapter begins by looking at the unique urban features of small towns' transportation networks. It then describes transit methods of connecting towns and cities and recalls the concept of Transit-Oriented Development (TOD) and offers strategies for designing mobility in small towns and ways of fostering walking and cycling. The chapter ends by describing a case study of a town in which retooling for active mobility took place.

Chapter 5 examines the design of new neighborhoods and rehabilitating existing ones. The first section reviews design principles of new residential environments where urban form, circulation and parking, open spaces, and architectural identity are articulated. The second part looks into the design of residences in already built areas where site selection, urban fit, and the choosing of suitable prototypes are discussed. Finally, a description of a new neighborhood design process is discussed.

Chapter 6 focuses on small towns' downtowns and their importance to the economic and social vitality of the town. The chapter offers ideas and strategies of how these places can be strengthened or revitalized once in decline and lists preservation principles to meet contemporary challenges. The urban renewal process of a small town ends the chapter.

Chapter 7 is about the economy of small towns. Their historical evolution, uniqueness, potential for tourism, cultural industries, and economic retooling strategies are some of the topics discussed. The chapter ends with a case study that describes an economic renewal process in a small community.

Finally, Chapter 8 examines human attributes of small towns and relates them to places. The urban manifestations of the term "social capital" are explored, the notions of places and place-making are studied, and selected gathering places and their contributions to the social fabric of a community are described. The chapter ends with a case study of a town that restructured its urban makeup by introducing unique meeting spots.

Small towns are an important part of any nation's urban tapestry. The success and evolution of such communities often depends on their ability to adapt to new times and emerging realities. It is hoped that this book will offer ideas, strategies, and tools to those who steer and plan their evolution.

Acknowledgments

The sources and the generating ideas that inspired the writing of this book span many years and include a number of research and design projects. My work over the years has involved many colleagues whose names are listed here and in the Project Teams section at the back of the book. My thanks extend to them all, with my apologies to those whose names I have accidentally omitted. I will make every effort to add their names to future editions of the book.

I was fortunate to work with a highly dedicated team of research assistants who helped me identify critical data sources, and relevant articles. They included Taleen Der Haroutiounian, Bryan Spatzner, Fouzi Quadhi, Laurie Bouchard, Jonathan Farkouh, Cailen Pybus, and Josie White. Many thanks to Josie White for her help in the preparation of the book's proposal.

Thanks are also extended to the elected officials, administrators, and public servants of the towns who invited me to consult them and are featured in the case studies. I appreciate my design team members, who are listed below for their utmost dedication.

Special dedication is extended to Jing Han (Jay), who drew all the illustrations in the book. His overall contribution, hard work, talent, and insistence on achieving excellence is truly appreciated and admired.

To Nyd Garavito-Bruhn, many thanks for preparing the material for publication.

To Professor Stuart Walker for the invitation to the UK and the tour of the Lake District.

To those in the McGill University, School of Architecture, who created the environment in which many of the ideas expressed here were born and for offering me a sabbatical leave during which this book was written.

To Nicole Solano, my editor at Routledge, who assisted with guiding the book's proposal through the various stages.

To Paloma Friedman, for her meticulous editing of the manuscript and her highly valuable suggestions in the process.

Finally, to my family: my wife Sorel, who accompanied me to many of the spots that are noted here, my daughter Paloma, and son Ben.

1
Affixing a Lens

The visitors' chairs in the small council chamber of Middlesex Centre's town hall were empty. I sat across from the six councilors and the mayor who govern the Municipality. A photo of her majesty Queen Elizabeth II hung on the wall behind them. On another wall there were photos of former mayors. I had been invited to present a report that I had authored for the municipality on economic development and branding strategies.

Located in the shadow of the city of London in the Province of Ontario, Canada, Middlesex Centre is a small rural community. Formal settlement of the area began in 1820 when the place was surveyed and divided into 100 acre (40.46 hectare) lots and laid out in parallel strips called "concessions" separated by roads. The Municipality, population 16,000, was formed in 1998 with the amalgamation of three small townships.

Cornfields and horse and dairy farms interrupted by urban hamlets make up most of the Municipality's land. Like many towns that reside next to a sprawling urban hub, Middlesex Centre saw the construction of subdivisions made up of large single-family homes for daily commuters. My suggestion that the Municipality needed to diversify its economy, which at present relies heavily on agriculture, by attracting industries, sparked a lively discussion. "Do you mean we should abandon our agricultural heritage?" a councilor asked. The response came from another elected official and the debate that followed captured the essence of what small towns are, and what their future may entail. Should they keep to a certain population size or actively seek newcomers and non-traditional land uses and other sources of revenue? Will expansion alter the cultural traditions of the place and offset its much accustomed social fabric? Is diversification an absolute necessity for survival and prosperity given current economic realities?

These fundamental questions are of value to settlements of any size; yet their implication on a small place can be significant and define every facet of their existence and evolution. Prior to delving into the heart of these issues, this chapter defines the unique characteristics of small towns.

Drawing Perimeters

A literature review shows that the lion's share of the research on the makeup and working of all settlements has been devoted to large metropolitan areas. The city and its many intricate concerns and forces have been the focus of writing by urban planners, geographers, and other social scientists. Small towns have often been left out, a point noted by several scholars (Ofori-Amoah 2007; French 2005; Partridge et al. 2008). The reasons are varied but they can perhaps be traced to the fact that many academic institutions and government seats of power are located in big cities. One will be hard-pressed to find the headquarters of a national or multinational media outlet or insurance company in a small town, for example. These enterprises may employ people who live nearby and commute daily, but the city will house the head office.

Small towns occupy only one of the spots in a fabric that ranges from a hamlet made up of a cluster of dwellings to a large urban metropolis. A "small town" can be defined by a variety of attributes such as demographic, geographic, or economics factors, to name a few. Those attributes will be closely examined in later chapters. Yet in the literature, population size seems to be an index most commonly used to draw their perimeter. Ofori-Amoah (2007) suggests that small cities are loosely defined as those with less than 100,000 residents. French (2005) refers to places with population of between 2,500 and 25,000 inhabitants. The Canadian Centre for Justice Statistics (2006) distinguishes them from rural places and defines them as "any urban area that has a minimum population of 1,000 persons and a population density of at least 400 persons per square kilometer." The European Union defines smaller cities as those with population between 10,000 and 50,000 people (European Union 2011).

"Mid-sized cities" or "mid-sized towns" are also commonly mentioned along with smaller ones. By some definitions those include urban areas with population between 50,000 and 100,000 people. In both small and mid-sized towns the population spans from 2,500 to 100,000, a range that will also be used as a yardstick in this book. My reference to "small towns" will, therefore, include "mid-sized cities" as well.

Small towns hold critical importance when it comes to where people live. Despite the fact that urban areas are still a draw, and the world is becoming increasingly urbanized, the share of those who live in smaller places has remained significant. A report by the United Nations Population Division (UNPD) (2005) suggests that 46 percent of all population growth will occur in relatively small cities. That percentage will likely depend on the development phase and evolution of a country. Similar to the migration pattern that characterized the Industrial Revolution, the proportion of agrarian-based living diminishes when higher paying manufacturing and service jobs grow.

According to the United States Census Bureau (2009), in 2006, 54 percent of Americans lived in cities with population between 10,000 and 250,000; of them, over 20 percent lived in cities between 10,000 and 100,000 (Figure 1.1). As shown in Figure 1.2, in Canada, 21.4 percent of citizens resided in small and mid-sized cities as per the above definition (Canadian Centre for Justice Statistics 2006; Statistics Canada 2005). In Europe, 38 percent of the total population lives in small and mid-sized cities and towns of between 5,000 and 100,000 inhabitants (European Union 2011).

These numbers have not been ignored by politicians and often lent small town and rural areas importance. Strong conviction, traditional values, and the loyalty that their citizens adhere to have drawn the attention of political parties. In some countries, policies and actions are often introduced to address their unique needs and gain favor. Constructing a road or locating government buildings in a sparsely populated area are some examples.

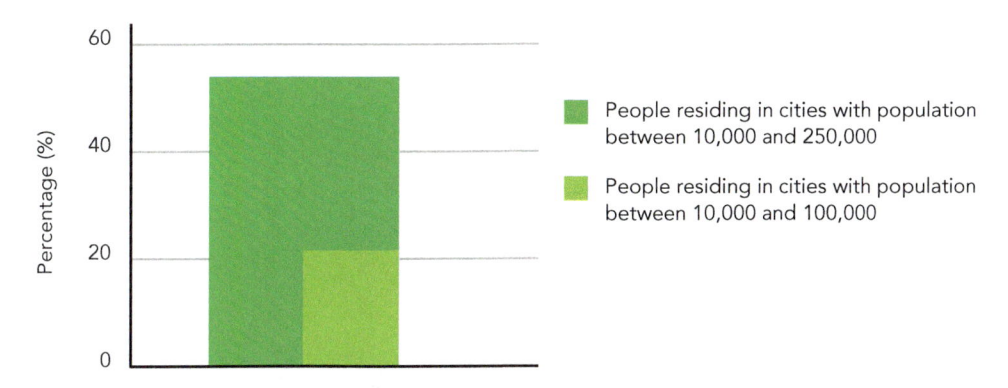

1.1 **Percentage of Americans who reside in small and mid-sized cities and towns**

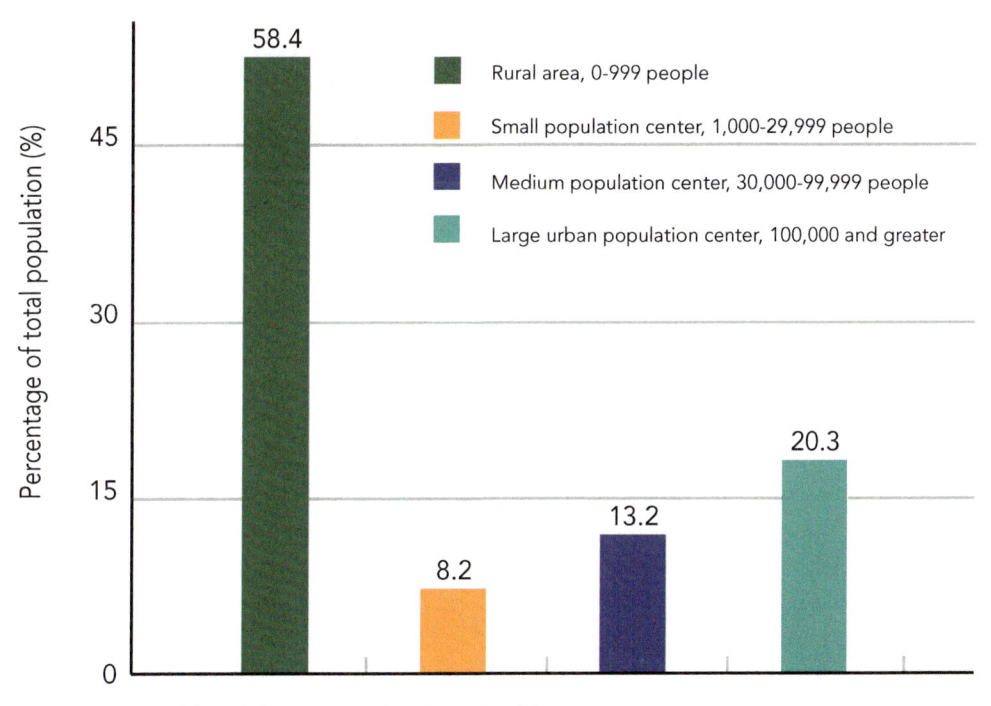

1.2 **Distribution of Canada's population by place of residency**

1.3 **Hot peppers on sale as natural Viagra in Positano, Italy**

In addition to demographic indexes, there are other non-quantifiable attributes that define small towns. "Sense of place" is one of them. It is an aspect that commonly refers to physical markings unique to each locale which give places, and indirectly the people who inhabit them, identity. The scene, noises, sounds, and smells of a busy urban hub are naturally different from those of a town (Figure 1.3). Their small scale and often reduced land mass also define their human side. Relaxed lifestyle, familiarity with each other, and established cultural traditions are some of the traits of these places. A popular perception often associated with small towns is that they are a place in which to raise a family, and with cities, as a place to foster a thriving career on one's own.

What makes people choose to reside and remain in small towns? Location theory suggests that people select their places of residency for diverse reasons. Employment opportunities, presence of relatives, availability and access to amenities, and housing affordability are some of the draws (Tabuchi et al. 2005). Filion (2010), for example, suggests that in Canada the urban system was first shaped by exogenous demand for staples and, subsequently, by the "dichotomy between an industrial heartland and resource-based hinterland." At times, unique opportunities, such as very cheap land, led to the migration to a place. In other times, small towns have attracted those who crave both traditional social values and unique physical environment.

Recent societal shifts that have affected governments and cities at large have not spared small towns. Some of these transformations are likely to have lasting social, environmental, and economic effects that will serve as a backdrop to this book and will be outlined below.

Societal Shifts

The outset of the twenty first century launched a "perfect storm" of societal shifts that are bound to affect and transform nations and municipalities. These transformations will require rethinking of currently followed planning policies and strategies. It would be of value to examine three domains where fundamental changes have taken place and affected urban systems: social, environmental, and economic. One needs, however, to note that variations exist in the manifestation of these aspects between continents, nations, and towns. The phenomena listed here can therefore be regarded as general in nature, yet present in most contexts, particularly western nations.

Social Transformations

Demographic trends can be looked upon and interpreted through various lenses. They include the age of the population, gender composition, and ethnic makeup, to name a few. The "graying" of small towns and the rise in the number of seniors, those aged 65 and older, is one such aspect, as shown in Figure 1.4. Born between 1945 and 1959, the "baby boom" generation will face retirement in the coming decades. The significant number of seniors is expected to put a strain on the social services of small communities where budget allocations for such sectors are often limited.

Residential mobility is another characteristic of aging. Some retirees are projected to trade a large, hard-to-maintain home with a smaller unit. Those who can afford it will move to regions with comfortable weather year-round and proximity to basic amenities, taking their wealth along with them. Those who stay will look for an apartment adjacent to or above shopping hubs or transportation routes. Demand for non-traditional dwelling types and intense remodeling activities will also rise as a result. There will be a growing interest in arrangements that accommodate aging in place, multi-generational homes, and assisted living. A growth

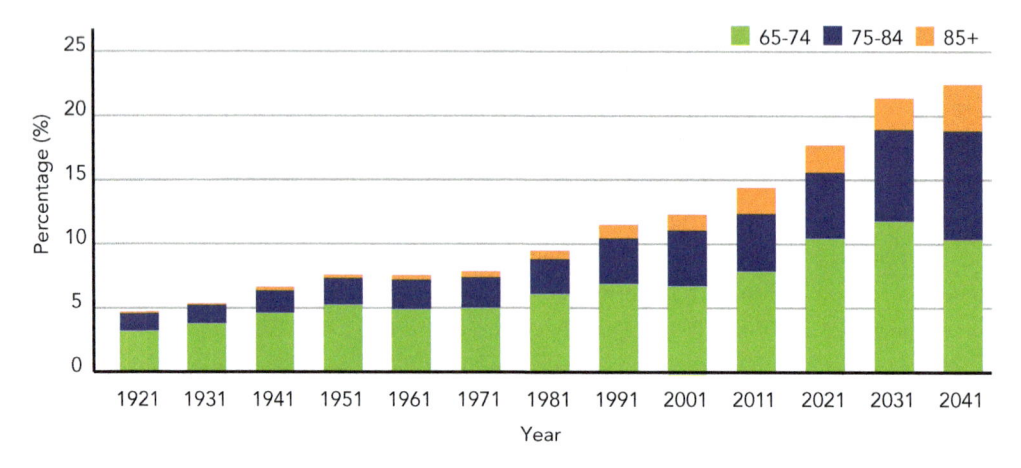

1.4 **Canadian seniors by age groups as percentage of the total population, 1921–2041**

in healthcare facilities and accessory services such as specialized fitness centers is also anticipated.

The rise in the number of seniors can offset the demographic continuum of small towns on account of young cohorts. To some degree, it is bound to adversely affect citizens' contribution to public life and the draw of some towns as "dynamic and growing places for all." Communal activities in many places are based on the contributions and participation of volunteers. These groups often meet in evening hours when older participants, particularly in cold climate areas, have difficulty getting to meetings. Once these social networks lack participants, they tend to function poorly or disintegrate altogether. The need to draw young households to small communities will therefore be critical in the years to come.

Younger cohorts are known to have a consumption pattern of products and services different than older households. Therefore, attracting families will be important to the economic

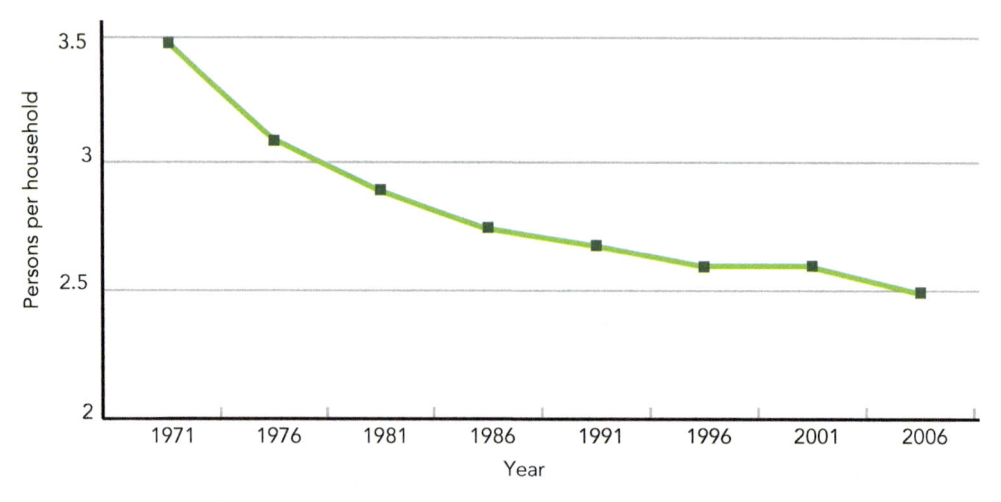

1.5 **Average household size in Canada, 1971–2006**

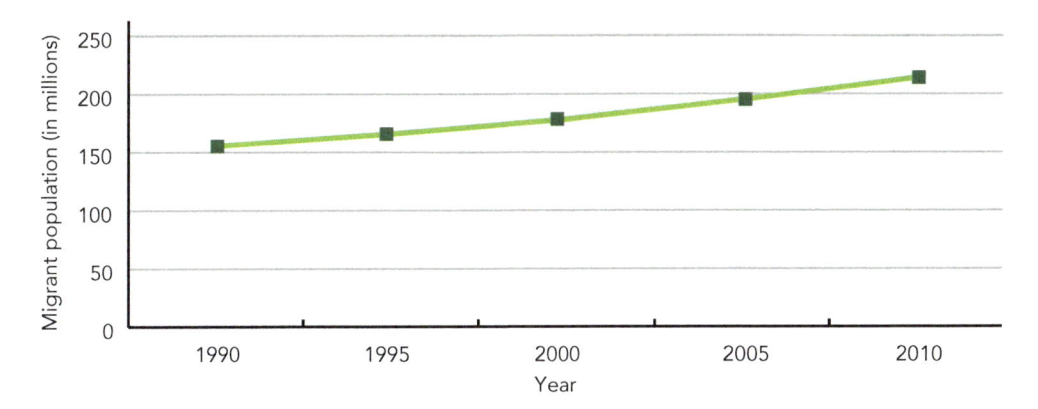

1.6 Trends in international migration stocks, 1990–2010

vitality of small towns as well. As shown in Figure 1.5, another notable demographic trend is a decline in the size of an average household. Coupled with housing affordability challenges, this may entail an increased demand for below-average sized homes and apartments.

Global and local migration patterns are another factor affecting communities as natural population growth in some countries declines, as shown in Figure 1.6. Researchers suggest that drawing immigrants to small towns is not simple, as witnessed by their identifiable, identical ethnic makeup. Hyndman et al. (2006) note that few immigrants are settling in small towns. Their study of several small towns in the Province of British Columbia, Canada, shows that despite an effort by local governments to draw immigrants to small places, large urban hubs were their focus. Employment opportunities and a desire to live next to people from their country of origin were the key reasons. These data are reflected in the ethnic composition of small town residents. According to Brennan and Hoene (2007), of small US cities near metropolitan areas that experienced rapid population growth in the 1990s, 76 percent were white compared to 13 percent that were black, 7 percent Hispanic, and 2 percent Asian. Yet the authors suggest that with the expected expansion of immigration to the US and primarily the growth of the Hispanic population, the present ethnic composition of small towns is also likely to change, which may bring about a need to amend social policies and programs.

Environmental Considerations

In recent decades, society has become aware and has acted to counter its toll on the environment. A link has been made between economic development, urban forms, and their environmental implications. Chief among the indexes that are used to evaluate a place's performance are the carbon footprint of a dwelling and a community. Amending policies is likely to have significant consequences on urban planning and the economies of small towns and is worth analyzing.

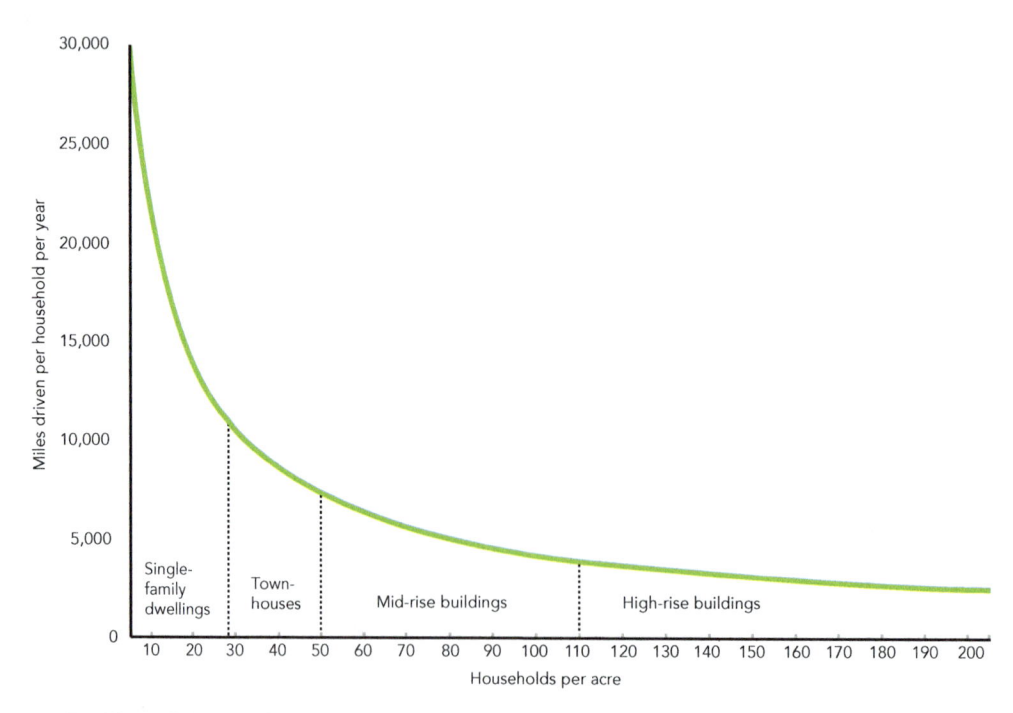

1.7 **Residents living in US communities with higher densities tend to drive one-third of the amount of those who live in neighborhoods with single-family homes**

The negative ramifications of developments made up of single-family homes and their resulting urban sprawl have given rise to a call for densification. As shown in Figure 1.7, in the US, residents living in communities with higher densities tend to drive one-third of the amount of those who live in neighborhoods with single-family homes. The main intention behind these calls is to reduce various forms of consumption and to justify investments in public transit and other costly amenities (Center for Transit-Oriented Development 2011). Increasing density is seen as a common sense approach to urban planning. Yet, densification is not easily achieved in small towns. As a designer, in public presentations in small towns of schemes made up of denser neighborhoods I have often encountered opposition. Citizens and elected officials argue that the reason they moved to or decided to remain in small communities is their spread-out nature.

The need to curb urban sprawl has also brought to the forefront a call for mixed-use developments. Living above or next to a store, as shown in Figure 1.8, implies, much like in earlier times, that denser communities will be planned from the outset with a wider range of land uses. It may affect commerce and mark a return to the scale of mom-and-pop stores and create what was coined "complete communities."

The negative effects of driving are another aspect with direct environmental ramifications. Residents of small towns commonly rely on distant urban centers for their upper level services which people reach using private vehicles. In 2005, the transportation sector in Organisation for Economic Co-operation and Development (OECD) countries consumed 26 percent of the total energy demand and produced 25 percent of the direct and indirect carbon

1.8 **Living above stores in Stratford, Ontario, Canada**

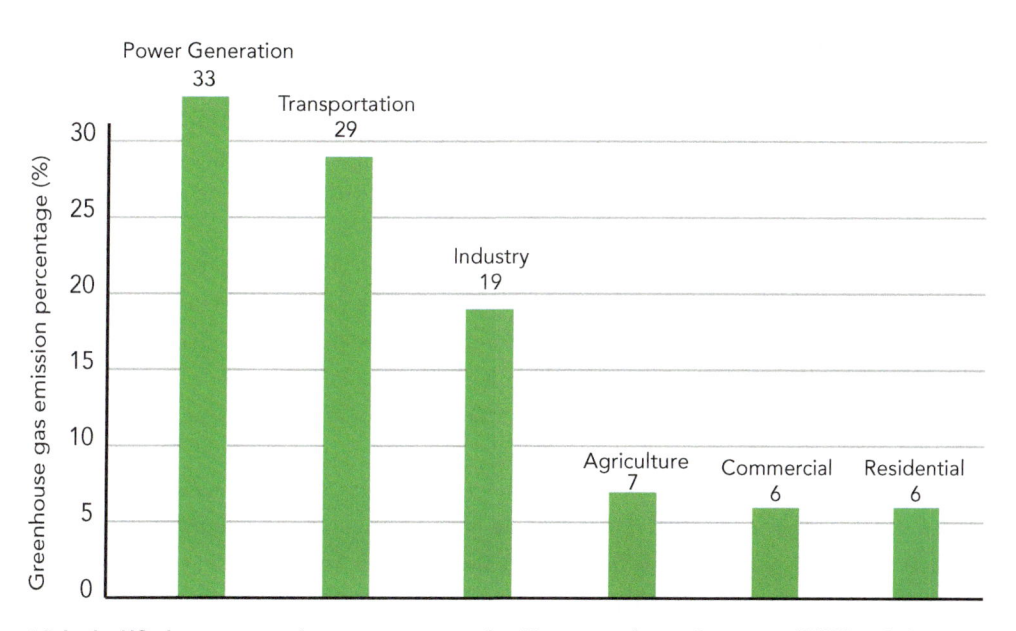

1.9 **In the US, the transportation sector accounts for 29 percent of greenhouse gas (GHG) emissions**

1.10 Solar-powered homes in Alkmaar, the Netherlands

dioxide emissions (and see Figure 1.9). A large portion of this statistic can be attributed to the extensive use of private cars. The United States Census Bureau (2009, 2011) found that the average daily commute to and from work in 2003 was 48.6 minutes. Locating employment hubs next to residential developments is seen as a strategic response to the need to reduce reliance on private vehicles in small towns.

Another area of environmental concern is the home itself. The need to rethink the design and construction practices of dwellings and align them with new environmental objectives has taken center stage in recent years. Many governments have established standards for building practices. These standards set strict building codes and efficiency criteria and act as an accreditation system by which projects are distinguished according to the scope of their environmental pursuits.

These trends are an indication that currently accepted standards are changing. The need to plan denser communities and design energy-efficient buildings is gradually taking hold. Developments with small carbon footprints, solar-powered homes, green roofs, recycled products, and water-efficient appliances will become the norm in big cities and small towns (Figure 1.10).

Economic Realities

Global economic transformations have taken their toll on wealth generation, labor markets, and on the lives of citizens in municipalities of any size. Governmental budgeting for deficit reduction has led to cutbacks in social services; international trade agreements have created employment in some countries and eradicated many jobs in others; recessions and sluggish economic growth have weakened the confidence of investors, employers, and everyday consumers. In addition, persistent high unemployment also suggests that other sectors of the economy, including manufacturing, are not generating wealth and are struggling to position themselves in a highly competitive world. These macro trends will trickle down to affect the economies of small towns and may require a retooling process of sorts, in adapting to this new economic landscape. Several trends may arise as a result.

The rise of "home grown" initiatives seems to be a natural outcome of these transformations. Establishing an economy least effected by global and national trends has always

1.11 **Locally made products are sold in a market in Tallinn, Estonia**

been a desire, and more so now, of many communities. It will be reflected in a drive by some cities to encourage people to shop and to use local products and services (Figure 1.11). One can also anticipate an intense competition between cities to expand their economic base and reduce their reliance on residential taxes as a main source of revenue. In a highly competitive climate, enterprises will choose locations that offer them the highest number of incentives. Existing business may leave small towns and relocate to regions, which unfortunately will upset long-accustomed loyalties.

The need to lower taxes to encourage private sector investment will stand in contrast to a desire by small municipalities to spend more money on enhancing public amenities. Since choices will have to be made between employment and amenities, balancing budgets will require greater economic diligence. It will entail careful attention to the sequence that begins when an employer moves to town, jobs are created, new households migrate in and new taxes are generated which lead to residential construction and a need for additional infrastructure and public amenities.

1.12 **WiFi Zone sign on a typical roof in the historic village of Alberobello, Italy**

New economic realities also put the single-family detached home beyond the reach of a growing number of first-time home buyers in many nations and, as a consequence, increase the demand for less expensive, smaller units. An affordability gap has emerged, where the rate of increase of house prices has far surpassed the growth of family incomes. This widening gulf in affordability in some regions can be explained by higher land and infrastructure costs that offer another argument for densification. It may also attract people to small towns where the cost of land is typically lower than in large urban hubs.

The need to foresee the evolution of commerce and the effect of a "hyper-connected" world are necessary to the understanding of the economies of small towns. The line between global and local has become blurred in recent years. Companies no longer need to be tied to a particular location but can run their affairs from afar using digital communication (Figure 1.12). As a result, the nature of commerce has also changed. It is hard to tell whether large format stores will be as trendy in the years to come or whether there will be a surge in a desire to shop in a more local, intimate, and personal setting. What has become apparent is that in recent years online shopping has expanded to rival in-person purchases. These trends are likely to affect the shape of consumption in many communities and as a result their economies.

Small Town Sustainability

The need to act upon the societal transformations that have been noted above has brought to the forefront the question: how should the needed changes be ushered in? In other words, how should small towns or parts of them be planned anew or retooled? Also, which policies are to be introduced to support their thriving attributes and the well-being of their citizens? Sustainability has been put forward as a philosophy and a guide for managing communities.

The proliferation of the term *sustainable development* and the conditions that brought it about can be traced back several decades. In 1972, the United Nations Conference on the Human Environment in Stockholm dealt with concerns that humanity is stretching the "carrying capacity of the earth" to its limits (Canada Mortgage and Housing Corporation 2000). The meeting served as a forum for the first international discussion on the relationship between ongoing environmental damage and the future of humanity. It was recognized then that population growth in some nations and overconsumption in others leave noticeable footprints in the form of land degradation, deforestation, air pollution, and water scarcity. Years later, this reflection led to the establishment of the World Commission on Environment and Development (WCED), an international initiative. In its 1987 report, *Our Common Future,* sustainable development was defined as "development that meets present needs without compromising the ability of future generations to meet their own needs." This definition established a conceptual approach to development, whereby any action taken must be pursued with its future effects in mind. The commission also created a paradigm for development whose main anchors are a need for social equity, incorporation of fair distribution of resources within and among nations, and the need to resolve the conflict caused by development pressures and the environment (Figures 1.13 and 1.14). Over time, these underpinning issues and the relationships among them have become the standard through which the success of all development activities is judged.

1.13 **People congregating in a market in Nyanga, South Africa**

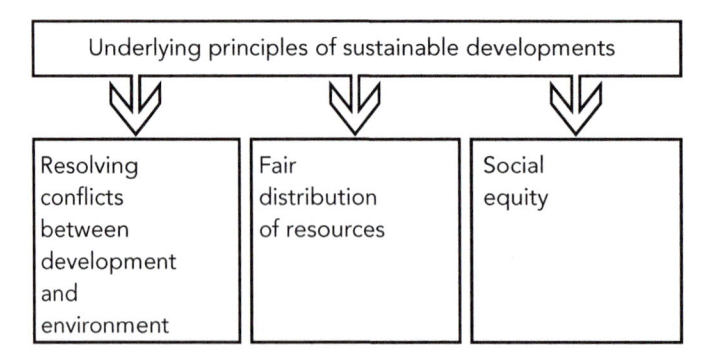

1.14 **The three underlying principles of sustainable development according to the 1987** *Our Common Future* **report**

The three original pillars of sustainable development were social, economic, and environmental aspects. However, it became abundantly clear that culture and governance must be part of any attempt to implement sustainability initiatives if the implementation process is to succeed. The first concern among these aspects reflects and responds to the social needs of a small town's inhabitants and their values. Social needs and equity are a broad, all-compassing concept that can be explained and interpreted in a multitude of ways. For example, when the creation of a sustainable healthcare system is an objective, ensuring that sufficient funds will be continually available is essential. A contribution to public health can be achieved by encouraging fitness. It has been shown that people with an active lifestyle are less likely to suffer from cardiovascular- and diabetes-related illnesses. It is, therefore, in the best interest of a small town that the neighborhoods in it are designed with bicycle and pedestrian pathways and that residential and non-residential functions are integrated.

1.15 **A narrow street in Saint-Valery-sur-Somme, France**

Promoting vernacular culture and preserving local traditions and heritage buildings also contribute to society in direct and indirect ways. Old buildings worth preserving are visible reminders of human history. People who pay homage to the past might contribute to the quality of future buildings. Conserving and converting old buildings also avoids demolition and helps reduce the consumption of natural resources that may otherwise be used in new construction.

Fostering economic sustainability is another objective with ramifications for small town planning. The aim is to avoid the transfer of costs that are the result of bad present decisions, to future generations. Building unnecessarily and excessively wide roads rather than narrow streets, for example, will have long-term economic implications (Figure 1.15). The streets will need to be resurfaced periodically, and more snow will accumulate and need to be removed in cold climate regions. When a development is privately initiated, the cost of wider roads will raise the price of each house, forcing buyers to borrow more money that they will have to repay over a longer period of time, thereby putting at risk their own financial sustainability.

Environmental sustainability is concerned with ecological attributes created by the construction and upkeep of a development, including its roads, open spaces, and homes. A "cradle-to-cradle" cycle assessment is necessary when planning a development. It regards not only the initial effect of choice of materials, for example, but also their long-term performance and their recyclability once their use has ended. Asphalt-covered roads will make rainwater runoff stream to manholes. Creating bio-swells at the side of roads will promote the growth of rainwater flora when it is planted, thereby saving runoff (Figure 1.16).

Governance is another vital aspect of sustainable development. Strategies and concepts, innovative as they may be, will not be implemented unless a municipal leadership can set appropriate policies and explain its long-term vision to the citizens. An effective political system will also draw new younger participants to public service creating a continuity of ideas and actions.

The five pillars critical to sustainable development can be viewed independently. Yet when one closely examines the inner workings of small towns that are designed and built on sound sustainable principles, you can see that the confluence of these aspects is critical in its effects on the built environment; this confluence is a focus of this book. These five overlapping issues are presented here as a way by which concepts will be formed and applications illustrated. It is important to recognize the interrelationships between these aspects. General principles are, therefore, articulated in the following sections to better recognize how these relationships can take place in small towns.

1.16 **A roadside bio-swell near Hoorn, the Netherlands**

Principles of Sustainable Systems

When crafting community development strategies for small towns, four principles can act as a guide (Figure 1.17). When exercised jointly, these principles can help articulate a vision and an action plan for a sustainable place.

The first principle can be referred to as the *path of least negative impact*. It is an approach that decision-makers of any planning endeavor need to choose to avoid or minimize negative impacts of an action on environmental, societal, cultural, and economic aspects. At the outset of any planning process, impact assessments should ensure limited short-term or long-term disruptive and costly ramifications.

An application of this principle is to establish an economic base that will not hinder future initiatives. Having a heavily polluting industry, for example, may not render a good image for a town that may want to develop tourism. Another example would be locating a school away from a residential area, which will limit walking or cycling opportunities by students.

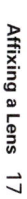

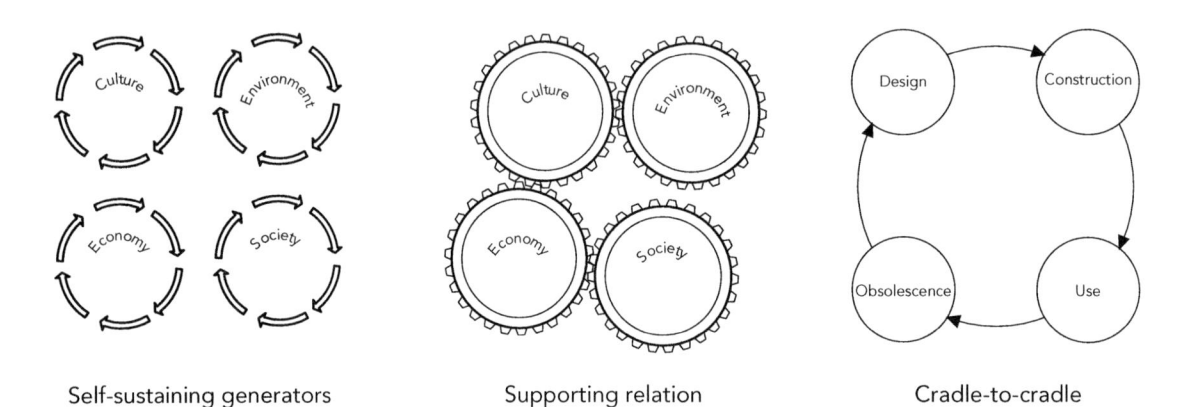

Self-sustaining generators   Supporting relation   Cradle-to-cradle

1.17 **Diagrammatic representation of sustainable systems**

Establishing a *self-sustaining system* is another principle. In a fluctuating economy, reliance on a single source of municipal revenue or energy is not sustainable. It places a town in a "survival mode" making long-term planning vulnerable. Another manifestation of self-sufficiency is patronizing local businesses. When this occurs, energy is not spent on transporting goods from faraway places, their cost is reduced and local jobs are created. This requires educating citizens to make them more aware of their choices and subsequent consequences.

Recognition of the *supporting relationships* between the five pillars noted above is another vital principle. For example, it is highly unlikely that enterprises will be drawn to a place with a municipal government that appears to be overly bureaucratic. Also, building smaller homes in a denser configuration, for example, will result in a reduction of urban sprawl. It will also save on cost of land and infrastructure that, when transferred to the eventual occupants, will result in production of affordable housing. Municipalities will benefit by attracting and keeping young, first-time home buyers in the community and ensure a much-desired demographic continuum.

The final principle for guiding a sustainable development is having a *lifecycle approach* and a long-term view of processes. It advocates that while maintaining the course of a chosen path, the overall strategy should, however, remain flexible to accommodate ongoing change as the need may arise. The process's elasticity and ability to adapt to various emerging circumstances are among its key attributes. When public facilities are designed for adaptability and can be easily modified to accommodate newer needs, investment in their future alteration will be smaller. A similar view should prevail, for example, when codes and bylaws are created. They ought to provide a framework for action, yet not restrict the introduction of amendments and changes when times and circumstances require them.

It is also essential to respect past decisions and have continuity of governance. Too often when municipal governments change and newly elected officials are appointed, a fresh set of objectives is set, with many of the sound old ones ignored. Tenacity is essential in following a strategy with long-term implications.

The principles that have been noted above are a prism through which the different aspects of small town vitality are considered in this book. Each element stands for a chapter that includes an in-depth examination of issues and case studies. The book not only sees the need to plan towns anew along proper sustainable principles, but to retrofit existing communities and sectors in them. Therefore, urban form can and should be regarded as a reflection of cultural identity, continuity, and heritage.

2
Form and Function

A stroll through the streets of Volterra in Italy feels like turning the pages of a history book. The Tuscan hillside town, population 11,000, is remarkably preserved. The place is also a telling story of why settlements were established where they were, how they evolved, and why they remained small.

With roots that date back to Neolithic times, Volterra began as an important Etruscan town. In the centuries that followed it was ruled by the Romans and feudal monarchs like the

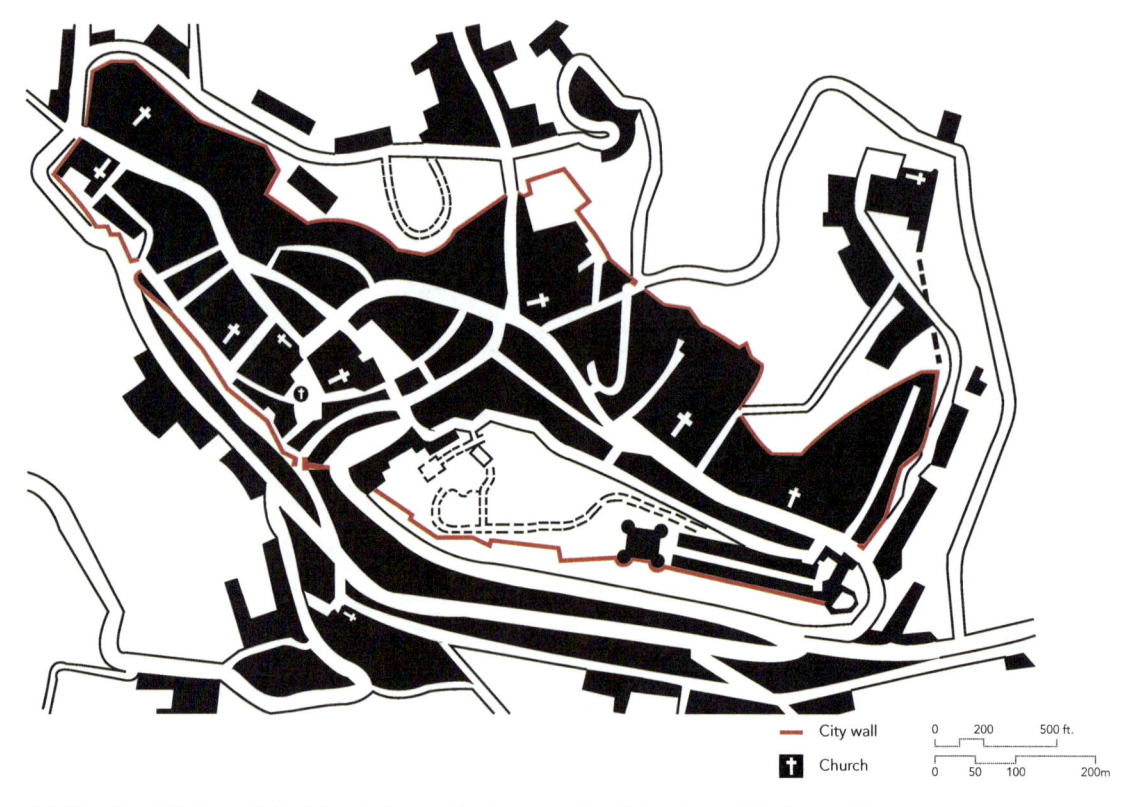

City wall
† Church

2.1 **The city of Volterra, Italy, is located on a ridge between the high valleys of Cecina and Era**

2.2 **Volterra rooftops demonstrate the city's organic growth**

Florentines and the Medicis, among others. Artifacts and edifices built in each period survived and are very much visible today. Its location on a ridge between the high valleys of Cecina and Era offered defensive advantages (Figure 2.1). With the help of defense walls that still encircle the town, it was possible to fend off attacking armies with varying success.

The walls also acted as a containment mechanism that forced growth within their confines. Existing buildings were added to and new ones were constructed on the footings of old demolished structures (Figure 2.2). It was an organic process that saw transformation and adaptation of the urban fabric to emerging political, economic, or demographic circumstances.

Narrow meandering streets cross Volterra's elongated shape and meet on squares near which churches or public buildings stand. Piazza Del Priori, the main square, is framed by the Town Hall and cathedral and serves as a main gathering place. Three- to five-story stone buildings that line most streets and have kept their original exterior markings with ground level shops house the inhabitants.

The surrounding fertile agricultural land was and still is the community's food basket. Volterra's economy has been linked to mining as well. In medieval times the place was known for its "alummines" production, a much needed material for dying cloth. Some of the town's labor force and its fortune are also related to the carving of alabaster, a translucent stone unique to the region. The mineral is still shaped into beautiful objects and sold in many of the shops that draw tourists, to support the local economy.

Volterra represents many of the geographic attributes that govern the establishment, form, and functional patterns of small towns. A reduced physical footprint makes it highly walkable and environmentally sustainable. It offers a prism, not only to the past, but teaching valuable lessons about future urban planning and adaptability. Form and function of small towns and their effect on sustainability is the topic of this chapter.

At the Beginning

A variety of opinions has been put forward about the origin of settlements. There have also been theories of why some have expanded while others, like Volterra, remained small. In general, settlements begin where people happen to congregate. In the *Economy of Cities*, Jane Jacobs (1969) suggests that the origin of towns is rooted in agriculture and trade. That lineage dates back to a time when most societies were made up of hunters and gatherers and survived on what nature could provide. People lived in bands whose population size and ecological footprint were determined by food supply. Schoenauer (2000) estimated that an area of 4,500 to 320,000 acres (1,800 to 13,000 hectares) per person was required to maintain an early settlement. This pattern was transformed and was replaced by permanent settlements with the invention of agriculture (Figure 2.3). Gathered or hunted food no longer decided the group's

2.3 **The stone-built Neolithic human settlement in Skara Brae, Scotland, demonstrates a permanent living arrangement**

size. When animals were domesticated, seeds planted, and crops harvested, there was sufficient food for the farmer's household, and leftovers for trade.

In addition to growing and harvesting food, the skills individuals needed in permanent settlements were diverse and remarkably different than in nomad bands. Some inhabitants specialized in tools or fabric making and others in the construction of homes, for example. The settlements whose economic base was anchored in surplus food production and trade were also physically organized and planned to support such activities (Figure 2.4). Farmers lived near their fields and animals on the outskirts, and tradespeople closer to the town's core often above their place of work. Trade also governed the choice of the settlement's location. Cities were built near or on places where produce or animals could be planted or raised, with aquifers for irrigation. When trade became a driving force of the settlement's existence, roads or waterways leading to it gained prominence. Traders, be they farmers or merchants from other posts, came to town to deal and housing them became an industry on its own.

Kostof (1991) challenges this theory. He argues that an "instrument of authority, rather than any particular form of activity was the gathering force of many towns." Distant seats of power or central governments initiated settlements and populated them with loyal subjects to spread their authority over vast territory. Volterra, for example, started as a regional outpost of the Etruscans and served a similar role for the Romans. In fact, many European towns grew from their Roman origins. In some, like the German city of Cologne, artifacts from the Roman era are still visible. As shown in Figure 2.5, in most Roman cities such as in Pompeii, the Cardo Maximus and Decomanus Maximus, the two main intersecting arteries, defined the planning pattern. In the North American Midwest, Kostof's argument is even more pronounced. Canadian cities like Fort Saskatchewan and Fort McMurray were started as policing outposts. The question of why some cities grow and others stay small still remains. The opinions are varied here as well. Some argue that the fortune of cities rises when a cataclysmic event triggers their growth and at times their decline. The Industrial Revolution had such an effect.

In 1820 only 7 percent of North Americans lived in cities, with the majority residing in either New York or Philadelphia, for example. Only ten cities in the US could boast populations greater than 10,000. As the Industrial Revolution spread from England, the populations of some cities that offered employment and attracted immigrants grew rapidly. By 1820 New York City was home to over one million residents, and seven other cities had populations that exceeded 100,000. By 1890 New York approached one and a half million people while Philadelphia and Chicago were each home to a million residents. Half of all the people in the northeastern US had become urban, as had a third of America's entire population (Jackson 1985).

Due to location, the entrepreneurial skills of their inhabitants, or the existence of natural resources nearby, or a combination of these, some places grew rapidly and drew people from other communities which remained small. Those small towns retained their core economic foundation, a chief reason for their establishment, which was as a trade and service center for the surrounding agricultural area.

Another urban pattern saw the agglomeration of several small towns into a single large one. Hamlets that started as residential enclaves expanded due to immigration waves to merge

2.4 **Grain grinding wheel in Ostia Antica, Italy**

2.5 **The Cardo Maximus in Pompeii, Italy**

boundaries and eventually become cities. Batty (2008) suggests that the process that drives agglomeration of small towns is identical to cities of average size. He also states that the inhabitants of peripheral towns are in effect making a trade-off between travel costs or distance and the cost of space, as in rent, house prices, and land values.

Sociologists have argued that interpersonal social relations and the rapid establishment of the networks that support them are key to urban growth (Adams 1960; Lampard 1965; Fischer 1982). Meier (1962) suggests that the invention of communication technologies and their rapid adaption have sparked the growth of some communities and kept others small. Cities that were powered by electricity and were quick to introduce telegraph or telephone links triumph over those that did not. However, one cannot single out one reason for growth. Ongoing immigration, for example, is as much responsible for the growth of cities as those other factors.

The post-World War II era marks the emergence of a new type of small city. The beginning of these small cities can be attributed to a massive outflow of people from large centers in search for a home to form "overnight" new towns as was the case in the UK for example (Figure 2.6). Whereas old settlements commonly grew over centuries by accretion,

2.6 **Post-World War II terrace homes near Shipley, UK**

post-World War II communities did not follow traditional urban patterns. A product of a highly skilled development industry, their planning thrust was based on efficient land subdivision. They were sited near highways and dependent on affordable car ownership and cheap fuel. Defined by cul-de-sacs and curvilinear streets, suburbia could not offer the sense of place of cities like Volterra. Such communities have been planned with a disregard for the local environment or sound sustainable principles. Coined *Edge City* in a book by the same name, Joel Garreau (1988) describes the process of their emergence:

> First, we moved our homes out past the traditional idea of what constituted a city. This was the suburbanization of America, especially after World War II.
>
> Then we wearied of returning downtown for the necessities of life so we moved our marketplaces out to where we lived. This was the malling of America, especially in the 1960s and 1970s. Today, we have moved our means of creating wealth, the essence of urbanism—our jobs—out to where most of us have lived and shopped for two generations. That has led to the rise of Edge City.

As noted above, the origin and outgrowth of old towns were the outcome of geo-political and economic factors, and the emergence of post-World War II towns was a result of a large-scale desire for home ownership. It is of value to know how the form and overall urban plan of both came to be.

On Urban Forms

Kostof (1991) suggests that cities follow two distinct patterns when it comes to urban forms. The first are *planned* or *created* cities: places whose form follows a charted plan much like post-World War II suburban towns. The second are *spontaneous* cities which, like Volterra, grow in a less-regulated fashion. Kostof also identifies four urban planning typologies which small towns are likely to follow, each with a different effect on appearance and function (Smith 2007).

First, he calls a layout whose growth occurred with no control *organic*. Many mid- and far-east towns as well as some medieval cities have such geometries. The town's formal planning was governed by key civic features such as a town hall or the building of a defense wall. Within this perimeter, due to limited buildable land, high-density construction was necessary. Frontal width was often restricted to between 13 and 25 ft. (4 and 8 m), a result of regulation coupled with the landlords' desire to maximize the number of rentable units along a street. Area could only be gained by increasing depth and height. As a result, structures ranging from two to five floors were built on long narrow plots. Property taxes were also levied according to the width. Heavily traveled streets, which housed shops, had the deepest and narrowest structures and commanded higher value. Encroachment onto the street was common, as seen in Figure 2.7, and corner sites with commercial activity benefited from a double-fronted façade (Quiney 2003).

The second type, a *grid* layout, is based on geometrical or orthogonal principles that are thought to have been initiated by the Greeks and spread by the Romans. Rooted in the *Milesian* form of town planning, neighborhoods were divided into relatively autonomous areas. Radiating out from the city center, those neighborhood units were identically organized. The concept did not differentiate the city core areas, where the civic institutions were sited, from perimeter and edge zones (Mumford 1961).

The third planning pattern is the *Diagram City,* whose design is based on formal geometry. According to Kostof, these shapes were the outcome of someone's vision of how the city should function and as a result how its inhabitants should live. A vision and a plan that foresaw a town along those principles and led to the planning of several towns were put forward by British planner Ebenezer Howard. In 1898 he published a book called *Tomorrow: A Peaceful Path to Real Reform,* better known as *Garden Cities of Tomorrow.* Ben-Joseph and Gordon (2000) suggest that such geometrical schemes often remained theoretical with many more ideal cities recorded on paper than built.

2.7 **Built encroachment onto the street in Rhodes, Greece**

The final category among Kostof's typologies is the *Grand Manner,* in which buildings, streets, and public spaces were arranged to convey the visual effect of grandeur and coherence evident during the Renaissance. A complete rebuilding of the fortification walls in some cities that saw rapid population growth was out of the question and would lead them to bankruptcy. Therefore, solutions, directed internally, necessitated the demolition of old decrepit areas and the introduction of wide boulevards. Such grand schemes were less evident in small towns and were often the outcome of planning intervention in big cities.

Another planning movement worth mentioning, this one contemporary, is *New Urbanism.* Bressi (2002) argues that it is a reform movement aimed squarely at the heart of architecture and, particularly, urban planning conventions and theories that have been

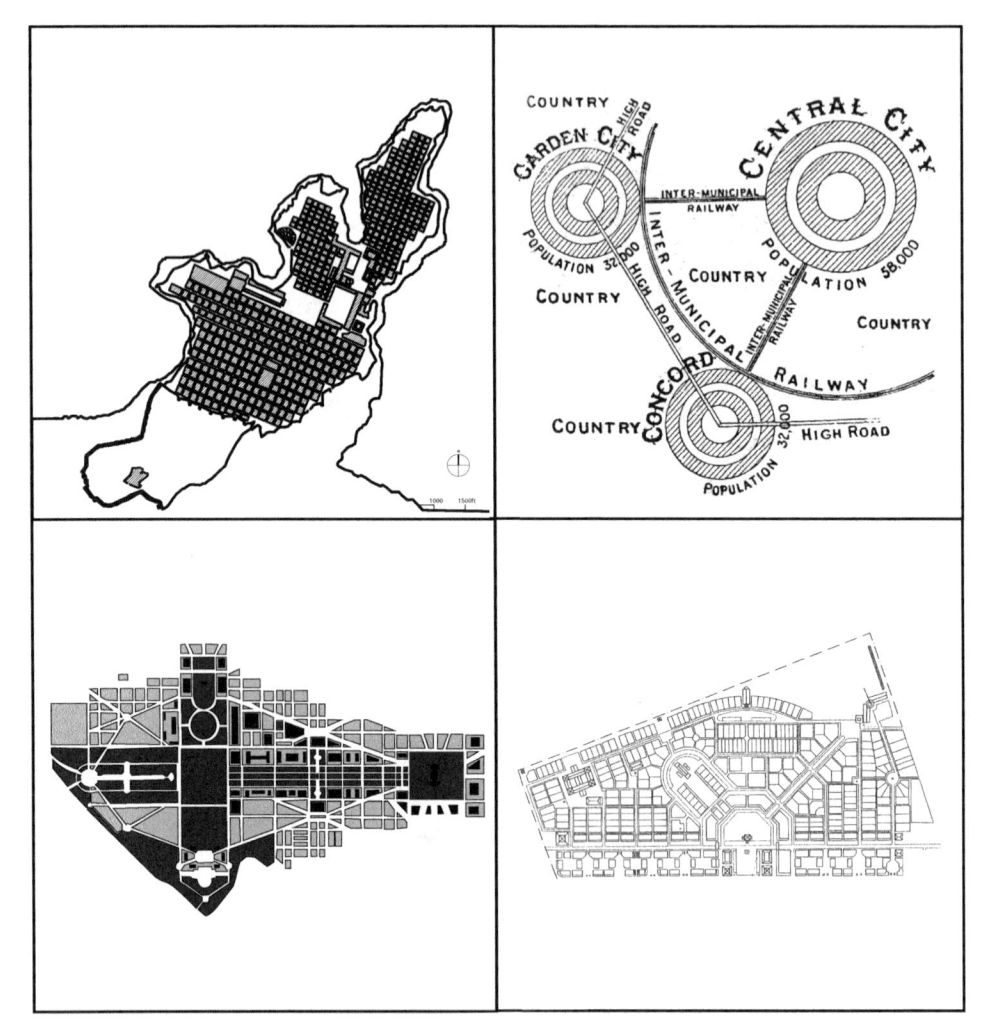

2.8 **A variety of urban planning typologies: Grid layout in the ancient Greek city of Miletus (top left), Howard's diagram of Garden City (top right), Grand Manner used in the planning of Washington, DC (bottom left), and New Urbanism in Seaside, Florida (bottom right)**

advanced over the last fifty to one hundred years. According to Duany and Plater-Zyberk (1991) the core and at times controversial premise of the movement is that traditional towns can offer rudimentary principles for new designs related to scale, urban design, and architectural expression. In essence, New Urbanism synthesized the core values of small town design, yet the question whether one can or needs to recreate the old has remained debatable. Talen (2006) suggests that the movement's experience has revealed that the "multidimensional approach to American urbanism, even if historically grounded, is exceedingly difficult to effectuate." Some examples of these approaches to urban planning are illustrated in Figure 2.8.

The Effect of Forms

A key question for small town design or retooling is about the relation between a chosen form and the place's function. As noted in the previous section, the urban form of a small town might have been the outcome of a preconceived vision or spontaneous organic growth. Each form will have defined physical characteristics which stand to affect its functioning differently. A critical attribute of urban forms and their evolution is how spread out or compact they are. In other words, how their densities affect walkability, use of public spaces, or social interactions for example (Figure 2.9). Do the citizens of Volterra live in a close-knit community compared to the inhabitants of a spread-out Midwest North American town? Can compactness and density be regarded as key defining aspects of small places?

Density, a numerical indicator of how crowded a place is, made its formal appearance along with the introduction of planning control mechanisms. One of the measures, gross density, divides the number of dwellings by the place's area, which includes streets and parks. Floor-area ratio, another index, looks at how well a plot is used by counting the enclosed space on all floors of a given structure and dividing it by the plot area. A tall downtown building will have a much higher floor-area ratio than a single-story small suburban shopping strip, despite the fact that both have a similar footprint. Densities can also be measured according to the number of people who live or work in a place. Each density will result in a unique sense of place and engages its residents and visitors accordingly. A good place to begin observing the effect of density on small town planning is by looking at the broader picture.

Often, one finds clusters of small edge towns primarily in the shadow of a big city. In her study Meijers (2008) asked whether in close-by cities of about 100,000 inhabitants, a similar extent of support for urban amenities can be organized as in a city of 300,000 inhabitants. After examining 42 Dutch regions, Meijers found that a municipality of 300,000 inhabitants has a greater financial base than the other three combined and the possibility of providing more amenities. However, what is often evident in small towns, based on my own observation, is a desire to stretch their economic means and have it all. There is a constant attempt to have the same type of facilities and amenities, albeit not the same number, that bigger cities offer to their citizens despite obvious financial limitations.

2.9 **A crowded street in San Gimignano, Italy**

	Old historic centers	High density	Low density	Suburban
Number of dwellings per hectare				
	475	155	21	8
Number of residents per hectare	2000	280	42	17
Average household size	4	1.8	2	2.2
Average dwelling area per occupant, m^2/sq.ft	10/110	60/650	60/650	60/650
Floor to area ratio	200%	200%	25%	20%

2.10 **Urban typologies and their respective planning attributes**

Each urban pattern, as illustrated in Figure 2.10, is likely to have its unique characteristics and behavioral aspects. Several researchers have studied attributes affecting social relations in denser communities, for example Matera, Italy, which is shown in Figure 2.11. Some list reduced travel by car, walkability, livable downtowns and less costly infrastructure as advantages while critics cite overcrowding and reduced park area as the key negative factors. Burton (2000) looked at the social equity dimension of "compact" towns. Her finding indicates that in them disadvantaged people have access to more stores and as a result greater economic opportunities. Inhabitants may have less green spaces but enjoy proximity to the countryside, greater access to public transit, report fewer mental illnesses, and are less likely to experience social segregation. On the other hand, Burton found that denser, more compact towns lack affordable housing, experience increased crime levels and, surprisingly, have a lower level of walkability and cycling. These findings indicate that not all preconceived notions about small town planning are valid and that compactness may not be a desired strategy in all locations.

Raman (2010) studied the effect of a town's physical form on social relations in neighborhoods. He suggests that densification is not the preferred solution in all planning initiatives and its acceptability will likely depend on the local social and cultural contexts. He found that in high-density neighborhoods respondents had smaller networks of friends but stronger social ties with few members. He relates those strong ties to the way those communities were designed. Compact places, according to Raman, can be poorly designed. Therefore, attention needs to be paid to planning attributes that affect the "values of spaces."

Once a place's urban form has been chosen and the density determined, the question is then how should the various land uses be organized in them? Land-use bylaws and zoning regulations like the one shown in Figure 2.12 are devised with input from urban planners and are enacted by elected representatives. They determine the type of permitted uses such as street widths, building heights, or minimum lot coverage. Often, as is the case in small towns,

2.11 **The compact historic center of Matera, Italy**

they prevent significant modifications to a place even if the demographic composition of the inhabitants has significantly changed and the homes no longer satisfy the needs of the new home-buying public. This lack of flexibility may affect a small town's ability to adapt to emerging socio-economic circumstances in times of change. Similarly, land-use bylaws dictate the ratio between commercial and residential development, based on principles of location theory which are also worth examining.

McDonald (2008) suggests several indexes that he refers to as the Landscape Matrix to quantitatively evaluate cities. *Land-use intensity* measures the number of people per unit area, *land-use heterogeneity* looks at the number of functional uses, and *land-use connectivity* at the degree of aggregation of the various uses. A theory about land location and use was introduced by Johann Heinrich von Thünen, an early nineteenth century scholar who laid the foundation for regional economics. According to the theory, a farmer's bid for a parcel of land declined as the distance to market increased and, as a result, crop transportation costs increased. Studies that followed also theorized that land would be converted from agricultural to urban use when the economic return from the sale of the land would benefit the farmer more than agriculture. William Alonso, a planner and an economist, developed a mathematical model of an urban land market. In Alonso's model, a range of economic players competed against each other to own land in the city, where the highest bidder was likely to get the land. The key features of Alonso's model were distance to the city center and expenses one would incur to get there (England 1980).

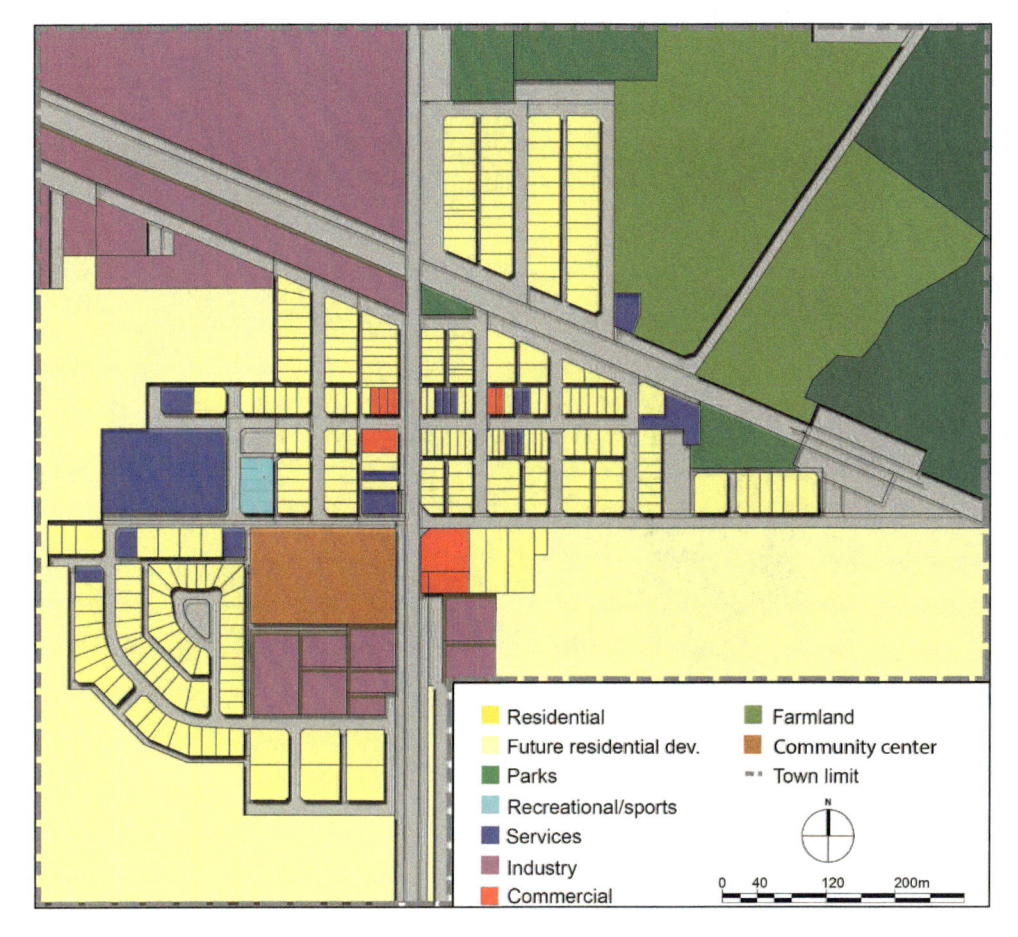

2.12 Land-use plan in Nampa, Alberta, Canada

Land development in small towns and the location of key functions and activities in them follow these principles. Commercial activities were commonly located in the center and residential areas in the periphery. In towns like Volterra, where the buildable area was restricted by a defense wall and challenging topography, builders had very few choices. Dwellings had to be layered on top of commerce or be constructed next to a church or a town hall. Layering was no longer a necessity in small post-World War II towns where vast tracts of land were relatively inexpensive. Their sprawl was guided by zoning that often segregated residential from commercial land uses. The gap between the two was beyond walking distance and mandated the use of cars.

In the core areas of many North American small towns such as Whitehorse, Yukon, Canada (Figure 2.13), there are often single- or two-storied commercial establishments. Layering residences above them was not welcomed by land developers who assumed that no one would want to live in them. To make matters worse, in the 1980s with the proliferation of large format retail shopping, many small towns saw the emergence of "new downtowns" on their edges with ramifications on their sustainability, a subject that will be discussed below.

2.13 **Main Street in Whitehorse, Yukon, Canada**

Sustainable Urban Forms

The planning, expansion, or urban renewal of a new town commonly begins by setting an overarching guide. As previously noted, sustainable development offers a broad vision anchored in the need to account for the long-term effect of present actions. Several researchers examined the relations between urban forms and their sustainable outcome. Their observations laid out principles and conclusions related to small town design and will be outlined here. A sketch of how a sustainable small town is envisioned in this book concludes this section.

McDonald (2008) suggests that globally "the form of urban development today will control resources use for generations to come." A chosen plan will also have a profound effect on ecosystems. For example, demand for fresh water is expected to increase several fold by both inhabitants of sprawling cities and industry thereby putting current supplies at risk. Yardsticks have been introduced to gauge a place's sustainability.

Ecological footprint is a measure that seeks to determine the amount of area that humans need for their survival (Holden 2004). It is an accounting tool consistent with thermodynamic and ecological principles (Chambers et al. 2000). Much like the land that ancient tribes needed for gaming, citizens need an area for their own existence. According to the *Living Planet Report* (WWF 2002), "the productive quarter of the biosphere corresponded to an average 1.9 global hectares per person in 1999." Holden (2004) found that human consumption of natural resources that year overshot the earth's biological capacity by around 20 percent. Following his research of Norwegian communities Holden estimated the ecological footprint of residents of small rural towns to be 10 percent smaller than those living in larger urban areas based on their travel patterns. Not surprisingly residents of small towns tend to travel less.

Other researchers looked at the relationship between social sustainability and urban form. According to Bramley et al. (2009) social sustainability encompasses two broad areas: social equity and sustainability. Social equity includes access to local services such as shops, schools, health centers, open spaces, public transport, job opportunities, and affordable housing. In their study the sustainability of the community was examined based on: pride of place, social interaction, safety, and satisfaction with the home, among others. The index, according to the authors, that is most likely to affect social sustainability is density; they argue higher densities may make access to services and facilities both easier and economically viable. It also means that people are likely to meet each other more frequently and have places to do so (Figure 2.14). In their findings Bramley et al. conclude that compact cities are not necessarily "win–win" on all dimensions of social sustainability. A reduction in greenhouse gas (GHG) emissions from

2.14 **A meeting spot in Frascati, Italy**

vehicles will have to be weighed against equally important social criteria. Urban forms, they suggest, "cannot be considered sustainable if they are not acceptable to people as places in which to live, work and interact or if their communities are unstable and dysfunctional."

Holden (2004), who looked at the relationship between urban form and its environmental consequences—particularly in regards to the residential environment—suggested that one also needs to look into the consumption patterns of inhabitants. Low-density neighborhoods tend to be greater consumers if these indexes are to be used. For example, consumption of energy for space heating and other everyday products will be more pronounced.

So, what should be the key indexes of a sustainable small town in relation to the ecological footprint? Holden (2004) suggests dense and concentrated housing design, shortest possible distance to the town center, and overall moderate geographic spread. These principles point to a possible conflicting argument about small town design that places compact planning ahead of a spread-out place, although the latter is often favored by residents.

The preferred planning strategy need not place these approaches at the extreme ends and force a choice between the two. The design of a town of any size can contain and mediate between both. As shown in Figure 2.15 the plan may designate areas to high-density dwellings that would economically justify introduction of commerce and public transit for example. On the periphery, the density can be gradually reduced to have more single-family homes. Lower density housing can be sited to make walking to a commercial hub no longer than 10–15 minutes for example. Small towns can maintain their "green" appearance and when designed properly still adhere to core sustainable principles.

Jabareen (2006) suggested a checklist of sorts for planning sustainable small towns with a reduced ecological footprint. He includes among them *compactness* that sees future areas built next to existing ones; *transport* that reflects the full social and environmental cost of its provision; *density* and *mixed land uses* that reduce the probability of using a car (Figure 2.16); *diversity* of dwelling types that creates a well-balanced socio-economic and demographic continuum; *passive solar design* that looks into microclimates, built form, and orientation among others; and *greening* that encompasses aspects associated with private and public open space including their vegetation.

When sustainable planning models are sought, Jabareen (2006) suggests *neo-traditional developments* which are modeled after nineteenth century neighborhoods and towns including those built along transit corridors; *urban containment* where a green belt has been introduced to halt urban sprawl; *compact cities,* which were described above and *eco-cities* that employ environmental management through institutional and policy tools. Each of these models will contribute differently to achieving sustainability and their choice will largely depend on the designer's objective.

Edwards and Haines (2007) sought to find out whether sustainable growth principles are observed in small towns or whether only lip service is paid to their implementation. They examined factors that included housing diversity, preservation of open space, and densification. They found that many of these initiatives and principles attracted less interest in small towns compared with larger urban hubs.

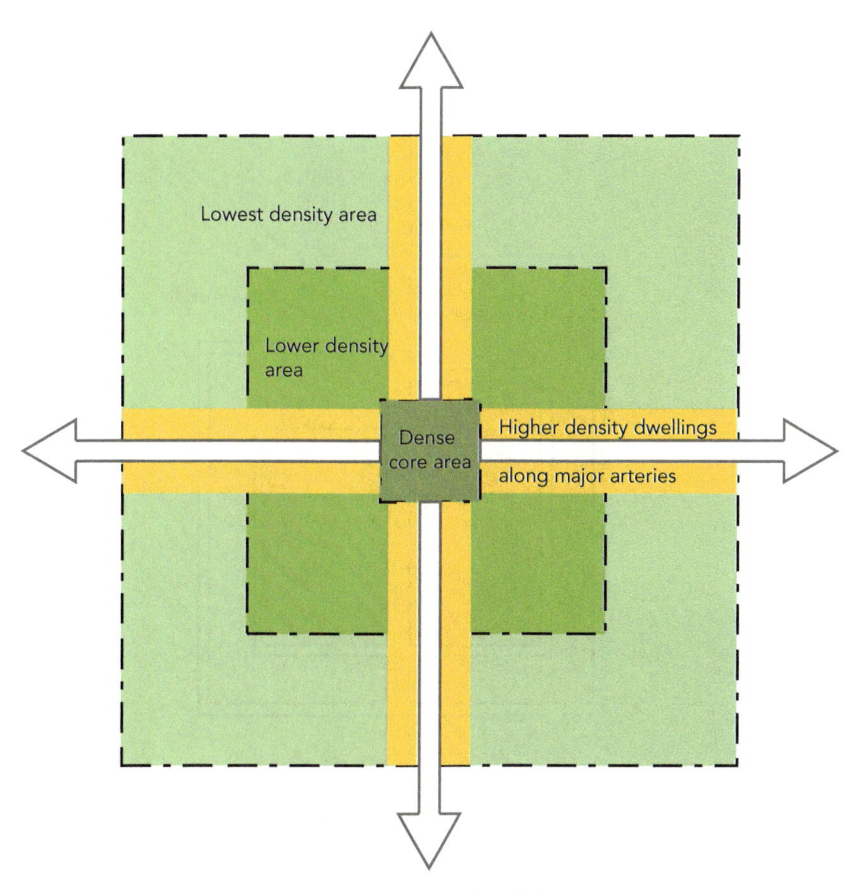

Labels within figure:
- Lowest density area
- Lower density area
- Dense core area
- Higher density dwellings along major arteries

2.15 In small town planning higher densities can be introduced along key arterial roads and in and around core areas

Planning sustainable towns or renewing them based on the principles outlined in this chapter represents a challenge. The designs need to propose a new paradigm for an economically, socially, and environmentally integrative approach. Yet the question still remains: What is a sustainable small town? Prior to an in-depth discussion and illustration of the different facets of sustainable design, a conceptual framework is drawn here.

In my view, small sustainable towns need to integrate people, land, and buildings. Environmentally, development patterns need to work around natural systems and features, which in turn can allow residents to enjoy the outdoors. Resource conservation also needs to be advocated and community ties called upon to encourage such efforts. Construction products should be minimally toxic during their installation and use, and be disposed of safely or recycled when no longer needed. Landscaping in private and public areas should be bioregionally appropriate and require little irrigation or harmful pesticides.

Socially, sustainable towns will accommodate diversity among their inhabitants. Residents of different backgrounds who share values and life experience should be able to live together successfully. Families are started, children move out and come home, and careers are

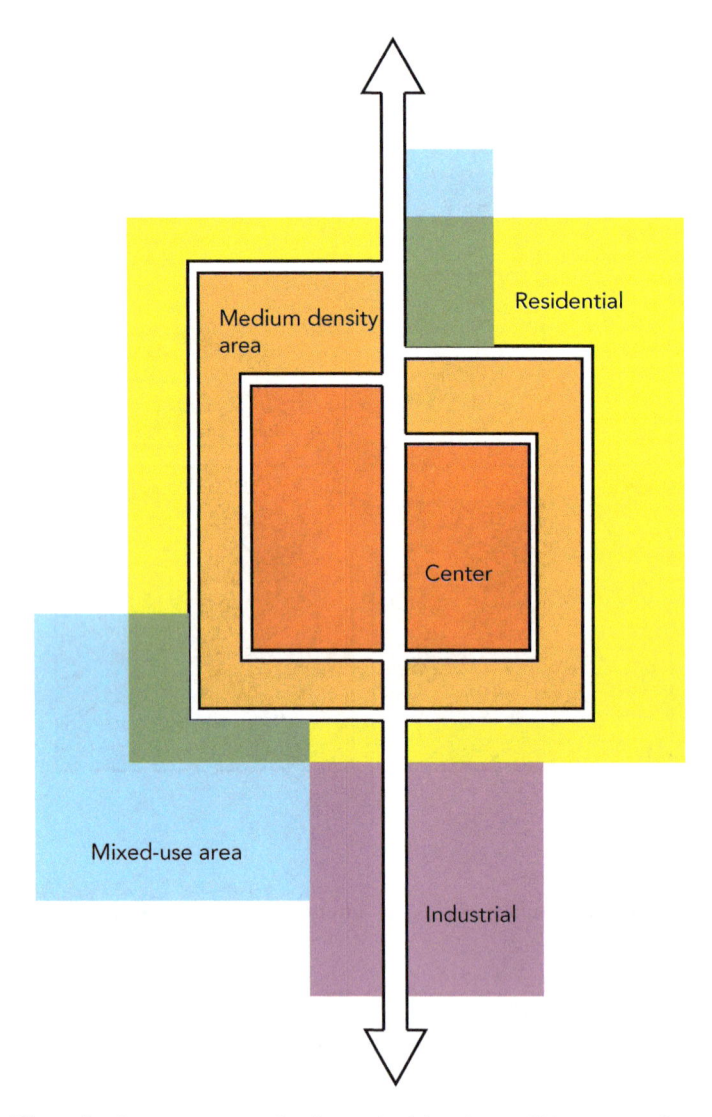

2.16 **Placing different land uses next to each other and mixing them will lower use of cars by residents**

switched and ended. Therefore, communities need to house residents throughout their lives by providing different housing types and easily modifiable layouts, as well as a range of services and support required by different age groups, family types, and occupants.

Residents need to be able to take pride in an attractive and orderly neighborhood, with areas for children to play, couples to stroll, seniors to chat, and locations for social gatherings (Figure 2.17). Public spaces in a sustainable town can be more like a well-used living room than a hallway or formal dining room. The community should also foster civic-mindedness. While architects and planners cannot solve political problems, they can certainly design streets and neighborhoods that permit and encourage neighbors to have friendly civic engagement.

2.17 **Summer festival in Marken, the Netherlands**

A sustainable town also needs to permit safe travel by foot, public transport, and bicycle. The use of cars should be given lower priority by accommodating pedestrians and cyclists with generous sidewalks and bike paths. Dwellings and public facilities need to be accessible to those with limited mobility as well, beyond simple ramps and handrails. As people age and face temporary or permanent difficulty in getting around, intelligent designs can ensure their continued access to and participation in the life of the community.

It is not always clear how to make the leap from general theories and aspirations to a specific site-oriented plan, but knowing what needs to be taken into account and considered is crucial for designers of new sustainable towns, sections in them, or their urban renewal.

Considering Urban Form in Ponoka

Located near a highway between the cities of Edmonton and Red Deer in the province of Alberta, Canada, Ponoka is home to 6,200 inhabitants. The town has a quaint core where mom-and-pop stores line the streets surrounded by homes (Figure 2.18). Unlike other small Albertan towns that experienced rapid growth due to a rising demand for oil, Ponoka witnessed a decline in recent decades. Few people migrated in and the downtown commercial center has had a hard time competing with larger regional businesses. Ponoka's leadership recognized that prior to adopting measures that will stimulate population and economic growth, a new vision has to be tailored for the place, one which will also look at the overall urban form and, in particular, pay attention to the relation between the core and the surrounding residential areas. It is with this background that I was invited to consult the town's administration.

2.18 **Images of Ponoka, Alberta, Canada**

History and Context

Ponoka was established in 1891 as a delivery point along the Calgary–Edmonton Trail. When a railway line was laid in 1893, the town was known simply as "Siding 14" until an unknown railway employee wrote the name Ponoka, an aboriginal term for elk, on a sign. The town was incorporated in 1904 and kept growing as settlers arrived from eastern Canada and the American Midwest. The core area features a wide range of heritage buildings, including a tiny

2.19 **Street façades on Chipman Avenue in Ponoka**

one-room store dating to the town's earliest years, well-preserved storefronts and signs from 1900 to the 1960s and western Canada's largest single-day livestock auction (Figure 2.19). A recent façade renewal program contributed to improving the appearance of buildings, but did little to fundamentally alter the town's fortunes.

Ponoka's urban evolution is reflected in its current land use (Figures 2.20 and 2.21). Industrial and commercial activities were located at its southwest corner and residential areas were initiated in the center and, as the town grew, spread to the north and east. The Battle River runs through and divides the town to create a central green buffer between the two sections. Over the years, Ponoka gradually expanded with the arrival of additional waves of immigrants and a residential subdivision was developed east of the river.

As for the core, in the early years it was made up of a mix of residences and businesses and offered services to the farmers who shop and use local services. In addition, the Stampede, a traditional western games ground, on the edge of downtown, went on to become a well-known regional draw. Some 70,000 visitors attend the games for two weeks during the summer.

Urban Planning Strategies

A close scrutiny of Ponoka's urban makeup reveals several advantages and some drawbacks that affect the town's future growth. Among the advantages one can recognize a convenient regional location, pleasant and vibrant core, a well-balanced demographic continuum, celebrated history, and a large stock of well-preserved heritage buildings and room to grow farther. The drawbacks are a rail line that divides the town in two, a disconnect between the core and the river, lack of a central focal gathering place, and absence of a physical link between downtown and the Stampede area.

The overarching objective of the new plan was to have more local residents and tourists patronizing downtown, close the gap between the west end and eastern sections, and lay the ground for future growth without furthering urban sprawl. When actual planning strategies were considered, it was recognized that a link between downtown and the Battle River should form a vital part of any concept. At present, there is no direct link and pedestrians must walk

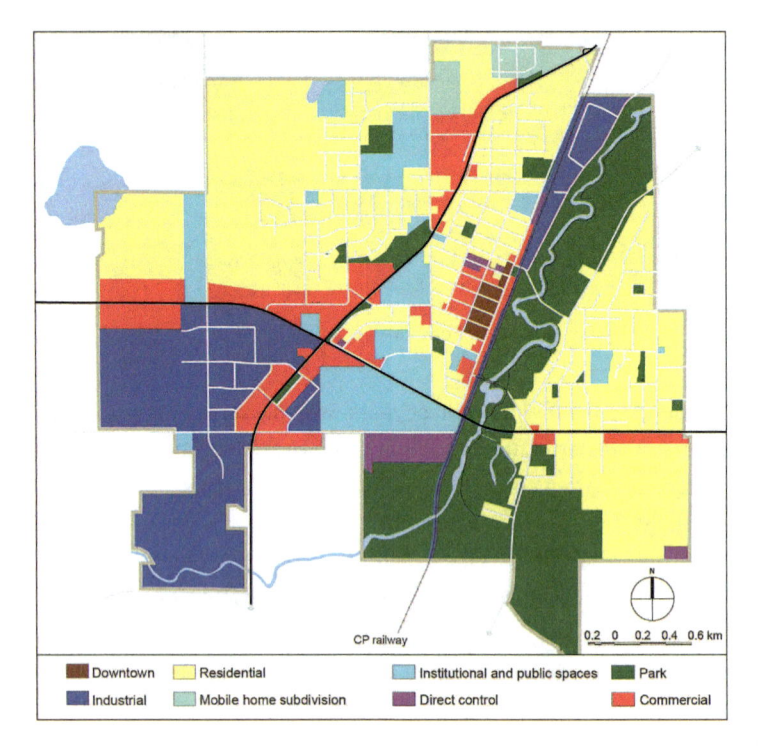

2.20 Ponoka's existing land-use plan is common in many small western towns

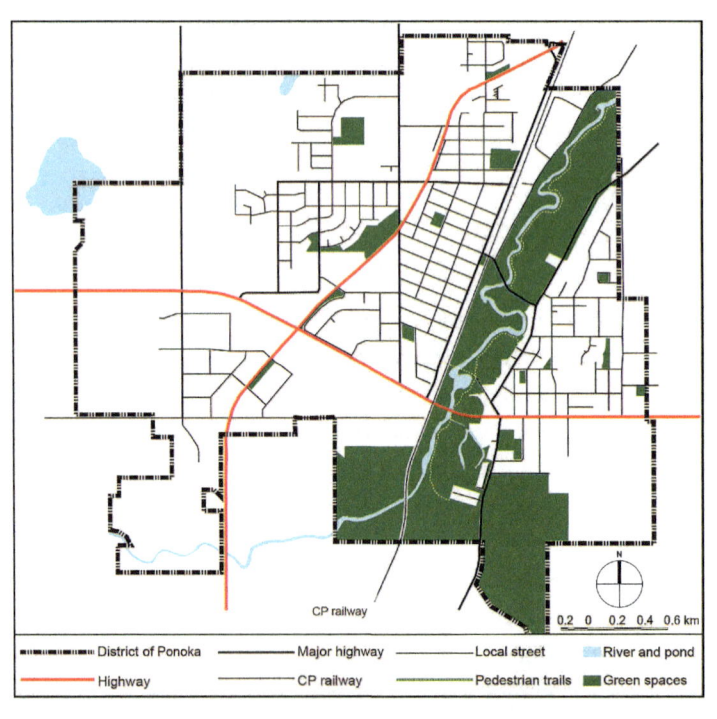

2.21 Ponoka's transportation networks

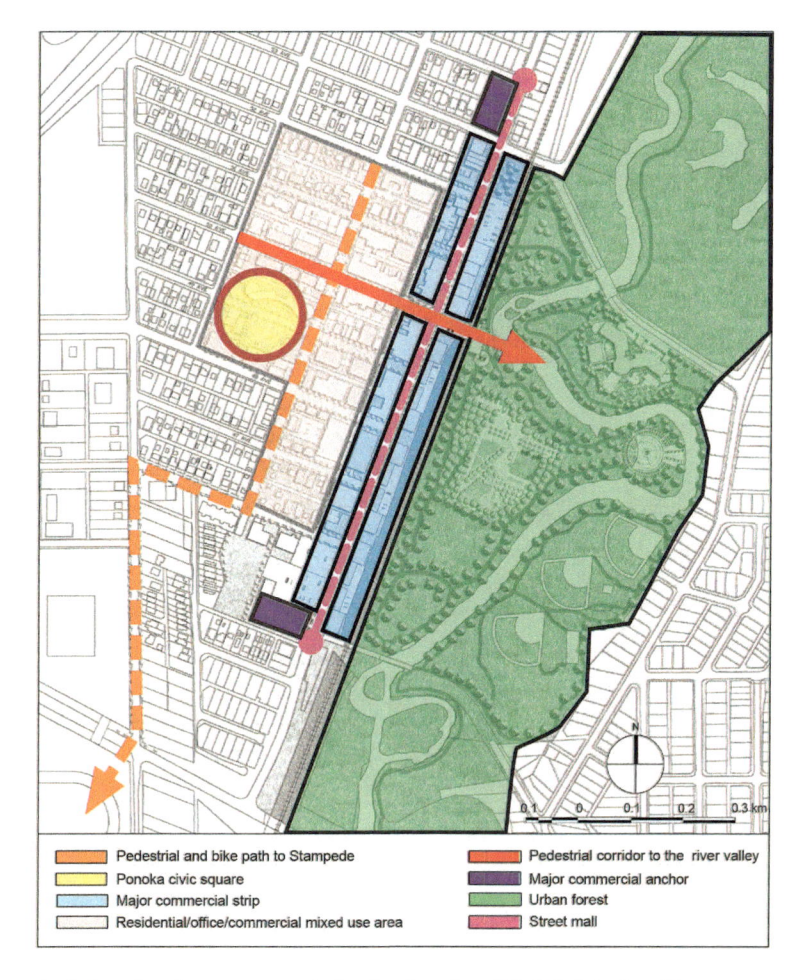

Legend:
- Pedestrial and bike path to Stampede
- Ponoka civic square
- Major commercial strip
- Residential/office/commercial mixed use area
- Pedestrial corridor to the river valley
- Major commercial anchor
- Urban forest
- Street mall

2.22 Conceptual plan showing new areas to be developed and their link to the old

around the rail line. If recreation, leisure, and tourist activities are to become one of Ponoka's future sustainable economic pillars, then building an attractive overpass or underground passage between the two is necessary, as shown in Figure 2.22.

To increase activity and to support local businesses in the core, the town must see its population increase. This can be done by constructing apartment buildings, with commerce on lower levels, or by adding floors to existing structures and building a main civic square (Figures 2.23 and 2.24). In addition, the Battle River with its green banks, one of Ponoka's main natural assets, can serve as a central pillar of any planning process. For example, initiating summer boating activities and winter skating events on the river and cultural and leisure destinations on its banks can turn it into a local and a regional draw. The process can be done in phases to accommodate gradual financial investments. Also, since at present downtown does not draw direct economic benefits from activities in the Stampede grounds that attract many spectators, a link was proposed between the two.

| | New buildings | | Renovated buildings | | Existing buildings | 0.1 0 0.1 0.2 0.3 km |

2.23 **A detailed plan for Ponoka's redesign**

2.24 **Rendering of a proposed civic square**

3
Green Small Towns

I parked my car in the belly of the huge ferry that took me across the Wadden Sea from the main land to the island of Texel in the Dutch province of North Holland. I knew little about my destination except that it was a place sought after by bird watchers. When the ferry docked I headed to my place of stay in the town of Den Burg, population 7,000.

While practicing sustainable planning, I often referred to 'green towns' or 'eco-cities' in presentations when explaining what cities can become if they were to adopt environmental policies and suitable actions. Den Burg was "green." Due to its remote location from the main land, its inhabitants have had to learn to live within the means that nature offered them, and over centuries they have used the available resources sustainably.

The town has a well-preserved historic center where once a week the main square plays host to a public market, as shown in Figure 3.1. Just-picked fruit and vegetables are neatly arranged in a colorful display for urban dwellers to buy. In the stalls you can also find clothing, soaps, and cheeses made in one of the many sheep farms that border the urban edge. The restaurants that frame the square serve local staples.

Den Burg's neighborhoods encircle the center. A short walking distance away you see brick cladded homes on small meticulously tended lots landscaped with native species. The clusters are connected to the center, each to another, and to the countryside by a vast network of well-marked bicycle paths. On the roofs of many homes one can spot sun harvesting photovoltaic panels and, in the distance, wind turbines catching the ocean winds that the island is known for. Along the coast there are bird sanctuaries for watchers who come here from abroad and fuel the local economy.

While strolling the streets of Den Burg, observing its homes, and traveling through its countryside, it dawned on me that most small towns are "greener" than big cities. Their physical impact, and as a result their negative effects, on the environment is naturally much reduced. Therefore, greening them further must be put in a different context. Introducing new policies, technologies, or planning concepts needs to follow parameters that weave old and new and dwell on the local. This chapter looks at these issues and outlines a number of strategies that can further improve the environmental performance of small towns.

3.1 **Market day in Den Burg, the Netherlands**

Small is Green

A place's ecological footprint is its productive area divided by the number of those who use it. The footprint of a community, for example, will include the entire crop and grazing land necessary to produce food and other resources that the place consumes, and the area needed to absorb the waste produce and the pollution emitted (The Why Factory 2010). Concentrating a large number of inhabitants, as big cities do, in a small area is likely to designate it as a place with a small ecological footprint. The authors of *Green Dream* argue that "today's eco-cities all have one thing in common: they are small." As an example they suggest that the City of London, England, has a footprint of 6.3 global hectares per capita, while the UK national average stands at 5.4. By those very same standards, in the year 2003 the *global* hectare per capita was 1.8 (The Why Factory 2010). The citizens of developed nations leave a big footprint compared to the world's other regions.

It is hard, however, to argue that all small towns have a reduced ecological footprint. The distinction will depend on the place's economy and location, among other factors. Edge communities whose inhabitants commute daily to work in a big city will have a larger footprint than towns whose citizens are employed locally. On the other hand, in small towns that are located in the heart of agricultural regions the cultivated land acts as containment of growth. It will be of value to reflect on the relation between towns and nature.

Since the Ice Age, human settlement planning and dwelling design have reflected vernacular responses to natural conditions. With the development of agriculture by about 7,000 BC, early civilizations began to modify landscapes. For the first time, trees, for example, were planted for shade and scenic and spiritual uses to foster a sense of place. This changed after the late nineteenth century. Increasing car ownership and higher standards of living rendered scenic rural landscapes attractive to those with the means to afford a secondary residence away from the crowded city. Farming villages, like Senneville, Quebec, Canada, with picturesque landscapes became the site of secondary homes for city dwellers (Figure 3.2). They not only generated agricultural produce to feed the city, but became a commodity by themselves.

The most significant development affecting natural areas occurred after World War II when low-density residential subdivisions consumed vast areas of farmland and attracted city people. Large-scale planning not only coincided with highway construction, but at times initiated it. Developers approached the environment with the notion that natural landscapes could be altered. Forests were unabashedly cleared and land made flat for ease of construction.

Those practices have been rendered unsustainable in recent decades. A question that still remains, however, is: what are "green" towns in a contemporary context? Several interpretations have been introduced to describe their key features. The general notion recalls places where

3.2 **A home built in 1880 for vacationers in the village of Senneville, Quebec, Canada**

planning strategies, policies, actions, and adopted technologies support an overarching intention to reduce their ecological footprint. In these communities one can also observe a collective attitude that aligns adopted practices and chosen lifestyle with environmental objectives.

An *eco-tech city* is a term used to describe communities that have adopted various means to achieve their environmental goals, like the city of Potsdam, Germany, which committed to reducing greenhouse gas (GHG) emissions (Figure 3.3). Ercoskun and Karaaslan (2011) suggest that these means include limiting the use of potable water and encouraging its harvesting and recycling and opting for non-polluting vehicles and sources of renewable energy, sustainable materials, and green roofs. They state that reducing oil dependency and fostering productive living arrangements is an inevitable direction for humanity. The chief objective of adopting such initiatives is to foster *resilience,* which is defined by Hopkins (2008) as the capability of a system, from individual people to a whole economy, to hold together and maintain its ability to function in the face of outside change and shock.

The environmental movement has progressed remarkably from its start following the publication of Rachel Carson's *Silent Spring* in 1962 to become a global force. Ideas were transformed into practices and products that saw a wide range of implementation. Digital means of communication and social media redefined "small." Ideas and new technologies can spring from anywhere and knowledge about them can be made available to a global audience rapidly. When discussing the introduction of ecological initiatives, the challenge for small towns is how to have citizens subscribe to this mindset when most believe that their place of living

3.3 **A poster demonstrating commitment to emission reduction in Potsdam, Germany**

3.4 **Sheep "mow lawns" in Oudeschild, the Netherlands**

is already "green." Compiling information that supports the town's goals to be used in social marketing can help community leaders gain a broad interest in their initiative.

Several studies have attempted to link the environmental performance of a place with some social science attributes. Looking at urban forests, Wolf (2007) found that people of all ages prefer natural views to built areas and that trees tend to enhance the visual quality of cities in the public eye. Commerce located in treed streets obtains greater patronage behavior and commands higher pricing, is easier to brand, tidier, and better perceived by shoppers.

Another factor affecting the economies of small towns is the relation between environmental practices and cost-saving (Figure 3.4). Building narrow roads will not only foster better human scale, it reduces the cost of maintaining them and thus municipal taxes. On the social front, Alessa et al. (2008) examined the concept of the social–ecological system (SES). They found positive linear relationships between perceived biological values and net primary productivities for three of six communities in Alaska. The communities that responded successfully to changing environmental conditions maintained a high level of functionality and demonstrated resilience. Dale et al. (2008) suggested that towns that adopted sustainable initiatives also demonstrated bolder community identity and a strong sense of place that "can result in mobilization for sustainable development initiatives."

These notions set the stage for the following sections where the conservation of land, energy, and water that support Low Impact Development (LID) will be discussed.

Managing Land

Green open spaces are essential to the environment, recreation activities, and the well-being of a town's inhabitants. Therefore, the responsible stewardship of these areas takes on an added importance. Such importance was recognized by several researchers who studied the correlation between landscape and built form. Bowler et al. (2010) reviewed studies on the effect of green areas on urban temperature known as the *heat island effect*. They found that parks and trees cool the environment at a local scale. Croci et al. (2008) studied urban woodlands as potential sites for biodiversity conservation. They found that such sites tend to accommodate over 50 percent of the species present in periurban woodland and effective management could even increase this number further. Liu et al. (2009) looked at changes to the landscape as a result of new development and road construction in China and concluded that, not surprisingly, natural patterns of flora and fauna change greatly once human intervention on a site begins.

How should nature be preserved and integrated into the development of new land in small towns? In general, no different than in big cities; yet there are still some marked differences between the two.

When designing new communities or retooling existing ones, the original topography must be preserved, because if it is altered, it may not be able to be restored and can forever change the local ecosystem and sense of place. Rivers or canals can be made part of the plan and roads and buildings can be sited with respect to slopes and to allow for the greatest sun exposure (Figure 3.5). For example, placing dwellings in rows at different elevations will not obstruct views to subsequent homes, will adhere to the lay of the land, and avoid casting shadows. A sloped terrain also allows for a simple, natural, and effective drainage system, and reduces construction costs. As well, a community that is located near a body of water can benefit from the tempering effects of evaporation. In the spring and autumn, the land becomes warmer than the surrounding water and a thermally induced circulating current is produced, providing a cool breeze.

Designers of new developments need to consider existing vegetation. Commonly, prior to construction, sites are cleared of trees and other natural features and re-landscaped when the buildings are complete. A plan that adapts and conforms to a site's existing features will reduce cost and retain uniqueness. Minimal disruption of the surrounding environment will also protect the ecosystem's biodiversity. Trees and other shrubs catch and absorb storm water

3.5 **Homes facing a channel in Almere, the Netherlands**

runoff and prevent soil erosion as shown in Figure 3.6. They also do their part in filtering out noise and offering privacy to homes. In the end, the planting of new trees should reflect the building orientation, height, setback, and fenestration.

Waste management and its disposal have become another land stewardship challenge and at times can affect small town economies. Despite the limited population of small towns, waste needs to be handled and disposed of. Mishandling it can also have serious public health ramifications and it can cause the pollution of groundwater. As a result of a steady increase in personal consumption, domestic waste has also been increasing, as well as its handling costs. Many mid-sized municipalities spend a significant portion of their annual budget to collect, transport, and dispose of waste (Statistics Canada 2005). In some small towns and rural areas where formal municipal collection does not exist, residents are often required to bring their waste to a local landfill and pay based on its weight. Therefore, waste management needs to be dealt with sustainably.

While the level of waste generated differs from country to country and even between households, it is hard to avoid creating any waste at all. The issue is not elimination but rather reduction and proper disposal (UNEP/GRID-Arendal 2002). When residential waste is discarded, it will eventually go through one of five post-consumer waste management processes. From

Setbacks are decided according to the location of the trees.

Road path parallel to the site's contours.

Roads follow clearances in the forest.

Cars park between trees.

Natural patch is left undisturbed.

Variety of housing types and locations according to the trees.

3.6 **Existing vegetation needs to be considered and integrated when a new development is initiated**

least to most sustainable, they are: landfill, incineration, anaerobic digestion, recycling, and composting.

Landfills produce greenhouse gases, including carbon dioxide and methane. Together with small amounts of nitrogen and oxygen and trace amounts of other gases, such as toluene, vinyl chloride, and benzene, they contributed to 3 percent of all greenhouse gases in 2002, for a total of 23.8 megatons (21.6 megatonnes) (Statistics Canada 2005). These gases are produced from organic and biodegradable waste. In a landfill pile, biodegradable waste does not receive sufficient oxygen and is forced to undergo bacterial or anaerobic decomposition. The amount of gas produced through this process varies depending on temperature, moisture content, and time.

Incinerators produce energy from the combustion of solid waste, which can be used to heat buildings or generate electricity in small towns. The energy, however, is only useful when it is produced from waste with a high heating value that burns without requiring additional fuel. Interestingly, many highly combustible materials that would make good fuel for incinerators, such as paper and plastic, are also recyclable and are likely to be diverted to recycling plants instead of reaching incinerators (Statistics Canada 2005).

New incineration methods, some of which have been introduced in Scandinavian countries, have mastered energy production by developing advanced filters that catch most polluting agents.

In *anaerobic digestion,* methane (CH_4) is purposely produced, collected, and burned for its energy value. Methane is produced by microorganisms breaking down biodegradable materials in the absence of oxygen. Although anaerobic digestion produces fewer gas emissions than landfill, greenhouse gases are still emitted since the methane conversion and the gas collection system are never 100 percent efficient. The waste left over from digestion is not toxic or contaminated and can be used as compost and tilled into solids (DeBruyn and Hilborn 2010). Both incineration and anaerobic digestion are illustrated in Figure 3.7.

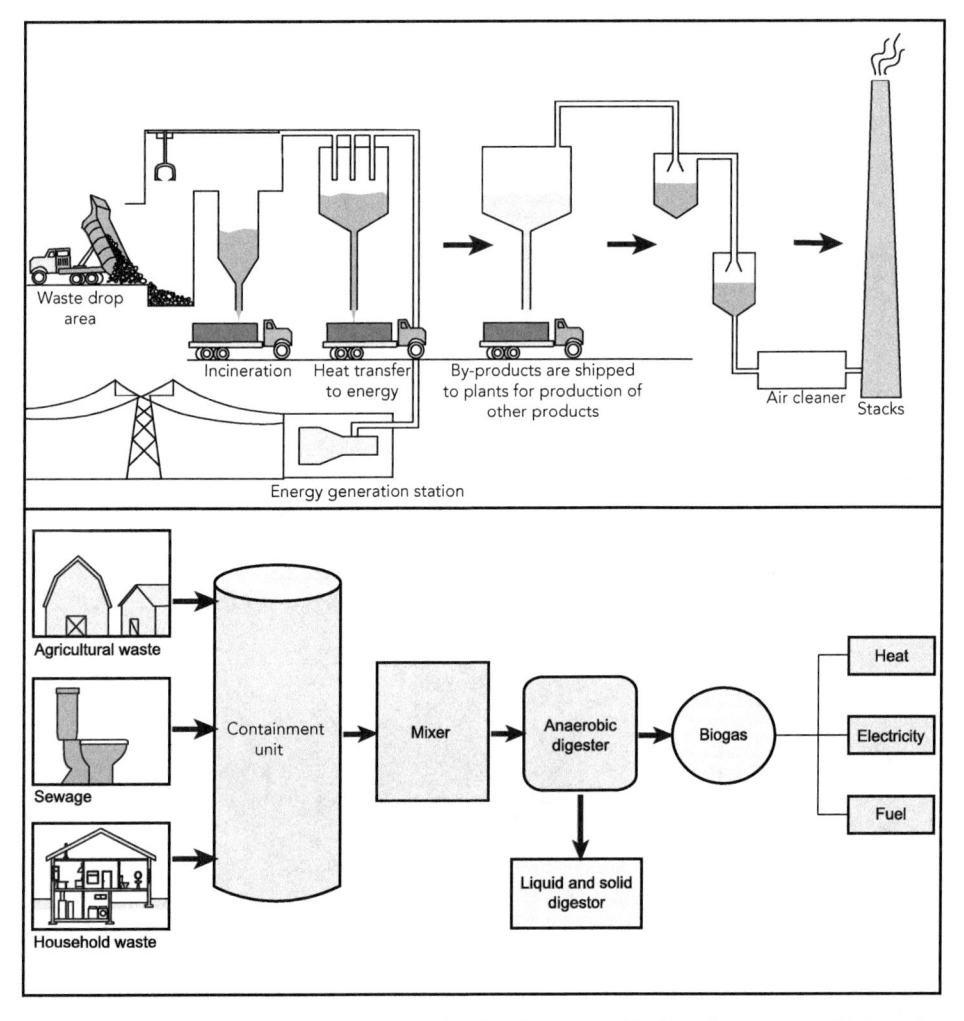

3.7 **Incineration plant converts waste to energy (top) and an anaerobic digestion process which produces biogas (bottom)**

Recycling involves the transformation of waste from commercial or domestic sources into other usable products (Figure 3.8). Collecting recyclable material requires transportation, which consumes energy and produces gas emissions. Yet the advantage is in reducing the amount of raw materials needed to make new products, and as a result air pollution and solid waste. For instance, when recycled aluminum instead of virgin bauxite is used to produce new aluminum products, energy consumption can be reduced by 95 percent (Statistics Canada 2005; Meisel 2010; Ecoworld 2007).

Composting is the biodegradation of organic matter by bacteria or other organisms in the presence of oxygen. When organic matter decomposes aerobically, the end products are mainly carbon dioxide and water, while the remaining solid mass can be used as fertilizer in soil. Since compostable materials originate directly or indirectly from trees or other plants, the carbon dioxide emitted from composting is not considered a pollutant but rather biogenic carbon dioxide (ICF Consulting 2005).

Food supply is another critical issue in small towns. Located away from large distribution centers, small towns often rely on in-trucking, a practice that puts at risk the community's food security and has negative environmental consequences. The cost of food has also risen in

3.8 **Recycling station in Porvoo, Finland**

3.9 **Farmers' market in Zhouzhuang, China**

recent years. According to Turner (2011) in December 2010 the United Nations Food Price Index hit an all-time high and the next month broke this record, and broke it yet again in February 2011. Encouraging local food production and vending has therefore become critical to the economy of small towns and the health of their inhabitants (Figure 3.9). Known as "edible landscapes," planting can take place in a variety of locations and scales. Individual production can happen in rooftops, gardens, or greenhouses. Neighborhood-based growing may take place in community gardens and large-scale greenhouses (Farr 2008).

A small town that has taken steps toward guaranteeing food security is the City of Armstrong in the province of British Columbia, Canada, population 5,000. Supported by a grant, the community started the Armstrong Food Initiative that included a pilot food-exchange program to connect those with extra produce from their gardens and orchards with those in need (de la Salle and Holland 2010). Central to the successes was the establishment of a food exchange. In a period of eight weeks, 5,000 to 6,000 pounds of produce (2,268 to 2,722 kg) were shared among 70 to 80 people. Other community organizations such as food banks also became the recipients of the exchange.

The initiatives that have been outlined above offer alternative ways to manage land in small towns with ramifications on policies and regulations. These initiatives form part of a communal effort to establish eco-cities.

Managing Energy

When the effect of urban design on energy efficiency in residences is considered, it is of value to recall past practices. Builders of ancient Greek and Roman settlements and dwellings knew how to take advantage of the sun's heat during winters and avoid it in hot summers (Oktay 2002). By knowing the sun's path, they oriented streets and buildings accordingly. Windows were positioned and roof eaves extended to reduce direct exposure. The designs also considered wind direction which determined the width of streets and sidewalks. In Roman settlements, for example, arcades were built on main streets creating comfortable environments for pedestrians (Goldsteen and Elliot 1994). Shepperson (2009), who studied the urban form of Mesopotamian towns in relation to the sun's path, points out that many of the streets were oriented north–south. Those streets were shaded most of the day with sun shining on buildings either in the morning or the afternoon which made the streets comfortable places to trade or congregate.

Contemporary planning for passive solar gain or cooling can be based on similar principles. When houses are oriented to "catch the sun," their occupants also enjoy a maximum amount of natural light. Therefore, homes oriented along the northwesterly axis in the northern hemisphere benefit from a shorter noonday shadow that otherwise might be cast if the same houses were oriented east–west. This principle guided the planning of Nampa, Alberta, Canada, illustrated in Figure 3.10. Moreover, additional units with or without solar panels may be erected upon the cusp of neighboring houses' shadows if dwelling design follows this layout.

Active solar methods, such as photovoltaic energy, have gained prolific use in many countries. It is a silent, reliable, renewable, and environmentally safe means of generating power in commercial and residential applications. Solar farms like the one near Lindos, Greece, shown in Figure 3.11, can be used to provide lighting and power water pumps and domestic appliances that service a home or an entire community. Although the price of photovoltaic panels is relatively high, the cost drops as demand rises. Solar cell arrays are being integrated into building elements such as roofs and cladding. In Switzerland, for example, arrays have been installed alongside highways to act both as energy sources and sound barriers (Ramage 1997).

Natural ventilation is another important aspect of sustainable design for energy conservation. Although wind patterns change from one season to the next, wind direction and speed can be estimated by examining the local topography, landscape, and weather patterns and by looking at a wind square (Brown 1985). For example, near bodies of water, the wind will flow from the direction of the water towards the land in the daytime but will reverse course in the night. Because of inertia, the wind will flow around objects and will sustain the same direction of flow. As a result, the vegetation in the surrounding area can greatly reduce wind velocity and deflect it from an object. During the cold months, trees can shield structures from winter winds that usually originate from the same direction. Favorable positioning will allow for cross-ventilation of homes limiting a need for costly and high-energy-consuming mechanical cooling means.

Whereas the planning principles listed above can be applicable to the design of any community, the introduction and use of alternative means of energy can be better implemented

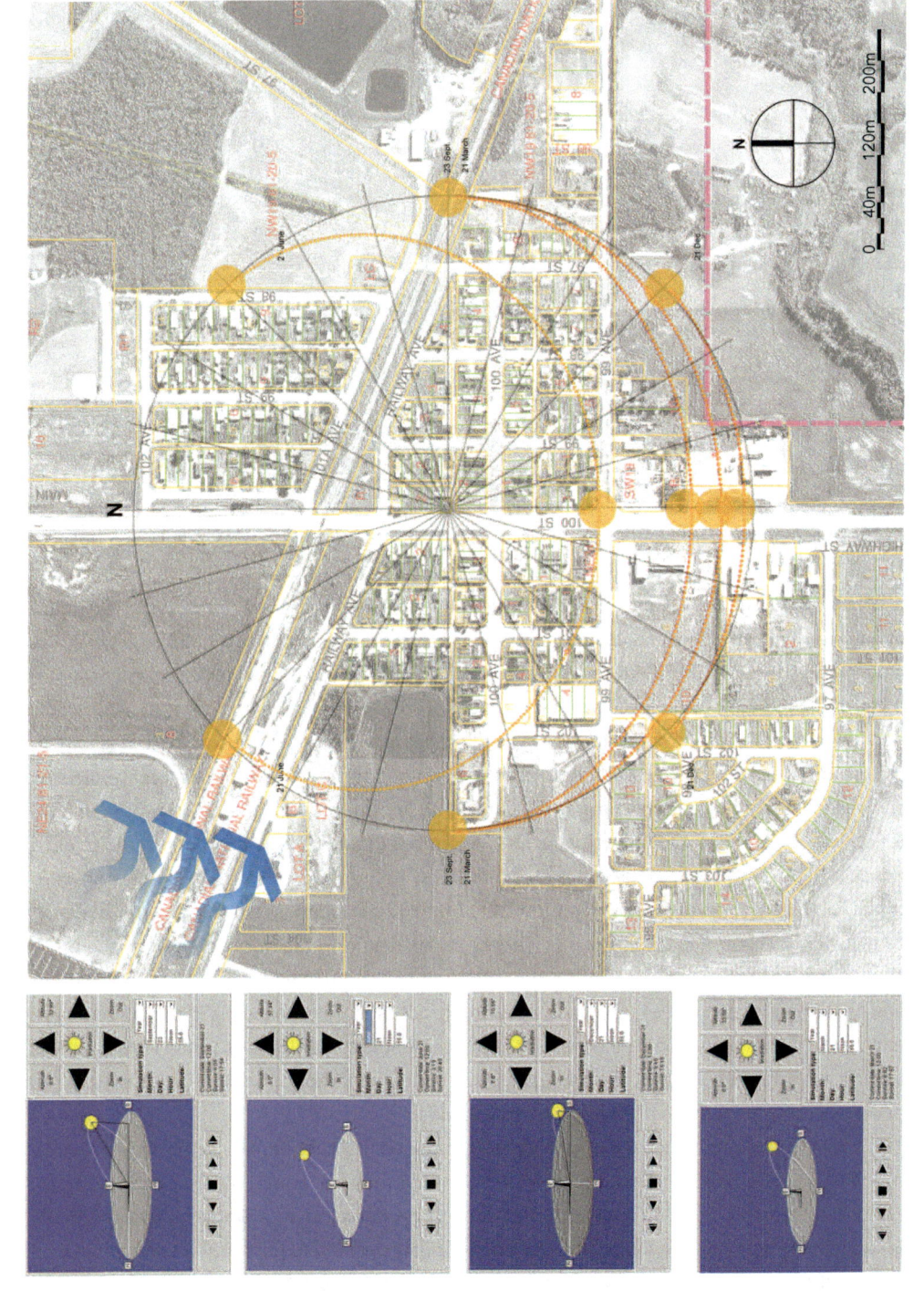

3.10 Wind directions and street orientations for passive solar gain were considered while preparing a master plan for Nampa, Alberta, Canada

3.11 **A solar farm near Lindos, Greece**

in small towns. The overseeing of policies and the towns' small size facilitates the introduction of alternative power sources. Some federal governments, like Scotland, and municipalities have made the production and use of renewable energy that includes geothermal heat, sun, tides, and wind their prime objective (Figure 3.12).

When a central, common source of heating powers a town, or portion of it, it is known as *district heating*. The Romans, for example, used hot spring water in their bathhouses as shown in Ostia Antica near Rome, Italy (Figure 3.13). The source can be of a renewable or non-renewable nature. The advantage of such a system lies in the savings that are offered to each household through economy of scale. Newman et al. (in Farr 2008) suggest that only one-third of the fuel energy input to a conventional fossil-fuel power plant is delivered to the end user as electricity. The rest is discharged to rivers and lakes and to the atmosphere. On the other hand district heating systems capture most of the heat and use it to produce steam and hot and chilled water. Known as *co-generation,* the process is made possible by combined heat and power (CHP) technologies that can serve dense population areas. According to the authors several aspects must be considered in the planning stage, among them the proximity of the power plant, transmission distance, and utility rates.

Several small towns have successfully introduced district heating. Some of those communities have set a goal to have their entire power supply generated by renewable sources. Lund and Østergaard (2010) describe the case of Frederikshavn, a Danish town of 25,000 inhabitants, where the city council in 2007 unanimously decided to pursue such an option. One of the actions taken was to expand the district heating grid from 190 gigawatt hours per year (GWh/year) to 236 GWh per year. In addition, in its overall strategy the municipality looked at

3.12 **Wind farm in Whitelee, Scotland**

3.13 **Clay pipes were used by the Romans to bring hot water from a central source to a bathhouse in Ostia, near Rome, Italy**

all its energy needs including transportation. The town converted its public transit fleet to biogas, expanded its geothermal production and introduced energy from wind turbines.

The German town of Ostritz, population 2,500, is another example of a municipal drive for use of energy from renewable sources. When the local environment was affected by pollution from coal-based power plants, the town decided to take action to reduce its ecological footprint and become energy self-sufficient. This meant a major transformation in local energy production and primarily the abandonment of coal power plants. The strategic decision was to supply heat to 75 percent of the town's dwellings from a biomass-based power station where the principal source was woodchips, a renewable source with low carbon dioxide emissions. Solar energy systems for water heating have also been installed to complete the energy supplies.

Another small community that followed an energy self-sufficiency path is Falkenberg in Sweden. The town introduced a comprehensive sustainable plan centered on energy and developed a windmill farm with ten turbines that produced a combined 12.5 GWh of electricity per year (James and Lahti 2004). In 1989 the town put into operation what was then considered the largest array of solar collectors in the world. Through a network of district heating, the energy is distributed to many of the town's homes, bringing the total amount of energy from renewable sources to 30 percent.

By adopting measures that include transportation efficiency, thoughtful urban planning, and alternative sources of energy some small towns demonstrate that their size can be an advantage in reaching energy self-sufficiency.

Managing Water

Along with fossil fuel, water has become a scarce and costly commodity in many countries. In addition, climate change has led to prolonged periods of drought with severe ramifications on agriculture. Small towns, primarily those whose economy is based on farming, have seen their fortunes decline.

Common contemporary town planning and development practices have not helped conserve water either. Sprawling low-density communities, which are built with extensive networks of asphalt roads and parking lots, not only contribute to the urban heat island effect, but their streets direct rainwater to storm drainage. The homes are sited on large lots whose front and rear yards are covered with turf that requires a great amount of water in the summer to keep the grass green. Many towns face another challenge. Once networks of water distribution and drainage have been constructed, they must be maintained, which can be very costly. Waste water needs to be channeled to energy consuming filtration plants for purification prior to being discharged to rivers. The environmental consequences of residential water consumption are also significant. According to Thomas (2005), to sustain a reasonable quality of living requires 26 gallons (100 L) per person per day. In reality, the average consumption ranges from 1.4 gallons (5.4 L), barely enough to live on in parts of the world that have low rainfall during the dry season, to 152 gallons (575 L) per person per day in the US (Figure 3.14). Much of this extra use is carelessly wasted (Green Living Tips 2009). In addition, when water is used for personal consumption it needs to be heated, at yet another cost to the environment and to each household.

The need to conserve and manage water at both the municipal and the household levels requires the adoption of a range of small- and large-scale measures. Storm water management strategies and bio-retention technologies were introduced in Prince Georges' County, Maryland, US in the mid-1980s (Urban Design Tools 2012). The measures were intended to address the growing economic and environmental limitations of conventional storm water management practices and became known as Low Impact Development (LID). LID approaches are rooted in the philosophy that storm water is a resource rather than a negative occurrence that must be dealt with. It suggests that urban forms should coexist with nature rather than work against it. ICF Marbek (2012) lists five principles that guide LID-based development: integration of existing natural systems, runoff prevention by using engineered techniques and natural preservation strategies, treating storm water as close to the source as possible, advocating the creation of

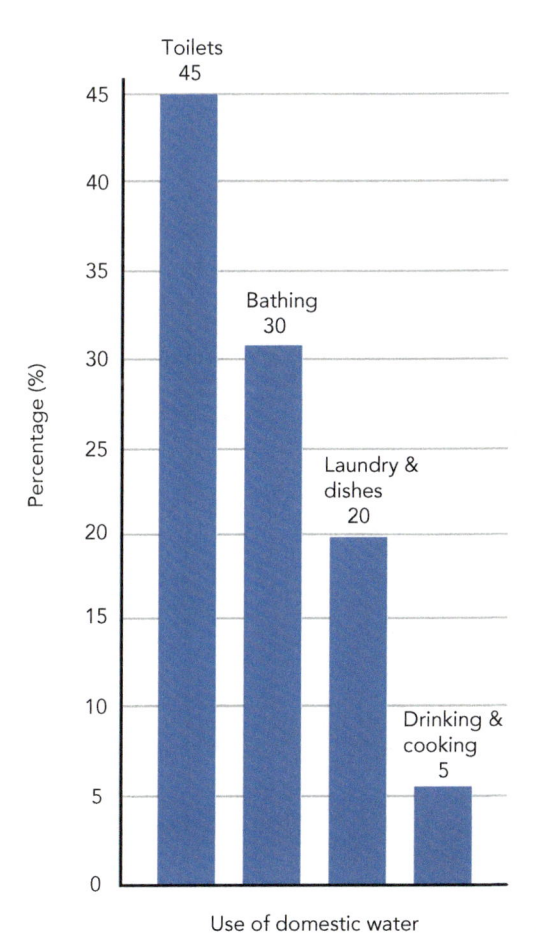

3.14 **Breakdown of domestic water use by an American household**

a range of landscape types to meet the water needs of natural ecosystems and, finally, educating stakeholders about the practices and their benefits.

LID is meant to serve a wide range of planning conditions and urban settings such as residential, commercial, or industrial in large urban areas or small towns. The initiatives have shown to have lower lifetime and off-site costs. In fact, it was suggested that the cost associated with site development, storm water fees, and maintenance can be reduced by 25 to 30 percent (Urban Design Tools 2012; Cirillo and Podolsky n.d.).

Several innovative applications of LID techniques have been implemented since their introduction. A common intervention is to have bio-retention planters at the side of main arteries. When heavy rain falls the planters collect rainwater rather than direct it to a drain. Known as *bio-swells,* similar techniques include planting hedges or trees at the side of the road to avoid drainage. Other strategies include the creation of retention ponds in the heart of neighborhoods to expand biodiversity. The introduction of permeable pavement in parking lots, streets, and private driveways, having smaller pipes and inlets, the use of green roof technology in public and private buildings, and rainwater collection and harvesting methods are some additional practices. A water harvesting system for plants' irrigation was used in the community of Västra Hamnen, Sweden (Figure 3.15).

3.15 **A water harvesting network used to water plants in Västra Hamnen, Sweden**

Several small towns have adopted LID-based innovative techniques. One of them is the Dutch town of Valkenburg, population 3,900. Situated below sea level, the Dutch had to employ many storm water handling strategies. In Valkenburg, it was decided to build a sustainable neighborhood where the prevention of future floods will be the leading planning principle. The city council decided to prepare the ground before construction started by ensuring sufficient soil bearing and accessibility. The excavation of the canals raised the ground level and increased the permeability of the soil. As a result, rainwater flowed directly from the roofs to collected surface water. Other municipal LID-based initiatives included the use of waste water to produce energy in Eva Lanxmeer in the Netherlands (van Timmeren et al. 2007) and in Hammarby Sjöstad near Stockholm in Sweden.

Water-saving practices are not limited to the urban scale; they can be implemented by individual households as well. They may include the use of fixtures such as low-flush toilets, efficient showerheads, taps, and appliances such as dishwashers. Other methods include gray-water harvesting and recycling.

Rainwater is usually cleaner than gray water and is less prone to contamination. However, it can be contaminated by dust as well as acidic atmospheric gases. Rainwater collection systems can be integrated in neighborhood planning. A group of dwellings or a single unit, for example, can collect and recycle rainwater from roofs and store it in large underground tanks for various later uses (Thomas 2005).

Water demand can increase by 50 percent or more during summer months due to plant watering. Excessive residential use of water for landscape irrigation can account for up to 40 percent of the total household water consumption (Regional Municipality of Waterloo 1990). Irrigation not only drains local aquifers but also pollutes groundwater with fertilizers, pesticides, or herbicides used in lawn maintenance. As such, some communities are adopting water conservation ordinances for landscape irrigation, limiting turf installation, or offering rebates to homeowners who install xeriscapes (McPherson et al. 1989).

Deriving from the Greek word xeros, meaning dry, *xeriscapes* promote water conservation through careful plant selection and integrated approaches to design and maintenance of land surrounding a home or group of homes. According to Ferguson (1987), without diminishing the aesthetic value or human accessibility, xeriscapes can save 60 to 70 percent of, or even eliminate, water requirements for irrigation.

Although the "payback periods" of xeriscaping alternatives are not immediate, the benefits of such landscaping are well worth the investment. Choosing local plants and promoting resource conservation and natural habitats are benefits to xeriscaping that escape typical cost-saving calculations. When implemented on a macro urban scale and in each home storm water can be put to good use and overall consumption reduced.

Placing Nature in the Center of Komoka

The Municipality of Middlesex Centre in the Province of Ontario, Canada, has witnessed growth since the 1990s. Most notable was the development of new low-density subdivisions ever closer to the city of London. As this trend is set to continue, the Municipality wanted to have a neighborhood built around the new Wellness Centre in Komoka, one of its former hamlets (Figure 3.16). As a result, I was invited to propose a plan for the land. While the specific objectives were gathered from a consultation with members of the community and council, the general mandate was for a mixed-use residential town center based on sustainable principles.

3.16 **Images of Komoka, Ontario, Canada**

Context and History

Located 14.7 miles (23.7 km) west of the City of London, Komoka has an area of 1.2 square miles (1.9 sq. km) and a population of 1,190. Its close proximity to London has made the place a bedroom community surrounded by a provincial park, a number of lakes and ponds as well as agriculture land. It is also a crossing point for three national railway lines. County Road 14 runs along the southern edge, joining it with the neighboring district of Kilworth (Figure 3.17). In Komoka, there are two large senior residences, two schools, and a community center. The new Wellness Centre offers an indoor gym, ice rinks, and a library.

Komoka's urban roots date back to 1798 when the first British settlers arrived and established mills that generated power using water from the Thames River. The construction of the Great Western Railway in 1857 was the main catalyst for residential and hotel development. Other factors adding to the area's prosperity were the many gravel deposits and the harvesting of dense forests of red and yellow pine. Komoka continued to be a railway crossing point, although it is no longer the hub it once was and the hotels have long since gone.

As for the site, its total area is 56 acres (22.63 hectares) made up of five parcels of a fairly flat terrain. A north–south road crosses the parcels leading to the adjacent neighborhoods. The plot west of the Wellness Centre included a filled-out former gravel pit.

3.17 **The project's site is located near the neighborhoods of Komoka and Kilworth**

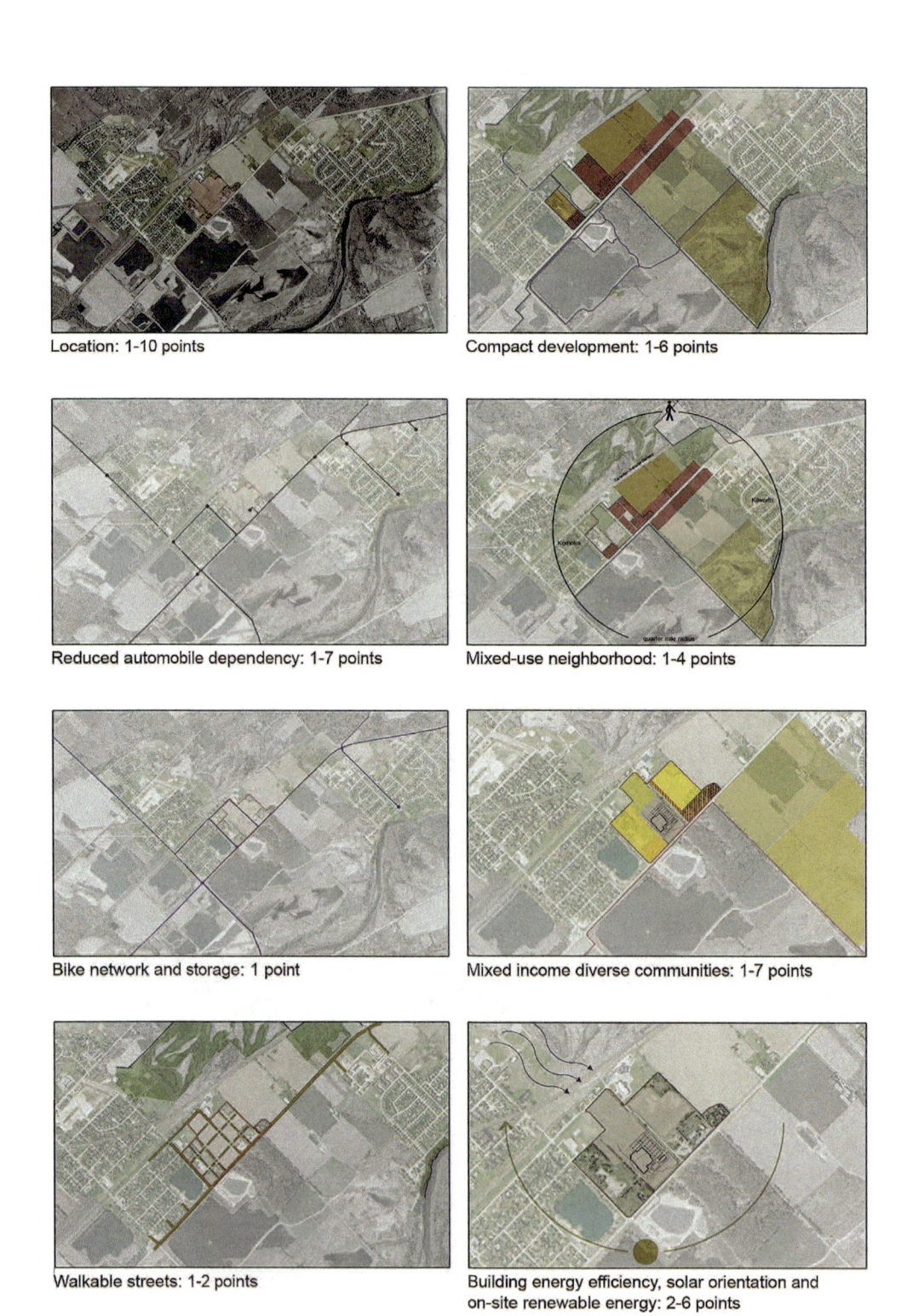

Location: 1-10 points

Compact development: 1-6 points

Reduced automobile dependency: 1-7 points

Mixed-use neighborhood: 1-4 points

Bike network and storage: 1 point

Mixed income diverse communities: 1-7 points

Walkable streets: 1-2 points

Building energy efficiency, solar orientation and on-site renewable energy: 2-6 points

3.18 **Some LEED criteria that guided the project's environmental performance and their ratings**

Setting Objectives

In setting design objectives we examined and accounted for Komoka's current and future needs as expressed during the various consultations. In addition, Leadership in Energy and Environmental Design (LEED) criteria were considered and suitable sustainable planning principles listed as shown in Figure 3.18. Key aspects with implication on our planning and environmental design strategies were: to reduce automobile dependency and design a walkable community by developing an extensive network of pedestrian and bike paths; consider and include the site's natural features; have medium-density, mixed-use, and diverse housing prototypes to accommodate people of all ages; offer easy connection between the dwellings, the commercial amenities, and the Wellness Centre; orient dwellings for passive solar gain and the possibility of add-on photovoltaic (PV) panels; include trees and native plants and landscaped xeriscaping as well as allow areas for community gardens and urban agriculture.

Sustainable Plan

Our three key planning features were to develop a "green" neighborhood, consider cultural, civic, and recreational activities, and follow Low Impact Development (LID) principles. As for the residences, it was decided that the majority of the housing will be medium-density single- and multi-family townhouses affordable for first-time buyers. Apartment buildings were located west of the Wellness Centre and will provide affordable accommodation for seniors. A small percentage of the land towards the north of the site was dedicated to single-family detached housing as well. The objective was to have a medium-density community of between 4 and 9 units per acre (9.8 to 22.2 per hectare) for a diverse population (Figure 3.19).

To provide services to the new neighborhood and to the municipality at large, commercial amenities were located along County Road 14. It was also assumed that the location of and the accessibility to the Wellness Centre would draw tourists and make them want to explore the town's other offerings. The land north of the Centre had been transformed into a communal park to include a variety of outdoor recreational attractions for residents and visitors.

A covered walkway was introduced to provide access from the back of the Wellness Centre to a row of shops and cafés. In the southwest corner we introduced a square, for civic events. A path for walking, jogging, and cycling looped the park to create a link with the recreational area. Along the path, visitors would enjoy a toddlers' water spray park, local history and art display boards, a sitting area in an orchard, an outdoor exercise equipment space as well as a children's play park. In addition, an outdoor amphitheater and a bandstand were located in the northwest.

Several pools of water from harvested sources ranging from reflection to natural ponds, will be featured in the park. Land surrounding the pools has been allotted for urban agriculture

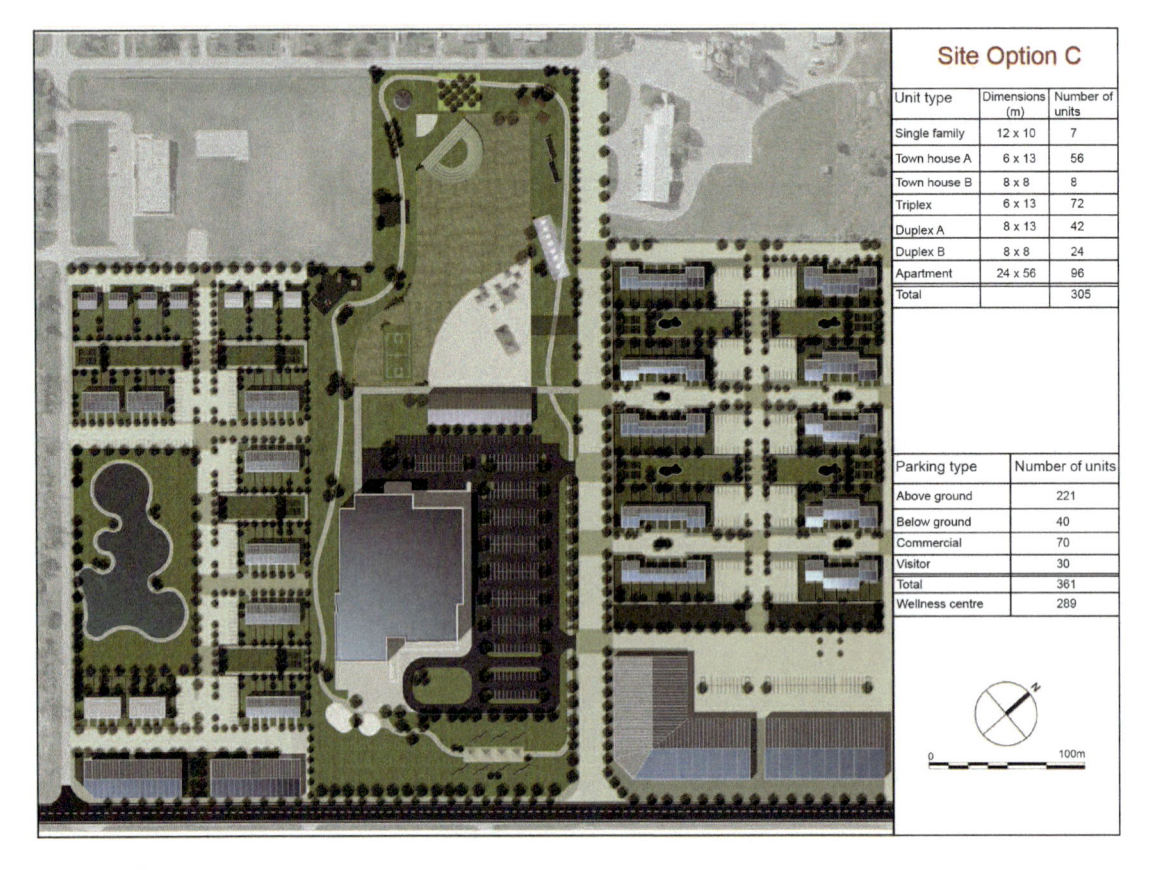

Site Option C

Unit type	Dimensions (m)	Number of units
Single family	12 x 10	7
Town house A	6 x 13	56
Town house B	8 x 8	8
Triplex	6 x 13	72
Duplex A	8 x 13	42
Duplex B	8 x 8	24
Apartment	24 x 56	96
Total		305

Parking type	Number of units
Above ground	221
Below ground	40
Commercial	70
Visitor	30
Total	361
Wellness centre	289

0   100m

3.19 **Site plan**

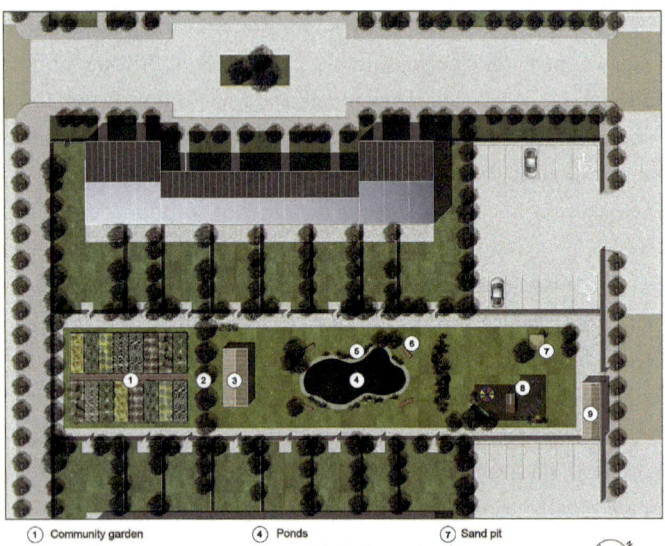

3.20 **The common green area**

① Community garden	④ Ponds	⑦ Sand pit
② Fruit trees	⑤ Shrubbery	⑧ Play park
③ Tool shed	⑥ Benches	⑨ Recycling centre

and the growing of crops (Figure 3.20). The water linking the pools follows a path reminiscent of the River Thames as a reminder of the town's unique sense of place.

All medium- and high-density housing has shared parking either behind or to the side of each residential block. It minimizes the amount of land dedicated to the car and improves the use and attractiveness of the street. All streets and lanes have been designed to be shared surfaces that prioritize the pedestrian and encourage cycling. In addition, a bike path runs the length of the neighborhood and connects to a bike path proposed for County Road 14 where traffic calming measures will be introduced. These measures will include a change of surface texture at the entrance to the town, planter boxes, sidewalk projections, and the inclusion of a bike lane. It was also proposed that the town considers having a "rent-a-bike" system, which will include a station at the Wellness Centre.

Architectural guidelines have been prepared to offer design principles of massing, exterior façade, windows, doors, streetscape, and parking. They were developed while considering the various housing types listed in the master plan. In addition, a separate set of environmental recommendations has been introduced to address orientation, nature, public health, urban agriculture, landscaping, and composting and recycling (Figures 3.21 and 3.22).

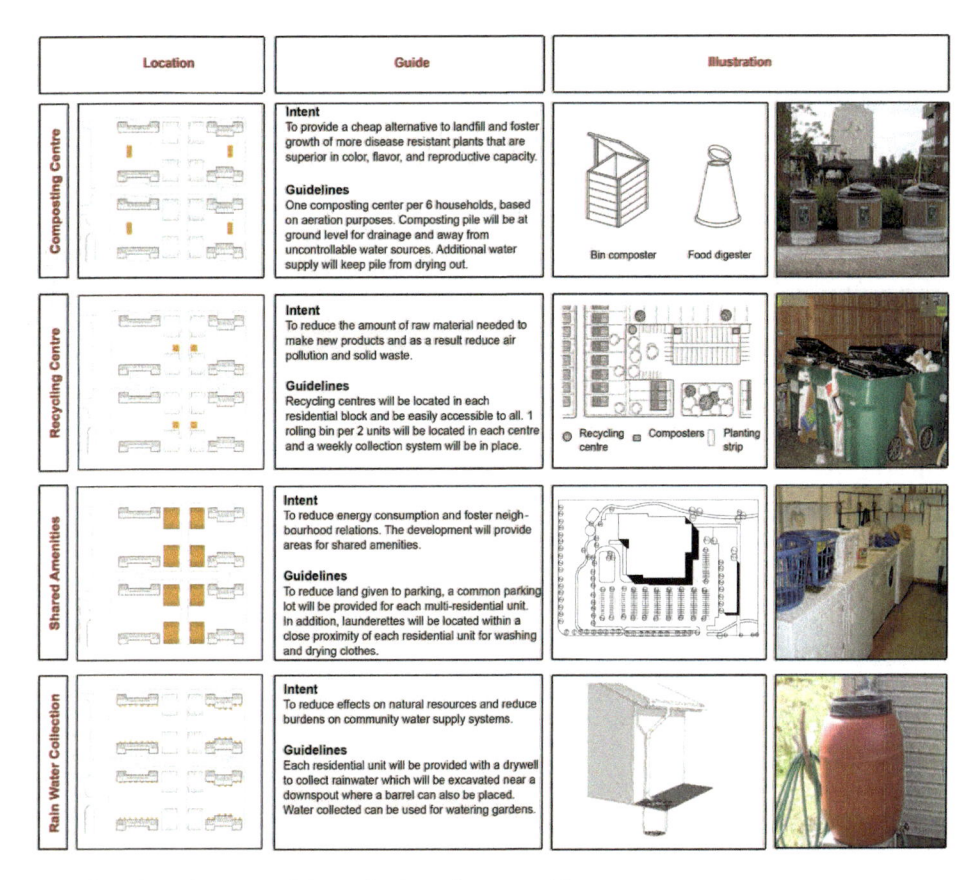

3.21 **Guidelines for some of the project's environmental features**

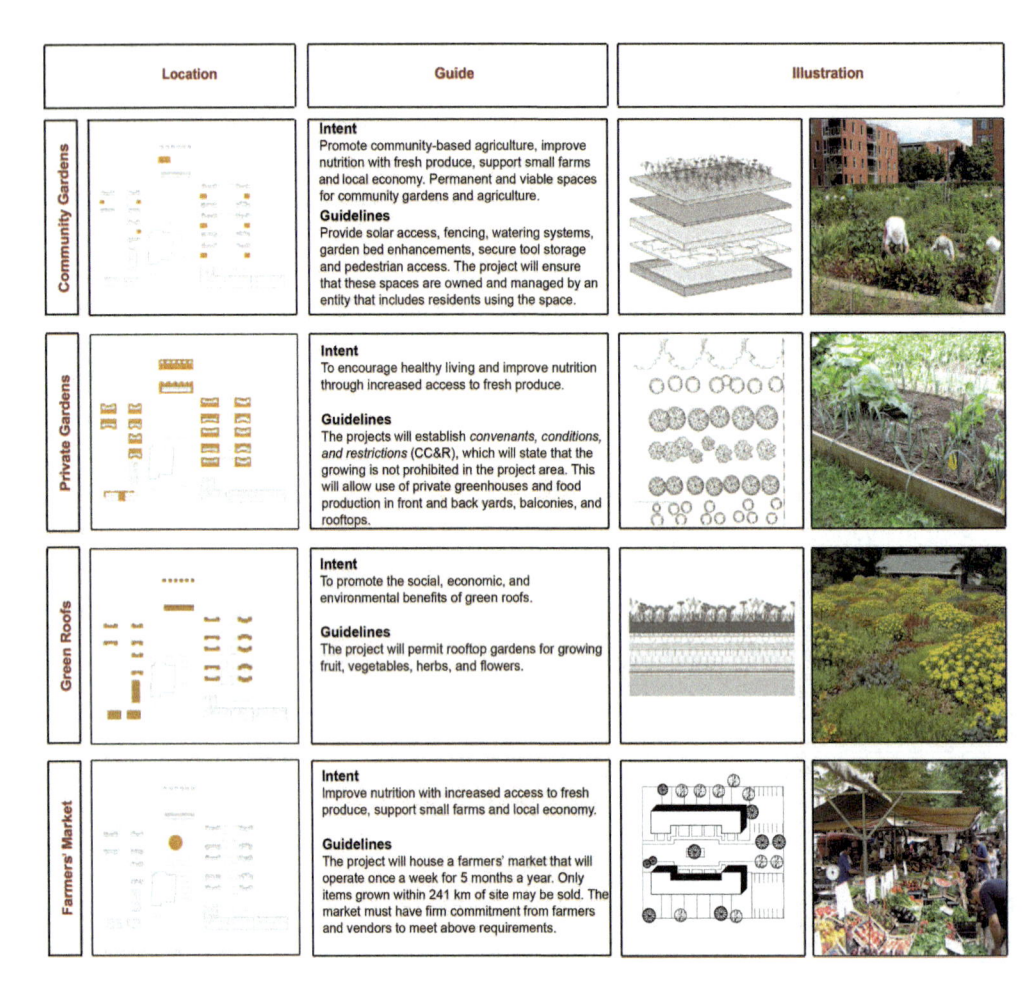

Location	Guide	Illustration
Community Gardens	**Intent** Promote community-based agriculture, improve nutrition with fresh produce, support small farms and local economy. Permanent and viable spaces for community gardens and agriculture. **Guidelines** Provide solar access, fencing, watering systems, garden bed enhancements, secure tool storage and pedestrian access. The project will ensure that these spaces are owned and managed by an entity that includes residents using the space.	
Private Gardens	**Intent** To encourage healthy living and improve nutrition through increased access to fresh produce. **Guidelines** The projects will establish *convenants, conditions, and restrictions* (CC&R), which will state that the growing is not prohibited in the project area. This will allow use of private greenhouses and food production in front and back yards, balconies, and rooftops.	
Green Roofs	**Intent** To promote the social, economic, and environmental benefits of green roofs. **Guidelines** The project will permit rooftop gardens for growing fruit, vegetables, herbs, and flowers.	
Farmers' Market	**Intent** Improve nutrition with increased access to fresh produce, support small farms and local economy. **Guidelines** The project will house a farmers' market that will operate once a week for 5 months a year. Only items grown within 241 km of site may be sold. The market must have firm commitment from farmers and vendors to meet above requirements.	

3.22 **Guidelines for the project's additional environmental features**

4
Moving Around

I strolled leisurely through the streets of Kfar Sava, a mid-sized city located in the eastern central part of Israel, enjoying the bright, warm winter sun. The upper floors of the four- to six-story white stucco apartment buildings that line the streets were terraced back, balconies were crowded with plants, and cars parked under an elevated first floor.

A sign pointing to a narrow path caught my eye. The paved 10-foot (3-meter) wide passageway ran between buildings with orange trees on one side and streetlights on the other (Figure 4.1). After a short walk, I entered a small square park, framed by buildings, with a play structure and tall broadleaf trees in its center. People stood on some of the upper-story balconies, watching the children at play. Two old men sat on a bench talking. Three young women occupying another bench facing the play area spoke with bold hand gestures, pausing from time to time to gently shake a stroller or shout at a child. The trees, the sounds, the conversations, and the sun added a warm backdrop to the setting.

I continued my walk, nodding to a passerby carrying bags of groceries. He seemed to have arrived from a busy commercial artery that I was about to cross. Several teenagers on their bikes passed me. I crossed the road and walked into the next inner court. A manmade grassy hill and play equipment formed its heart. The path took me to a pedestrian mall where people sat around tables under arched colonnades in a café. A meticulously landscaped civic square with a performing arts center and a library lay in the distance.

I arrived at Kenyon Arim, Kfar Sava's main shopping mall. The fashionable stores on various levels and the ground floors cafés were crowded. People on balconies of upper level residences watched the commotion below.

It had taken me 15 minutes to traverse the six-block stretch. The path connected neighborhoods, offered opportunities for exercise, and for turning strangers into acquaintances. Walking in Kfar Sava, I also experienced the intimacy that I could not have had if I had driven. I could view details and read people's expressions because of the slow rhythm in which the information revealed itself. I appreciated the original thought process that left a sliver of land between apartment buildings for pedestrians and cyclists. It was a fitting design for a small place that tied movement and human relations.

4.1 **A pathway in Kfar Sava, Israel**

Introducing pedestrian paths and considering mobility and connectivity aspects in planning have taken on an elevated importance in recent years. The need to curb urban sprawl, reduce dependency on private vehicles, and lower emission levels are among the facts that make planners rethink network design. One can, however, wonder whether strategies that are applied to transportation design in large urban centers are applicable to small or mid-sized towns like Kfar Sava. Small towns have unique characteristics worth noting along with recent trends in transportation planning.

The Effects of Mobility

One of the distinguishing features of small towns is their relatively reduced land mass. The distance between key community anchors, such as residential districts or public amenities, is often short which, of course, depends on the town. For example, in European historic centers those distances can be very small, whereas in North American or Australian towns they might be stretched out.

Another aspect of towns is their small population size, which affects the economic viability of public transit. Providing a regular bus service faces a reality of a reduced number of users. The service may not be provided at all or would only reach some areas. When no or partial transportation is provided, citizens are likely to use their own cars, further diminishing the viability of the service. Lack of transit service often affects those who need it most, such as seniors and lower-income groups leading to health and social challenges. It would be of value to list some of these challenges beginning with health.

The amount of time that people spend at the wheel has, regardless of their place of living, grown significantly. For example, in Canada, some 75 percent of the population use a car on a typical weekday and spend on average an hour a day commuting to work. Overall, 72 percent of those who live within 5 miles (8 km) of their destination never choose cycling as a mode of transportation. The effects on personal health are also significant. A Canadian Heart and Stroke Foundation (2005) survey found that since people who live in smaller towns and rural areas walk less, they are often at a higher risk of heart disease and stroke than their city-dwelling counterparts.

A similar conclusion was reached by Badland and Schofield (2006). In their study of the relationship between town size and physical activity level, they noted that in less compact residential areas people are less likely to utilize non-motorized travel modes. In comparing larger and small New Zealand cities they recommend that interventions developed in smaller regions need to focus on local infrastructure rather than the traditional focus on social support.

An outcome of physical inactivity is the rapid rise in obesity. Freeman and Quigg (2008) noted that car dependency among children in small towns with no public transit can affect their physical development, leading to obesity and lower self-esteem. The habit of driving children to school rather than having them walk or bicycle also predisposes them to a culture where being driven is the norm. Further, a study by Minster (2010) citing a German project called "Go to School on Foot" found that children have reduced the time they spend outdoors from four hours a day to only one half-hour per day. More of those who used a private car rather than the bus to get to school were overweight or obese.

According to the United Nations Children's Fund (UNICEF), children now account for one-third of all settlement dwellers, about one billion people, and are generally excluded from the decisions that shape the physical environment around them (Torres 2009). Cities are commonly planned for adults with cars which deprives children of an opportunity to be autonomous. Also, in rural settings, until children become adolescents and learn to drive, their mobility is limited. Their parents exercise control of the trips and the means of travel they use. Torres (2009) suggests that one can see how the problem can become circular: children are driven because it is dangerous, but it is dangerous because the world is adapted to automobiles.

Another outcome of mobility that has health and environmental ramifications is the level of emissions, as shown in Figure 4.2. The negative effect of the growing number of vehicles equals more health risks, greenhouse gas (GHG) emissions and global warming. Although the particular composition of motor vehicle exhaust varies according to the type of fuel, the primary constituents that pose health risks are present throughout. Carbon monoxide (CO), nitrogen dioxide (NO_2), ozone photochemical oxidants, and suspended particulate matter all contribute to the deterioration of urban air quality (Schwela and Zali 1999). A 2010 report by the US

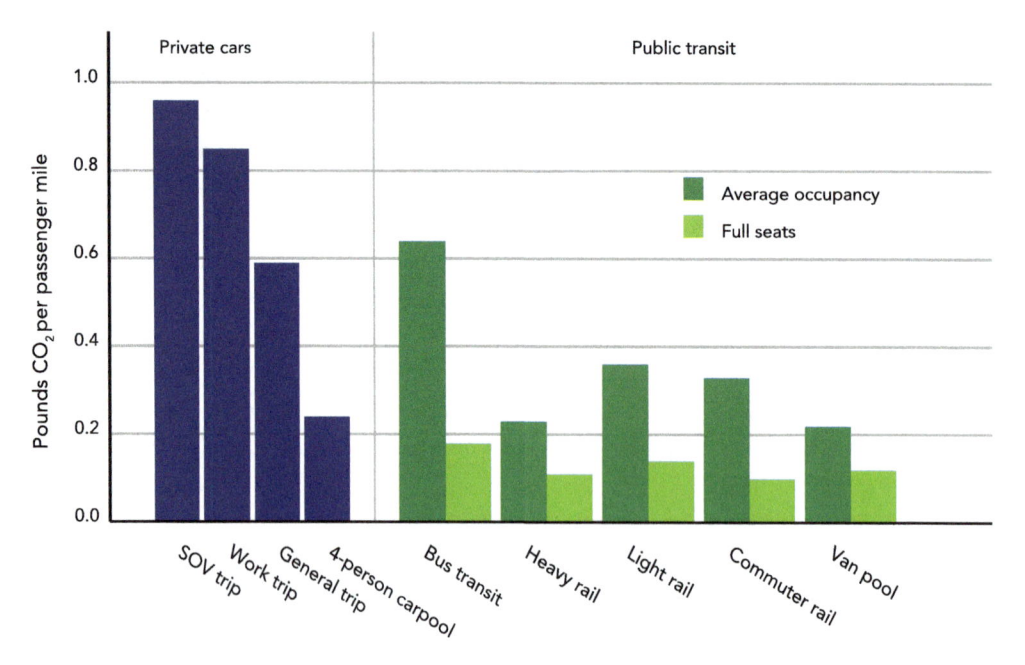

4.2 **Tailpipe emissions of common transport modes per passenger mile**

Department of Transportation after examining transit-related research, identified that public transportation can reduce GHGs in three principal ways: providing low emission alternatives to driving; facilitating compact land use, which reduces the need for longer trips; and minimizing the carbon footprint of transit operations and construction (Hodges 2010).

An aspect that can be regarded as the outcome of poor mobility and connectivity planning is the diminishment of sense of place. When people are driving to places and not walking or using public transit to reach them, the likelihood that they will meet other people is reduced. As a result, the social fabric, vital to a community and in particular small towns, can be eroded.

The economic impact of mobility is also worth noting. Litman (2009) writes that creating good walking conditions tends to be undervalued and unaccounted for in typical planning, as shown in Figure 4.3. The effect is a shift of resources from pedestrian and cycling to automobile-oriented land-use patterns. A study of consumer expenditures in UK towns found that those who walk to and from downtown shopping districts spend about 50 percent more per week supporting local retail establishments (Litman 2009). Meanwhile, the study suggests that spending on fuel and vehicles tends to contribute relatively little to local employment or business activity.

Recent societal challenges have given rise to new transformative ideas and, as a result, new enterprises. Whereas large capital is required to translate those ideas to products, at times, small investment is needed to develop them. In fact, many consumer products that have come to change our daily functions were home-based inventions. Having affordable housing for young entrepreneurs in small towns along travel corridors can support the creation of future jobs and wealth.

4.3 **Making places walkable: signage (top left), accessibility for people with reduced mobility (top right), changing street texture (bottom left), and prohibiting all except for local vehicular traffic (bottom right)**

Connecting Towns and Cities

For residents of small towns that depend on large metropolitan areas for employment and services, a daily commute by private car to the big city is common. The negative ramifications of such a practice are significant and include pollution, traffic congestion, and ongoing investment in infrastructure. In an era of greater environmental awareness and high cost of fuel the need to consider alternative transit systems has become urgent. Those alternatives will be discussed below.

Studies demonstrate that when new roads are constructed, people who used public transit switch back to driving their own cars (Hansen and Huang 1997). Research also shows that between 60 and 90 percent of new road capacity is consumed by new driving within five years of its opening. Several transportation principles are grounded in the idea that movement of people and cars should be regarded as an interconnected system to which various modes of transportation contribute, as illustrated in Figure 4.4. By encouraging people to travel in common, the number of cars and the need for new roads is reduced.

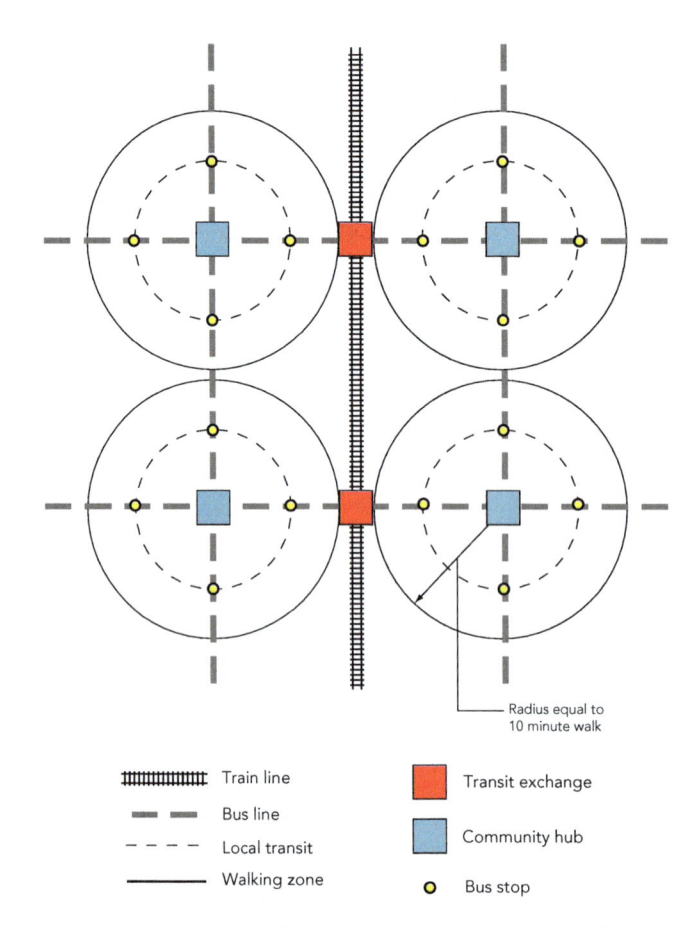

Radius equal to
10 minute walk

  Train line   Transit exchange

  Bus line

  Local transit   Community hub

  Walking zone   Bus stop

4.4 Movement of people and vehicles should be regarded as an interconnected system

Creating cost-effective transportation links between small towns and large centers has become critical to the prosperity of smaller places. In fact, recent years have seen significant resurgence in such systems in many countries (Kuby et al. 2004). Among the mass-transit methods introduced, are those known as the Bus Rapid Transit (BRT) that includes longer buses for which a special traffic lane is dedicated (Figure 4.5). There are also conventional and high speed trains that run more frequently during rush hours (Deng and Nelson 2011). The effect of these transit methods on small towns is significant. According to Garmendia et al. (2008), residents of small towns who would otherwise move to big cities choose to stay put. In addition, city dwellers who are looking for affordable housing move to small towns from which they commute. According to the authors, this contributes to the local housing market and fosters growth and vibrant economic activity. A planning pattern that sees communities built along transportation arteries is known as Transit-Oriented Development (TOD).

TOD is a strategic urban approach that argues for weaving various modes of commuting with residential and commercial land uses (Calthorp 1993). In recent decades, TOD has emerged as a leading concept in responding to some of the challenges that small towns located on transit corridors face in moving and housing their citizens. TOD was initially proposed in the mid-1990s as the shortfalls of past planning practices grew evident. It underwent its first iterations by 2004, when a new wave of projects proceeded after the founding of the US Center for Transit-Oriented Development (Dittmar and Ohland 2004).

Some of the benefits that are associated with TOD are enhanced access to the transit network by households of all incomes and reduced transportation costs, improved public health due to increased walking and cycling, improved access to local and regional amenities and job opportunities, increased transit ridership, creation of a sense of community and place, and the use of transit as an organizing development principle.

In recent years, TOD has gained support as a tool for promoting growth of towns while minimizing the effects of sprawl, leveraging economic development, and catering to changing lifestyles and market demands. According to Cervero (2008b), it responds to a desire for reduced car ownership and to provide more affordable housing. It has been appealing in its focus in linking and coordinating public transit, housing policies, and sustainable urbanism.

4.5 **A Bus Rapid Transit stop near Vijfhuizen, the Netherlands**

As of 2007, over 100 such developments exist near American transit agency property (Cervero 2008a). Though the emergence of TOD has been advocated over the last two decades, the approach on which it is based derives from old urban planning principles.

In small communities TOD seeks to adjust planning practices and make them functional, economic, livable, and accessible. Congregating people within walking or cycling distance of a major public transit route that lets them reach, using multi-modal methods, other places, is seen by experts as a means to achieve significant reduction in the number of car trips taken by citizens. By combining residential and commercial land uses, "complete communities" are established where people can live, shop, work, study, or be entertained.

A chosen transit technology commonly defines the TOD corridors; yet, they also depend on the system's design and quality. A high quality, high frequency service along dedicated lines provides certainty to investors that it will not be suddenly abolished. TOD potential is also determined by the walkability or bikeability of an area, as well as the presence of retail amenities and the performance of the housing market (Center for Transit-Oriented Development 2010).

There are essentially three transit corridor types: *destination connector*, *commuter*, and *district circulator*, which are illustrated in Figure 4.6. This is a useful generalization, yet actual corridors tend to have a more complex structure and are usually composed of a mix of types. Destination connectors accommodate ridership in both directions throughout the day because they serve employment centers and other public or residential destinations. Yet, the most significant contribution to the planning of TODs at the corridor level is that it benefits not only the region, but also the towns along them.

Building advanced transit systems using the latest modes and technologies requires large investment (Figure 4.7). Such costs can only be justified when those systems are well used. A large number of paying users will render these systems economically sustainable.

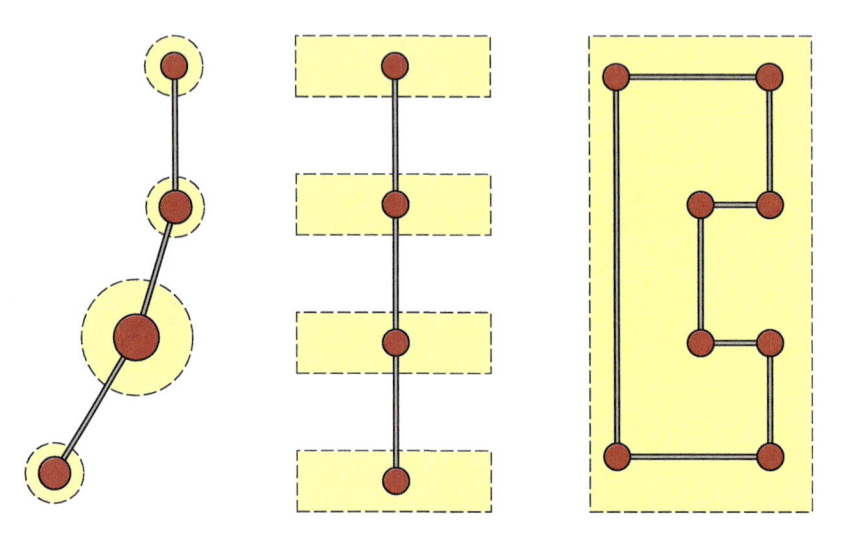

4.6 **The three Transit-Oriented Development (TOD) corridors are: destination connectors (left), commuter (middle), and district circulator (right)**

4.7 **Driverless transit technology connects Ørestad and Copenhagen, in Denmark**

When considering successes and failures of public transit systems, economists shift the emphasis to accessibility. They argue that a system is as good as its number of users. Investing in unused networks does not make economic sense. In addition, when a new transit system can have subsidiary advantages such as job creation or expanding the stock of affordable housing, investments are further justified. In other words, a transit system needs to be sustainable on all fronts.

Planning Mobility Networks in Small Towns

The amount of driving by an average household in the developed world has increased significantly regardless of location. Yet, Ewing et al. (2003, in Higgins 2005) suggest that wise urban planning that considers the roads network can greatly reduce the rate of oil dependence

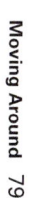

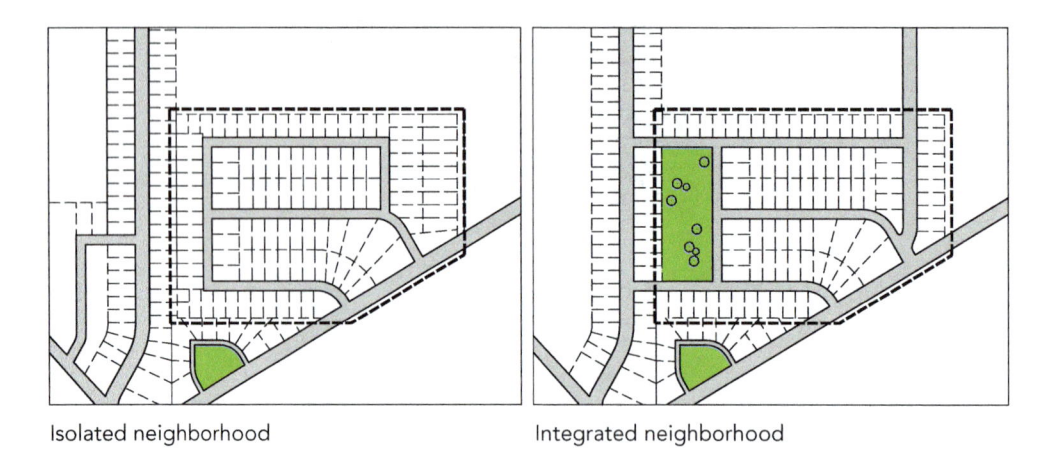

Isolated neighborhood   Integrated neighborhood

4.8 **A town's roads network needs to integrate new development (right) rather than force unnecessary longer driving distance (left)**

and carbon emissions as well as increase people's activity level of exercise (Figure 4.8). This section outlines macro and micro planning strategies to improve mobility in small towns.

One can argue that an initial planning decision that determines a town's urban form will also greatly affect its mobility patterns. For example, residents of a development on a town's edge will likely be forced to drive to the core. While evaluating travel patterns, Turcotte (2008) found that at over 6.2 miles (10 km) from the city center the housing density of a neighborhood will have little effect on residents' car use. In other words, beyond a certain distance, people will not attempt to reach their destination by foot or bicycle. Unlike spread-out metropolitan areas, small towns need to grow organically around a core and include connection between their districts as well as between them and the center.

A sustainable planning strategy in small towns that has been noted above is to increase density. It was demonstrated that people who reside in compact communities tend to drive less, as illustrated in Figure 4.9. The question is: what level of density would foster greater walkability? The typical twentieth century urban form has two distinct densities. The first, is lower density with an average of 7 units per acre (17 units per hectare) commonly associated with sprawl. In contrast, a city's average would be 31 units per acre (77.5 units per hectare).

By combining the planning features of both, urban forms suitable to small towns or parts of them can be introduced. Such a design may average 22 units per acre (55 units per hectare), with rear private parking and yards. Minimal, though acceptable, widths will separate the houses. The new design will mix traditional with contemporary planning ideas to foster better mobility.

According to Van der Ryn and Calthorpe (1986), many of the trips taken daily by drivers are to non-residential destinations and can be avoided if these functions could be closer to homes, as illustrated in Figure 4.10. Badland et al. (2008) found that people who reside close to their place of work or study are more likely to perceive they can engage in transport-related physical activity, or actually do. Therefore, a chosen strategic urban location and the clustering of key community amenities will make it easy to visit several of them in a single trip. When

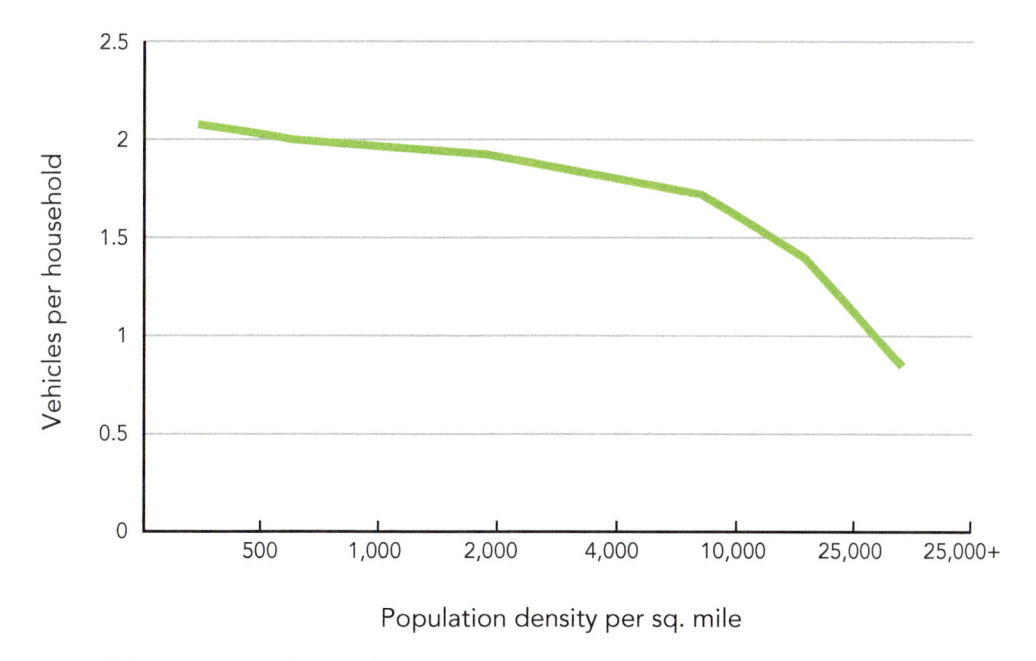

Population density per sq. mile

4.9 **Vehicle ownership per household decreases with increased residential density**

possible, having commercial and residential uses in one building will help some citizens reduce their travel pattern altogether.

The proliferation and use of the Internet have enabled the introduction of home businesses. They can contribute to the reduction of travel time since they will be used by nearby residents. The placement of schools in the community's heart can also foster a culture of walking or bike riding among children. The same school can also house a library or a sports facility that is open to all citizens after hours. These assertions are supported by Cao et al. (2007), who found that land-use policies designed to put residents close to destinations and provide them with alternative transportation options will actually lead to less driving and more walking.

Another aspect to consider while developing mobility networks in small towns is public transit. Most municipalities argue that the system needs to be economically self-sustaining, an objective that is hard to achieve with fewer riders. Yet, it was recognized that public transit contributes to housing affordability and social equality, as it prevents the need to own and maintain a car. A bus service, or at the very least partial service, therefore, needs to be an integral part of the planning process. When designing a public transit network, it should be done in conjunction with streets and paths in mind for maximum use. The system can be hierarchically organized, allowing residents to easily reach other buses or trains that connect with major urban centers.

Cost-saving measures may include smaller buses that use alternative sources of energy like the ones used in many European cities such as Urbino, Italy (Figure 4.11). Also, the service can be offered on demand and special vehicles can be provided for seniors and people with

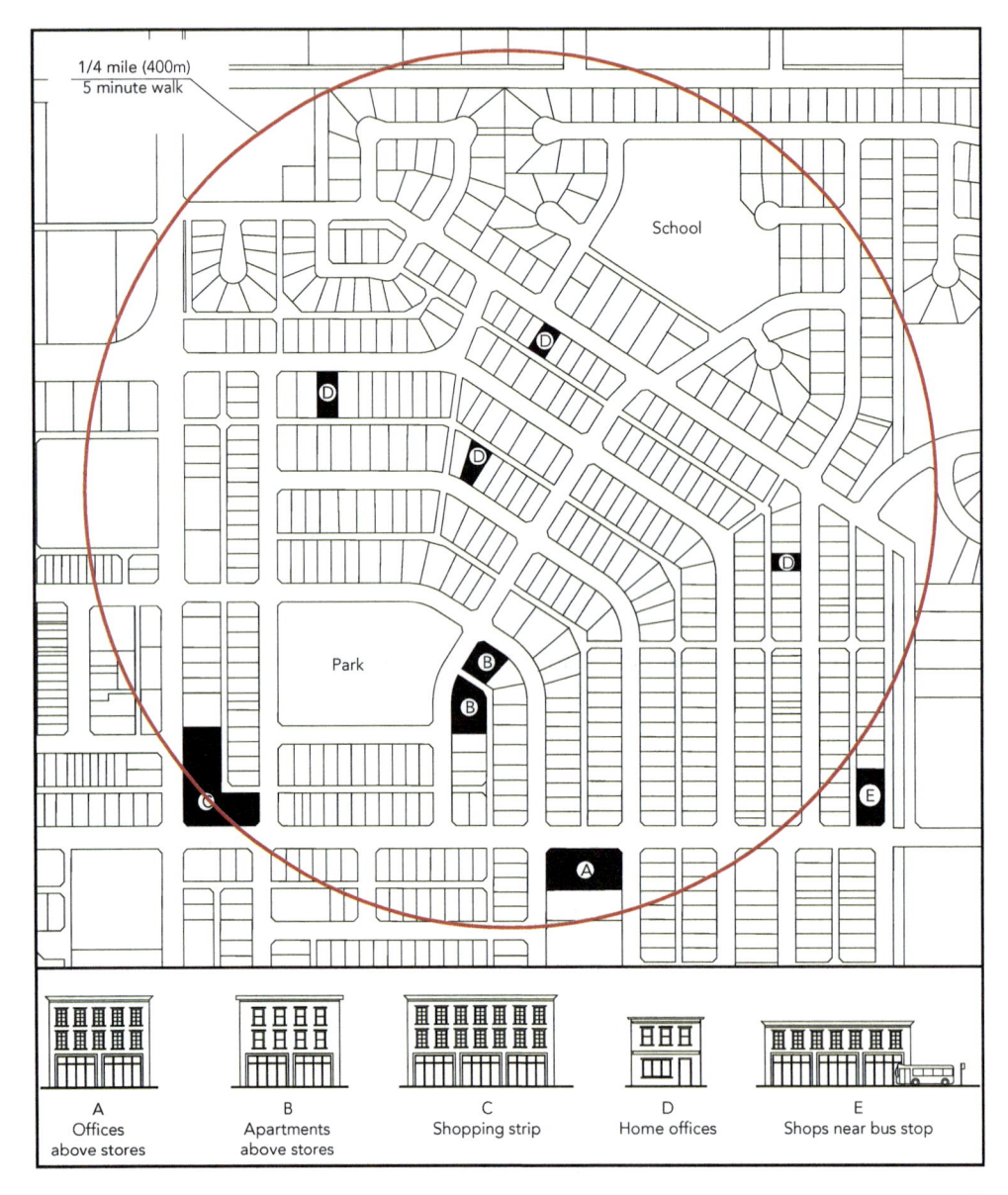

1/4 mile (400m)
5 minute walk

School

Park

A	B	C	D	E
Offices above stores	Apartments above stores	Shopping strip	Home offices	Shops near bus stop

4.10 Weaving residential and non-residential land uses will help reduce reliance on private cars and will render a place more sustainable

reduced mobility. In sparsely populated areas, the service may be offered at rush hour only. Public transit also needs to correlate between the frequency of service and the type of users. For example, in neighborhoods with younger families more buses can travel during morning and afternoon rush hours when schools are in session.

Providing free shuttle buses is an idea that can also be considered in small towns. The City of Langford in the Province of British Columbia, Canada, introduced such a service which

4.11 **Cost-saving measures in small towns may include the use of shorter buses, like this one, in Urbino, Italy**

connects residential with commercial areas (Figure 4.12). The cost of the service is offset by advertising, voluntary contributions by passengers, and the city. The advantages to the community were numerous, including stimulating local economic activity, reducing traffic load, and fostering a healthy lifestyle.

Parking is another issue that affects mobility in small towns. Since residents are often traveling by private vehicles, parking becomes a concern primarily in core areas. In their article "Parking at Mixed-Use Centers in Small Cities," Marshall and Garrick (2006) studied parking patterns in several small New England towns and found that the number of parking spaces required by zoning regulations is significantly greater than the number being used, even at peak use days. Large expanses of common parking areas or a succession of street-facing garage doors also has poor aesthetic, as well as negative health and ecological ramifications. When more outdoor area is devoted to parking, less is allocated to parks and streetscape, and it is simply not pleasant to walk through or live near.

4.12 **A trolley stop in Langford, British Columbia, Canada**

Fostering Walking and Cycling Habits

Cycling is no longer a fringe mode of transportation. Pucher et al. (2011) noted that over the past decade, there has been a large increase in funding pro-bike policies and initiatives by central governments and municipalities (Figure 4.13). In this regard, the relatively limited area that small towns occupy and the fewer vehicles that travel on their roads make them highly suitable for active moods of mobility.

Rohrer et al. (2004) looked at the health aspects of walking and found that people who perceived that they had no place to walk were significantly less healthy than those who thought they had at least one place to walk to. They suggested that support of walkable neighborhoods, streets closing to vehicular traffic, and education of patients about options for walking may be in the best interest of health promotion officials in communities (Figure 4.14). While examining walking to public transit, Besser and Dannenberg (2005) concluded that walking to and from public transportation can help physically inactive populations, especially low-income groups, attain the recommended level of daily physical exercise.

The question is: how should small towns align themselves with and act upon these fundamental shifts in mobility? It is hard to offer a template response for all locations, yet some researchers have offered various observations.

4.13 **Various measures can be taken by municipalities to make riding a bike convenient and safer**

4.14 **Closing downtown streets to vehicular traffic in Burlington, Vermont, US**

When one recalls the names of North American places that have dedicated street lanes for bicycles or bike-sharing programs, few small towns make the list. In fact, in their paper "Factors Correlated with Bicycle Commuting: A Study in Six Small US Cities," Handy and Xing (2011) cited 2005 US Census Bureau data that suggested only 0.4 percent of workers regularly rode bicycles to work. Turcotte (2008) also noted a marked difference between large Canadian urban centers and smaller towns. He found that in 2001, 81 percent of the residents of smaller communities with populations under 250,000 went everywhere by car—either as a driver or a passenger—compared with 69 percent of residents of large cities.

In studying "Sidewalk Planning and Policies in Small Cities," Evans-Cowley (2006) noted several challenges. They include lack of pedestrian activity, sidewalk maintenance, pedestrian planning, financial support, and technical capacity. Therefore, the introduction of active means of mobility may require a targeted approach that considers the scale and resources of small towns.

Fostering better coordination between motorized traffic and walking and cycling was argued by Jacobsen et al. (2009). They recommend interventions with small cost implications such as traffic calming measures, 15 km/h or 30 km/h zones, congestion charging, bicycle lanes on major streets, and giving priority to the rights and safety of vulnerable road users as opposed to vehicles, as shown in Figure 4.15. A similar suggestion was made by Dumbaugh and Li (2011) who found that factors associated with a vehicle crashing into a pedestrian and cyclist are largely similar to those resulting in crashes between vehicles. Therefore, increasing safety, through either design or policing, needs to be a first step in introducing modes of active transportation.

Another measure that can be introduced in small towns with a relatively small price tag is improvement to the built environment itself. Winters et al. (2010) suggested that well-marked paths, signage, traffic calming devices, and road markings tend to foster biking and walking. Similar strategies were introduced by Dutch, Danish, and German cities to support cycling (Pucher and Buehler 2008). Such strategies include: bike parking facilities, coordination with public transport, traffic education and training, and the enactment of supporting traffic laws (Figure 4.16). In an attempt to promote bike use the same countries offered simplified access to bikes through sharing programs, bike trip planning, and public awareness campaigns. Driving cars was made difficult by reducing the automobile speed limit, increasing parking charges, automobile taxation, and strict land-use policies.

4.15 **A sign accommodating pedestrians in a French community**

4.16 **Bike attachment to a bus in Thunder Bay, Ontario, Canada**

4.17 **A high street closed for vehicular traffic in Kent, UK**

Accommodating pedestrians can also be achieved by introducing safety awareness programs (ITE 2005). They include simple and relatively inexpensive educational interventions aimed at making walkers and motorists take note of each other. Other measures with a higher price tag can be introduced in denser areas which are known to be more walkable (Saelens et al. 2003). Shared streets, where cars travel at a reduced speed to compensate for the vulnerability of cyclists and pedestrians and that also enhance interactions between neighbors, is such a measure. Known in the Netherlands as *Woonorf* or Streets for Living, these arrangements can suit small towns. On these streets, furniture and plants are combined to let motorized traffic take place on the terms of the non-motorized users. A lack of differentiation between the roadway and sidewalk creates unified streets, while strategically placed parking spaces and landscaping reduce vehicular speed. This concept can also be applied to existing streets without major reconstruction expenditures.

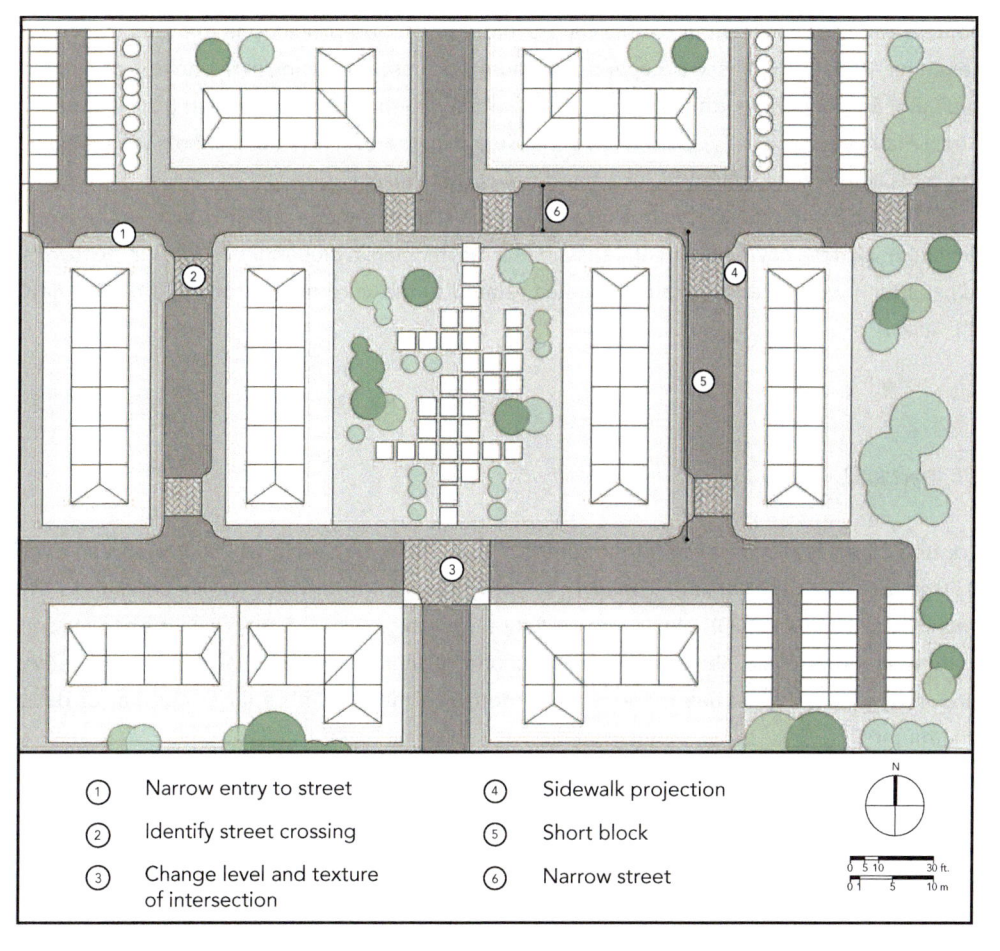

①	Narrow entry to street	④	Sidewalk projection
②	Identify street crossing	⑤	Short block
③	Change level and texture of intersection	⑥	Narrow street

4.18 **Traffic calming measures**

Road bumps can also reduce speed, or highly textured driving surfaces can be used. The bumps can be placed at the entrance to a street to indicate an increase in residential density and the need to slow down. Stamped concrete or cobblestone segments can also be effective while emphasizing gateways and entrances. A technique that is particularly useful when dealing with heavily traveled streets is to raise the level of the road at intersections. As a result, the continuous and uninterrupted crosswalk ensures that pedestrians will have priority. Some traffic calming measures are illustrated in Figure 4.18.

Retooling for Sustainability in Stony Plain

External circumstances can act as a catalyst for change. This was the motive that triggered my invitation to the town of Stony Plain, in the Province of Alberta, Canada. The town has seen its population and building activity increase significantly and needed to address these. Most notable were the newly built residential developments, and projections that this trend will continue. Alberta's oil-based prosperity, the increased cost of housing in the nearby provincial capital of Edmonton, and the quality of life offered were the main causes that drew people to Stony Plain. Lower density, lush green parks, low crime rates, and good schools were among the aspects that were valued by locals and newcomers alike (Figure 4.19).

A desire to maintain this quality of life, yet usher in a managed growth, was the overarching goal in the development of a sustainable master plan, a blueprint of sorts, for the town's expansion. I was asked to examine issues related to the current land use and offer a new direction.

Context and History

Located 20 miles (33 km) west of Edmonton, Stony Plain, population 15,000, is spread over 6.56 square miles (17 sq. km). The town is linked via two route ways, which cross it, to the capital region (Figure 4.20). Along with neighboring Spruce Grove, Stony Plain is a service and commercial hub to 60,000 inhabitants of mostly rural agriculture-based hamlets. Relative proximity to the capital has made it a bedroom community with a large number of daily commuters.

The town's settlement dates back to 1881 and the establishment of the first homestead in the area. In the early 1900s, Stony Plain was part of the Canadian National Railway network, for which it served as the western terminal. The railway stop was also the catalyst for the town's economic expansion. Its urban evolution began in what is today the historic core with gridiron street layout typical of early twentieth century mid-west towns. There were parallel residential streets and a main artery along which commercial and institutional amenities were built.

4.19 **Images of Stony Plain, Alberta, Canada**

With successive population growth waves after World War II, rapid residential developments began, and new neighborhoods were built off the core. Developers who owned land often dictated the direction of the town's expansion. As a result, the community east side saw accelerated building activity. With the proliferation of cars, new subdivisions could be located further away from existing ones, and the organic growth pattern characteristic of earlier periods somehow diminished. The development of Meridian Meadows marks a change in Stony Plain's urban evolution, as for the first time a neighborhood was built across the highway.

The town's current land-use plan demonstrates a pattern consistent with its size. Commercial as well as light industrial activity is placed parallel to the highway. Commerce is also permitted in various zones within the town, most notably in the center. Residential land use, mostly low density, constitutes the majority of the municipal area. Land reserved for future

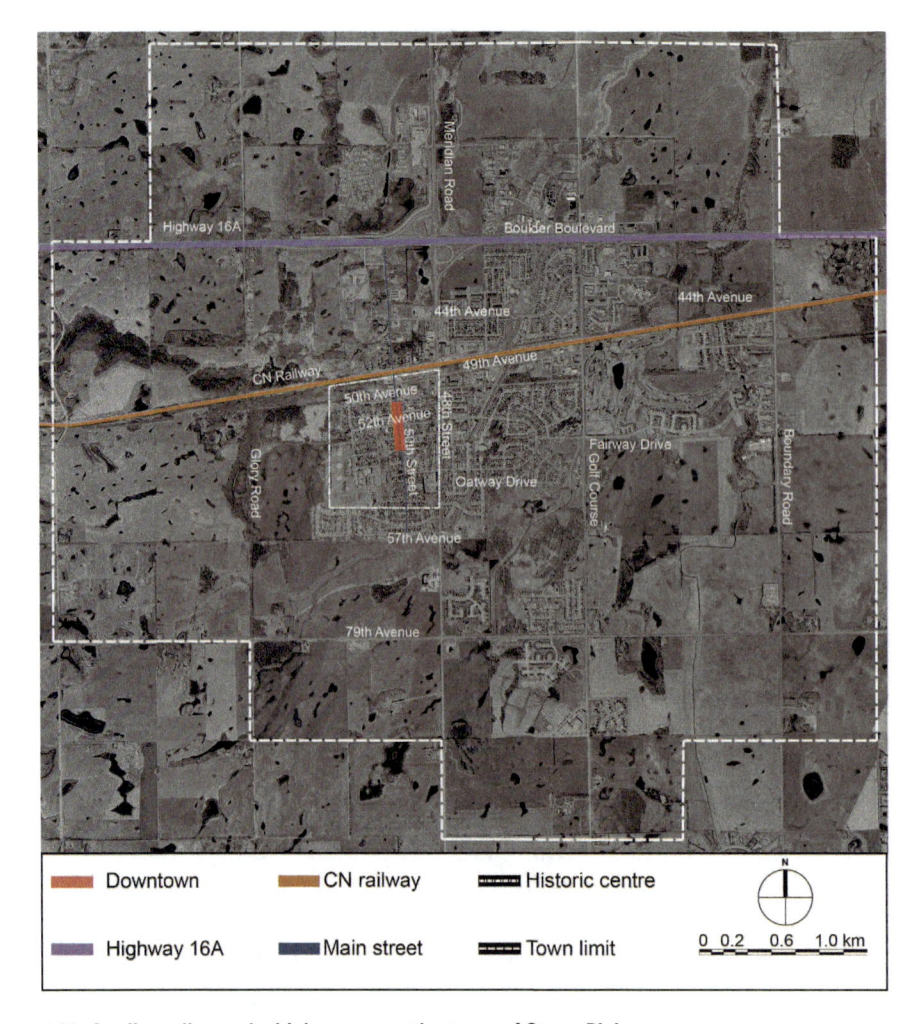

4.20 **A railway line and a highway cross the town of Stony Plain**

expansion is located in the south, east, west, and north across from the highway. Other notable features are a well-developed and used recreational trails network of which the citizens take great pride and several municipal parks that reflect the high quality of life that the town's residents enjoy.

Planning for Sustainability

To chart Stony Plain's future urban development along sustainable principles, we considered strategies that strengthen its economic performance, environmental conditions, social profile, and cultural attributes. The plan's key features are described below. On the foundation of the existing land uses we reformulated the town's master plan. In the new proposal, illustrated in Figure 4.21, we preserved some of the former land uses and made adjustments to residential, commercial, and industrial areas. The new plan proposes to place a less dense residential area on the town's northwest and denser neighborhoods south of the highway.

In recent years the town permitted development of neighborhoods in a decentralized fashion disconnected from downtown and from one another. We recommended that Stony Plain will grow organically around its core. To maintain its country image, it was suggested that corridors with medium-density housing will be established parallel to arterial roads and in some instances on the periphery of existing neighborhoods. We also suggested a mixed-use medium-density area east of downtown (Figure 4.22). Expanding downtown and increasing its population would help revitalize the area and support local commerce.

A demographic forecast indicates that Stony Plain will see significant population increase and building activity which stand in contrast to a desire to maintain its "small town" character. In our view this can be achieved if more land, greater than the required 10 percent, is allocated to green public spaces in future neighborhoods.

To foster walkability, it was recommended that future services and commercial amenities will be located at the intersections of arterial roads that border several developments (Figure 4.23). It would also support local economic activities. Rather than locate new schools on the edge as is currently the practice, we suggested siting them in the heart of some neighborhoods.

To strengthen the core, we recommended that the town limits the building of "big box" stores south of the highway and encourages the construction of taller apartment buildings with ground floor businesses. Encouraging work–live opportunities was also recommended. As the core becomes a draw, more effort will need to be invested in its appearance. Downtown needs to have architectural design guidelines to ensure harmony of forms, materials, colors, and proportions. To broaden its tax base, diversify its economy, and reduce the daily commute to Edmonton, the plans suggest development of a new light industrial area off the highway for the many companies which service the oil industry and are currently seeking locations.

A meeting place for a town's people is a public square. At present, Stony Plain does not have one. We recommended that the town construct such a gathering place across from city hall. Preferably, the square will be framed by tall buildings and have apartments above ground floor businesses. To foster better integration among residents of different ages and backgrounds, housing types will be mixed in neighborhoods and bi-generational homes for extended families will be encouraged. The design of future homes will conform to new design guidelines that will foster greater consistency of appearance.

As part of its effort to draw to the town young families, we saw a need to increase the affordable housing stock. As a result, the town will require developers to allocate a certain percentage of all built units to affordable housing as part of its neighborhood planning.

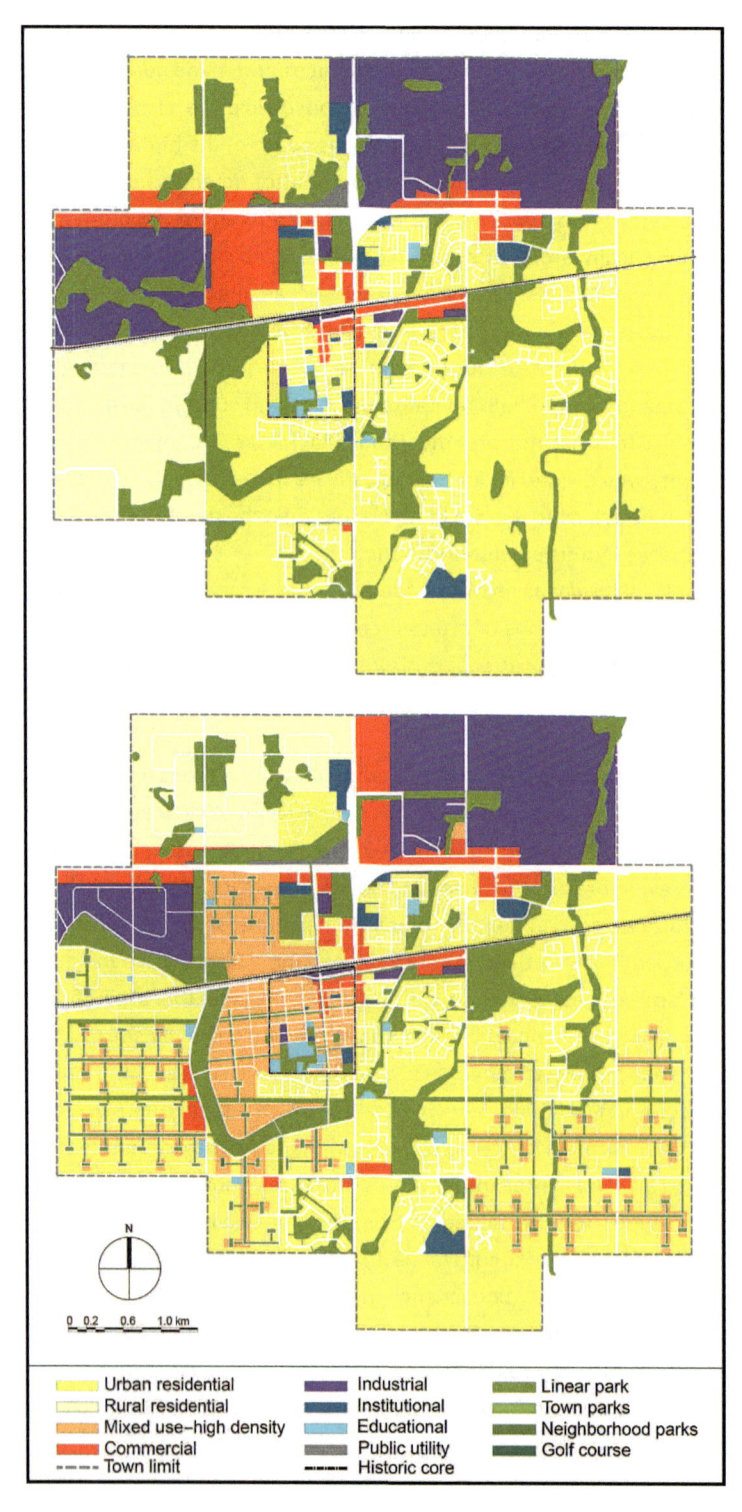

Legend:

- Urban residential
- Rural residential
- Mixed use–high density
- Commercial
- Town limit
- Industrial
- Institutional
- Educational
- Public utility
- Historic core
- Linear park
- Town parks
- Neighborhood parks
- Golf course

0 0.2 0.6 1.0 km

4.21 **Existing land use (top) and proposed (bottom)**

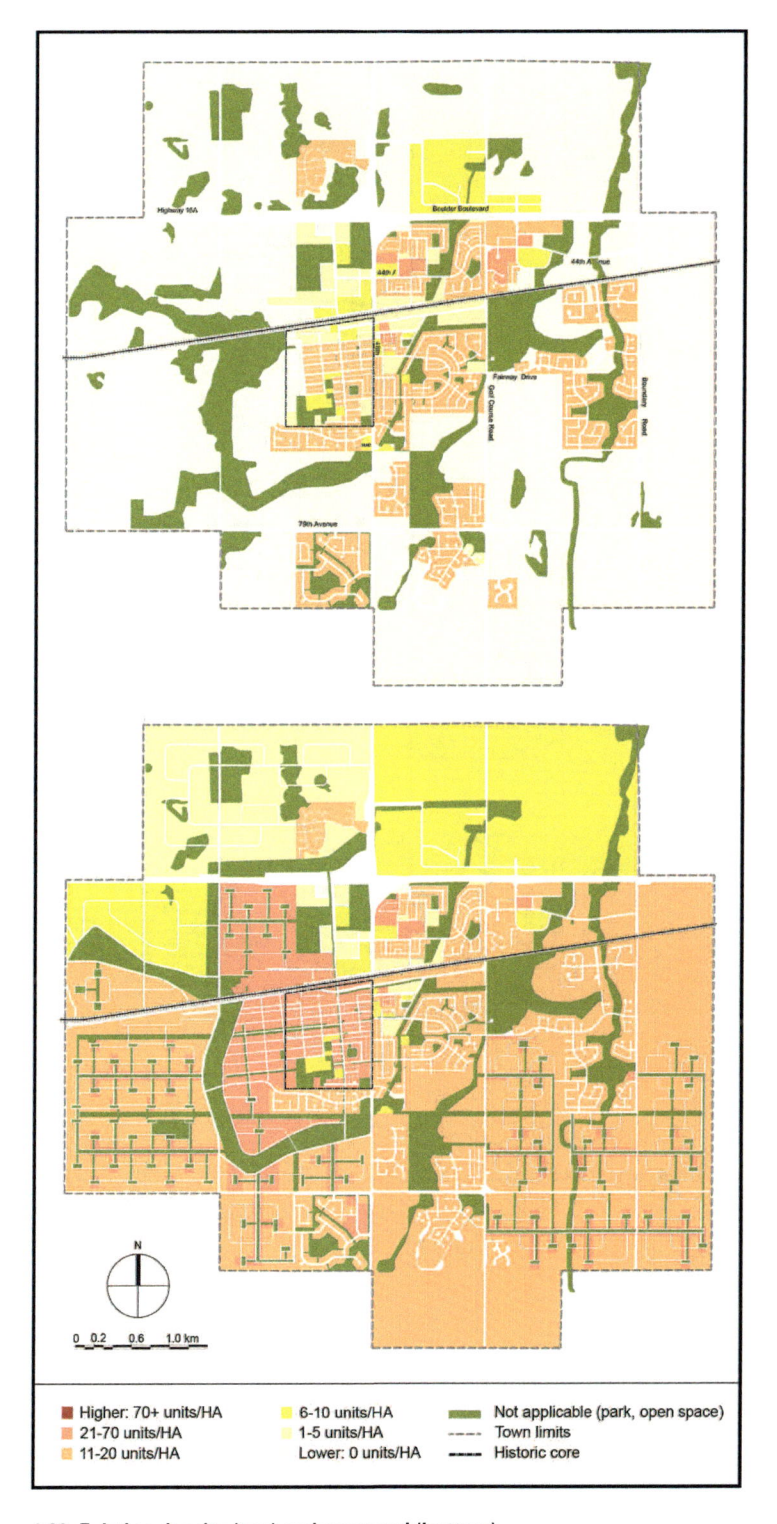

Higher: 70+ units/HA 6–10 units/HA Not applicable (park, open space)

21–70 units/HA 1–5 units/HA Town limits

11–20 units/HA Lower: 0 units/HA Historic core

4.22 **Existing density (top) and proposed (bottom)**

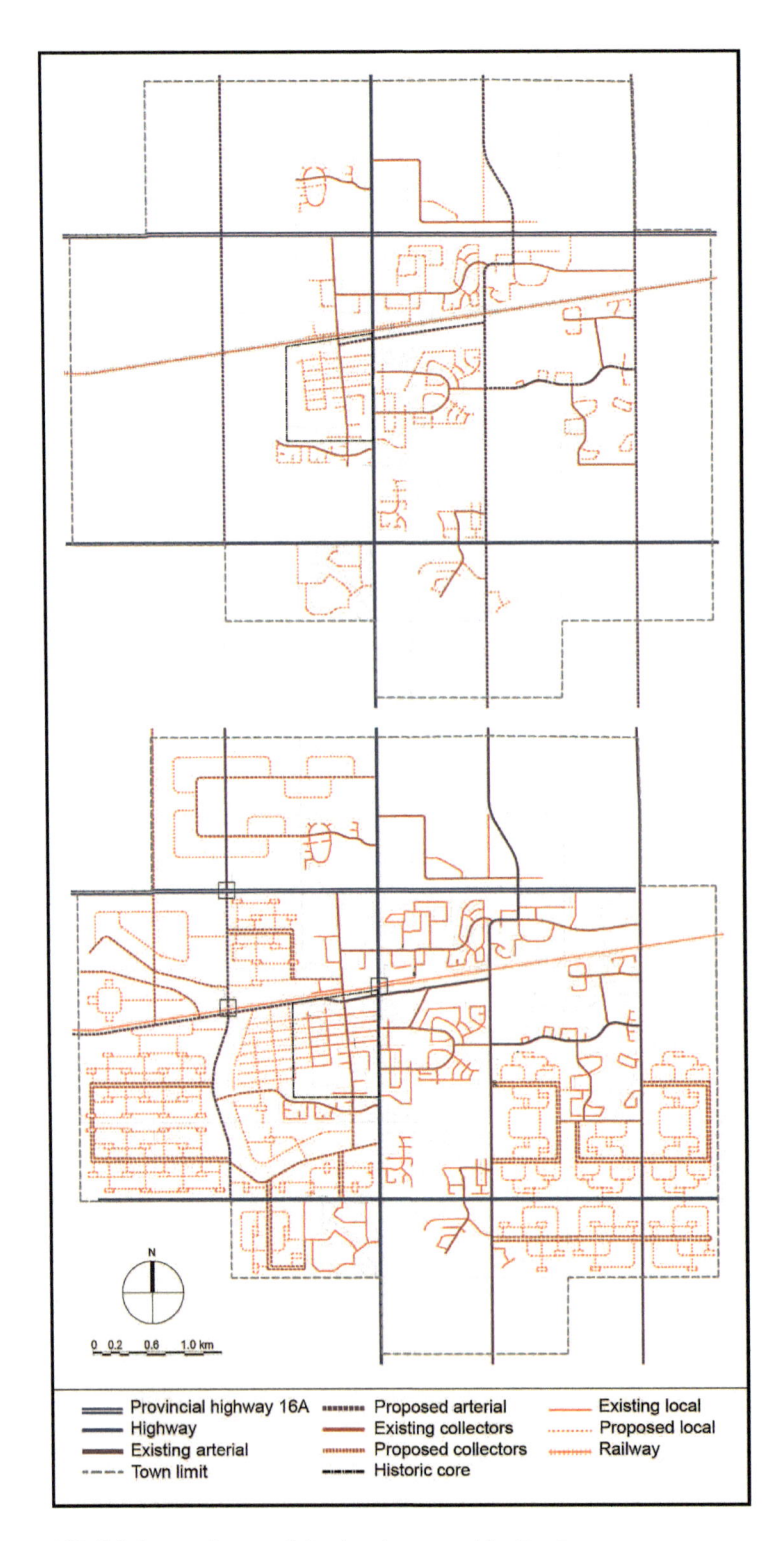

Provincial highway 16A Proposed arterial Existing local
Highway Existing collectors Proposed local
Existing arterial Proposed collectors Railway
Town limit Historic core

N

0 0.2 0.6 1.0 km

4.23 **Existing road network (top) and proposed (bottom)**

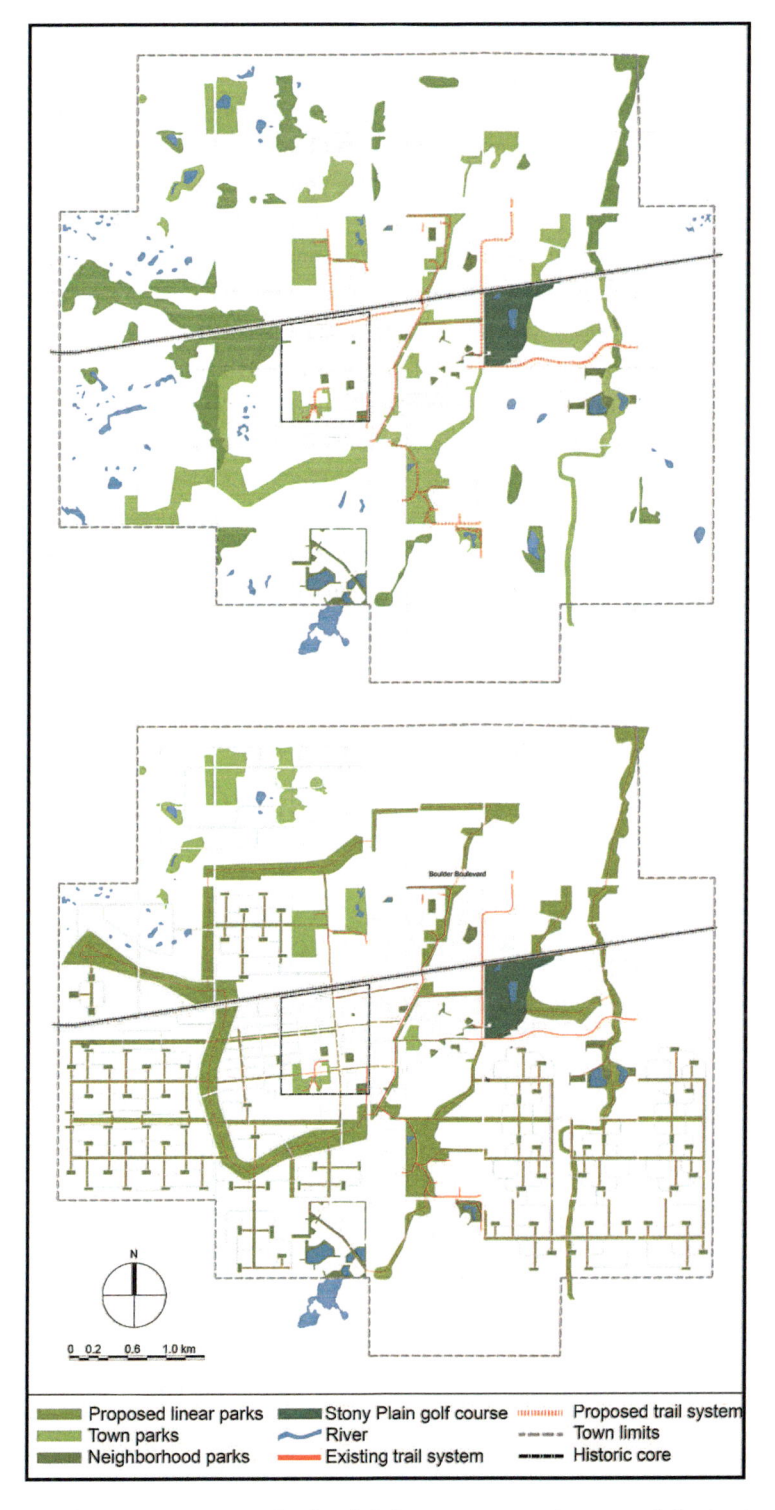

Proposed linear parks   Stony Plain golf course   Proposed trail system
Town parks   River   Town limits
Neighborhood parks   Existing trail system   Historic core

4.24 **Existing open spaces (top) and their use as commuting network (bottom)**

Green Areas and Transportation

Since Stony Plain intends to extend its highly attractive trails and park system to several residential areas, our proposal suggested that all neighborhoods, new and old, will be linked to this corridor. We envision the establishment of a hierarchical system made up of principal linear parks and a secondary network of neighborhood green spaces. Since the linear parks currently have a bike and pedestrian path, it can also act as an alternative active mobility network (Figures 4.24, 4.25, and 4.26). We also suggested that the town will adopt a policy and see that every new street will have a sidewalk on at least one side.

Due to economic reasons and similar to other towns of its size Stony Plain does not have a local transit service. It puts a strain on those who need it most and cannot drive, such as the seniors. Our recommendation was to explore the introduction of such a service. To sustain its economic vitality it may run small buses mostly during rush hour with on-demand service for the elderly. In addition we recognize a need to alter the current road network to reduce speed and encourage pedestrian and cycling movements. In cooperation with neighboring towns a rapid bus service will be introduced between Stony Plain and Edmonton to the benefit of daily commuters.

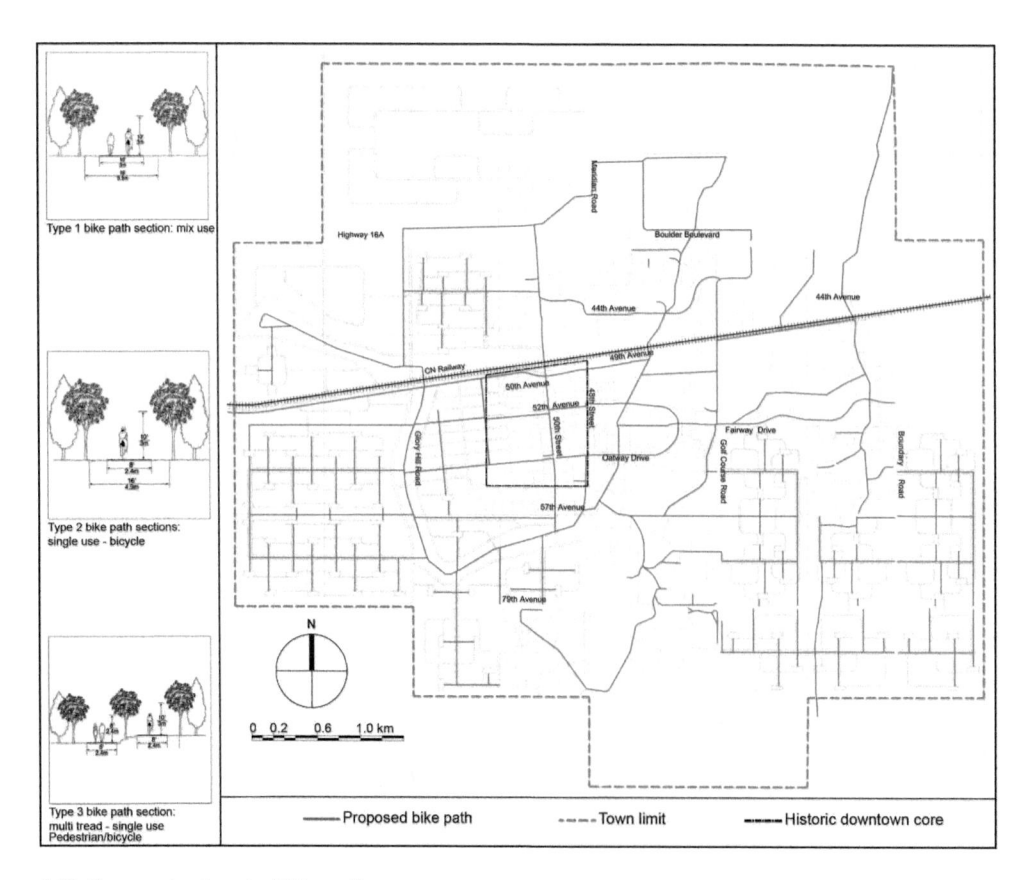

4.25 **Proposed network of bike paths**

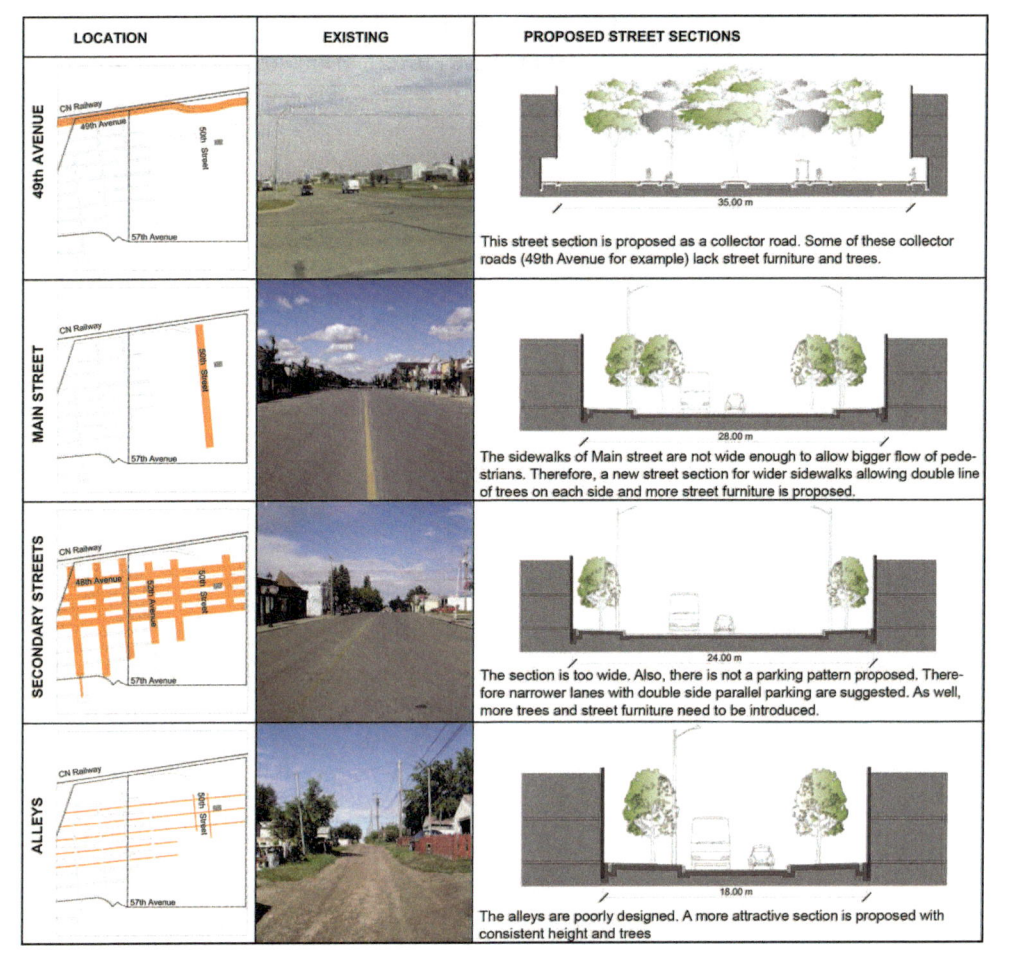

LOCATION	EXISTING	PROPOSED STREET SECTIONS

49th AVENUE — 35.00 m — This street section is proposed as a collector road. Some of these collector roads (49th Avenue for example) lack street furniture and trees.

MAIN STREET — 28.00 m — The sidewalks of Main street are not wide enough to allow bigger flow of pedestrians. Therefore, a new street section for wider sidewalks allowing double line of trees on each side and more street furniture is proposed.

SECONDARY STREETS — 24.00 m — The section is too wide. Also, there is not a parking pattern proposed. Therefore narrower lanes with double side parallel parking are suggested. As well, more trees and street furniture need to be introduced.

ALLEYS — 18.00 m — The alleys are poorly designed. A more attractive section is proposed with consistent height and trees

4.26 **Proposed street sections**

Environmental Considerations

The need to address global and local environmental concerns requires taking steps to ensure the adoption of suitable practices. Stony Plain will therefore adopt commonly used environmental guidelines for homes and neighborhoods. As an official policy the town will explore the possibility to require that developers of all future residential and commercial buildings will conduct impact assessments prior to planning.

In addition, we argued that the town needs to lead by example and have all its public buildings energy-efficient and use low-emission alternative power sources. The need to lower energy costs also requires a new approach to the design and construction of new communities and homes by fostering environmental sensitivity in planning and orienting new neighborhoods and homes for passive solar gain. To further reduce the impact of its development and conserve water, the town will pay attention to existing patches of green areas and encourage water-saving xeriscaping practices and use of native plants and limit the use of turf in its own public parks.

5
Dwelling in Small Towns

Helsinki's tourist office directed me to Porvoo when I inquired about a small quaint town in the area. Located 31 miles (50 km) east of the capital of Finland, Porvoo, population 49,000, has a mix of old and new buildings. With urban roots that date back to the fourteenth century, the place has a well-preserved historic core adjacent to the Porvoonjoki River that runs through it. While walking in the town's old section I noticed contemporary dwellings across the water. I walked to the river's other bank and stood near a row of houses painted green, saffron, and ocher lining the street.

I pushed open a gate, entered a courtyard and stood in the middle of a group of homes. There was a marked difference between what I saw and the scenes I was so familiar with in North America. The place had features that, I considered, every neighborhood should have: diversity of dwelling types, sensible density, properly scaled public spaces, opportunities for outdoor activities, no vehicular traffic, and humble beauty. Nothing called for your attention.

Single-family detached units, row housing, and apartment buildings stood side by side next to meticulously landscaped paths. The homes respected a color scheme, which lent the place a coherent appearance. At the core of the neighborhood there were covered parking structures which cars entered from perimeter streets. No cars were allowed elsewhere.

At the heart of each cluster there was a play area with a sandbox and swingset for toddlers, recycling and composting centers, and laundry hanging facilities. There was a seniors' center and I could see a school in the distance to which a bike path led.

There are no set standards of how a neighborhood in a small town should be planned or what it should look like. Yet, if I am to articulate the features of one, it would be inspired by the "Modern Wooden Town of Porvoo," as the place is known. It had many of the attributes that make a community sustainable on all levels. It put the interests of people ahead of vehicles. There were no huge garage doors, extravagant front yards, and oversized fenced-in rear yards. It offered sufficient privacy, yet it was open for everyone to see and enjoy (Figure 5.1).

This chapter attempts to learn from Porvoo and looks at designing and rehabilitating neighborhoods in small towns.

5.1 **The Modern Wooden Town of Porvoo**

Designing New Neighborhoods

As a result of urban sprawl some small towns have seen their edges expand. At times, peripheral growth took place at the expense of the core's decline. When visiting new developments in small towns, there is no noticeable difference between their planning pattern and those of the suburbs of large cities. Should there be any? Do the guiding planning principles of neighborhoods in small towns need to be different? Two key reasons to answer yes come to mind.

The first has to do with an overarching desire for a sustainable existence that forces planners to think innovatively about the form and function of any built environment, including residential. Aspects that have been elaborated above that affect urban form, nature, and mobility must be considered in the conception of all communities. The second has to do with the unique nature of small towns, their sense of place, and social fabric, which need to be reinforced and preserved by design. Powe and Hart (2011) suggest that small towns stand for a compromise between the advantages of "urban" and "rural" locations. They offer access to town services and employment, yet, are perceived to provide an acceptable level of peacefulness, safety, and closeness often associated with villages and hamlets. Small towns, and primarily those with a reduced land mass, can have better linkages between their districts, and those areas and the town's center. When planned correctly, their chosen form can also strength and enrich their *social capital*.

In their article "Social Capital and Quality of Place: Reflections on Growth and Change in a Small Town," Hanna et al. (2009) argued that places can be seen as a materialization of social capital based on their ability to offer a proper backdrop for relationships to sprout. Lack of spaces for connectivity to happen, both deliberately and spontaneously, can shape people's perceptions of social capital in their community.

This statement offers a view that social and urban fabrics are intrinsically linked. Knowing one another and having a close-knit social web are features of small towns that ought to be maintained. Therefore, residential planning in small towns needs to forge a delicate balance between traditions rooted in a local culture and the advent of contemporary design concepts and technologies.

Several key guiding pillars to the planning of communities in small towns can be listed. First, new neighborhoods may be planned to have a broadly equal area and a similar number of units. Having wide discrepancies between subdivision areas may lead to social and physical tensions. Second, a variety of housing types would address the space and economic needs of households with diverse demographic backgrounds and incomes. Third, a need to somewhat increase their density, voiced above, will also arguably strengthen their social web and reduce their environmental footprint. These principles will be further elaborated below.

Choosing a Form

The designated areas for new neighborhoods will be the outcome of a planning process and will be elaborated in a master plan. In the process, attention will commonly be paid to land ownership, proximity to and connectivity with key municipal institutions, and the town's amenities, to name a few attributes, some of which are illustrated in Figure 5.2.

Determining the form and the perimeters of a development is another valuable part of the process. An existing natural or scenic feature that marks an edge can be of particular importance in small towns. Van Rensburg and Campbell (2012) suggest that a green edge will make a town more compact and limit urban sprawl while protecting the environment. Including existing natural assets in the plan rather than clearing them out is a valuable principle.

Similar planning strategies have been used in the Scottish town of Inverurie, population 11,000. A combination of preserving existing patches of forested areas coupled with new planting contributed to the preservation of the local sense of place and wildlife corridors, as illustrated in Figure 5.3.

Once the location of a neighborhood has been chosen, and its edges drawn, the desired density will be considered next. With an overall drive to curb urban sprawl and increase density, several researchers looked at the relation between higher density and liveability. Shibu (2010) noted that more than the overall density, what affects social interactions in a community is

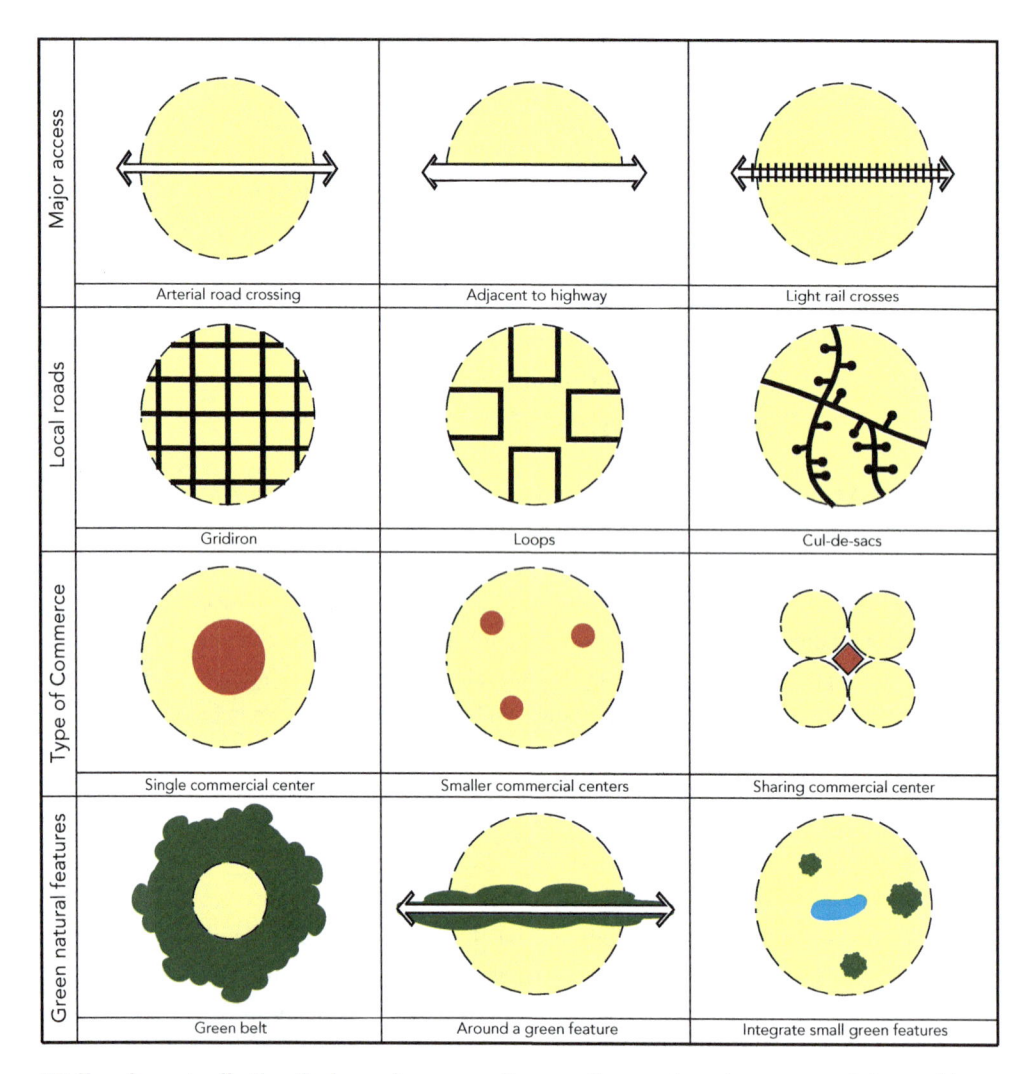

Major access	Arterial road crossing	Adjacent to highway	Light rail crosses
Local roads	Gridiron	Loops	Cul-de-sacs
Type of Commerce	Single commercial center	Smaller commercial centers	Sharing commercial center
Green natural features	Green belt	Around a green feature	Integrate small green features

5.2 **Key elements affecting the form of a community are: adjacency to major access and thoroughfares, local roads, type of commerce, and natural features**

how those places have been planned. Such a view was supported by Lovejoy et al. (2010) and Howley et al. (2009), who found that what affects residents' satisfaction is not whether the planning follows traditional or suburban principles but aspects such as housing types, schools' standing, noise, lack of community involvement, traffic, and absence of amenities.

As for compactness, several factors determine what would be considered a low-, medium-, or high-density neighborhood in a small town. For instance, choices made with respect to the average size of dwelling, type of parking, and the amount of private outdoor space will all affect the resulting densities, as shown in Figures 5.4 and 5.5. For example, attached units can be mixed with detached houses to elevate the overall density and limit sprawl. The attached dwellings can provide owners with privacy, affordability, and help foster

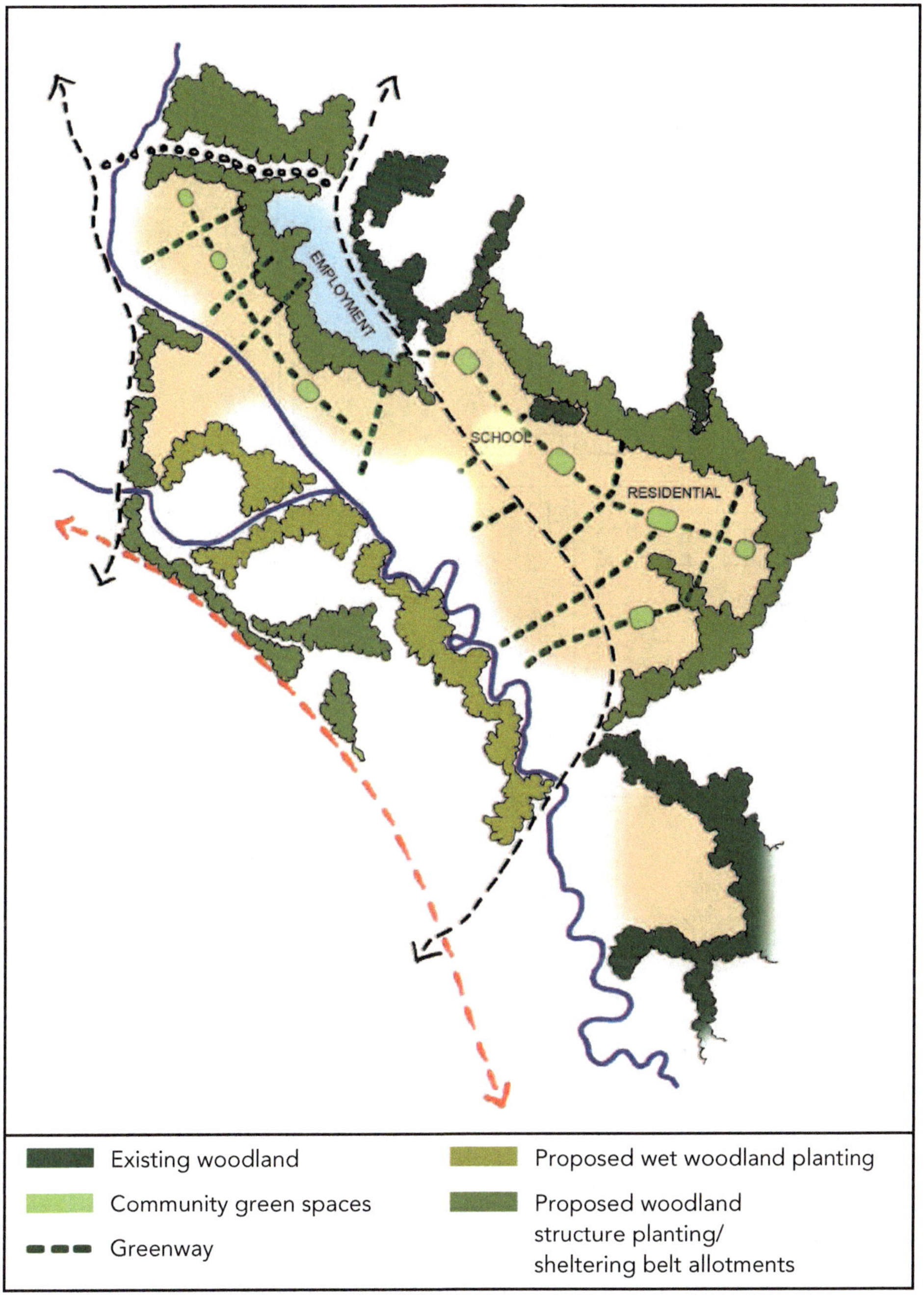
EMPLOYMENT
SCHOOL
RESIDENTIAL
Existing woodland
Community green spaces
Greenway
Proposed wet woodland planting
Proposed woodland structure planting/ sheltering belt allotments

5.3 **The Scottish town of Inverurie integrated existing patches of green areas and new planting in its design**

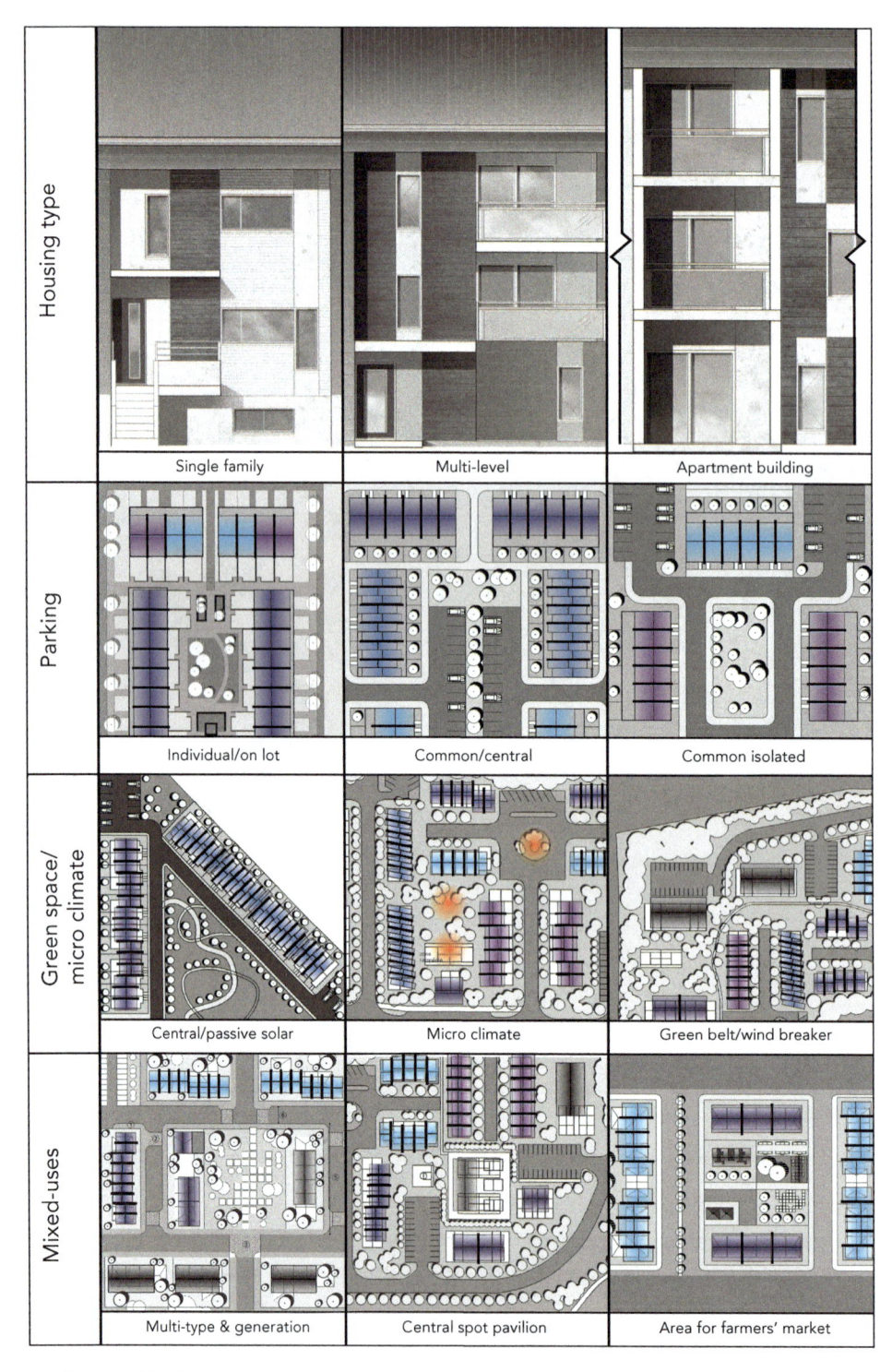

Housing type | Single family | Multi-level | Apartment building

Parking | Individual/on lot | Common/central | Common isolated

Green space/ micro climate | Central/passive solar | Micro climate | Green belt/wind breaker

Mixed-uses | Multi-type & generation | Central spot pavilion | Area for farmers' market

5.4 Factors affecting the overall appearance of a neighborhood are choice of housing types, parking, green spaces, and non-residential land use

Dwelling type	1 Single detached	2 Semi detached	3 Row house	4 Triplex	5 3-story walk-up apartment	6 Combined apartments & row houses	7 Slab block apartment	8 High rise point block apartment
Isometric								
Plot plan								
Dwelling units/acre (dwelling units/hectare)	8 (20)	14 (35)	19 (47)	21 (52)	65 (160)	84 (207)	90 (222)	120 (296)
Floor area ratio % open space	0.24 76%	0.38 81%	0.56 72%	0.60 80%	1.36 55%	1.92 62%	1.78 62%	2.62 87%
Unit area in square feet (unit area in square meters)	1200 (111.5)	1200 (111.5)	1200 (111.5)	1200 (111.5)	800 (74.3)	800 & 1200 (74.3 & 111.5)	800 (74.3)	800 (74.3)

5.5 **Dwelling types and their representative urban planning attributes**

a sense of place. The higher density also lowers the need for individually owned vehicles since the increased number of residents makes public transit economically viable.

Grant (2002) studied the application of mixed-use theories into practice in the Canadian context. She found that despite their notable advantage, making mixed-use communities work was difficult. The commercial segment of the development remained empty for a long time prior to occupancy. It is a challenge that developers in small towns can expect.

Circulation and Parking

Designing mobility networks while suitably integrating streets and parking is central to the planning of communities in small towns, primarily in higher density neighborhoods. Thought must be given to the typology and hierarchy of streets to reduce the amount of through traffic while giving priority to pedestrians and cyclists. The lengths, widths, and construction of roads should respond efficiently to residents' needs and be safe and cost-effective. It is common to see streets in North American low-density subdivisions with proportions that far exceed the needed requirements.

Streets should also be designed to accommodate public transit, control noise, and spare motorists from driving long distances unnecessarily. Curvilinear circulation, with loops and cul-de-sacs, is often present in the residential areas of small towns. Unlike the gridiron, this pattern adapts well to a site's topography and natural features. Also, through traffic on loop and cul-de-sac roads is minimal since they only provide access to homes on those streets thereby creating quieter and safer roads. Additionally, studies have demonstrated that they consume smaller amounts of land (Tasker-Brown and Pogharian 2000). The core of the cul-de-sac can be part of shared streets onto which dwelling units face, and offer opportunities to foster a local sense of place.

Before designing parking, specific requirements must be considered. The type of users, size of dwellings, form of tenure, location, and proximity to public transportation will determine the amount of parking needed. A circulation network's visual impact—very wide roads, and vast asphalt-covered parking lots, long series of repetitive garage doors, for example—can be reduced when parking is integrated with landscaping (Figure 5.6). Several smaller screened parking areas will result in lower visual presence. Depressing those areas or berming their perimeter combined with appropriate landscaping are effective methods for concealing them.

5.6 **Not having garage doors on front elevations will contribute to better street appearance**

Open Spaces

Public and private open spaces are essential to the quality of life of each resident and the community as a whole. They cannot be treated as mere leftover areas and need to provide fresh air, let in sunlight, and foster identity, while guarding privacy and offering a stage for a healthy social web. At the outset, a planner needs to determine if an area shall be divided up among units, be a shared green public space, or a mix of both.

Private outdoor spaces can be used for a variety of purposes. For example, front yards form transition zones between a home's private and public realms, as shown in Figure 5.7. They can be planned to support a more enjoyable community experience. Lindsay et al. (2010) advise that the design of front spaces and their relationship with the street needs to ensure the residents' privacy. In the rear, hedges, screens, and trellises will offer enclosure for personal activities. Yet erecting overly fenced areas is not advised either.

5.7 **Shared front open space in a project in North Vancouver, Canada**

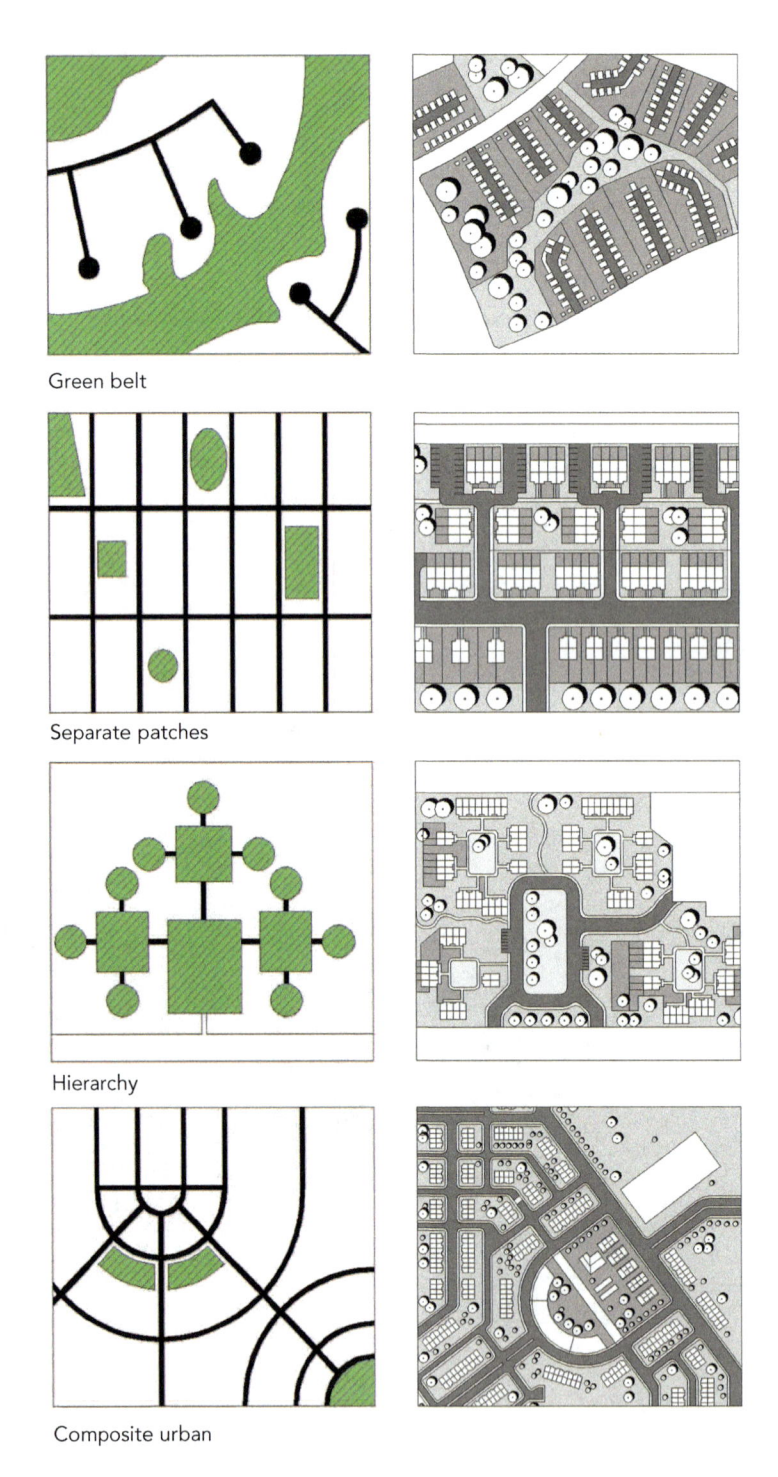

Green belt

Separate patches

Hierarchy

Composite urban

5.8 **Open space distribution in a town can consist of a green belt, separate patches, hierarchy, and composite urban patterns**

Public open spaces are central to establishing community identity and opportunities for social interaction. The planning of these spaces must occur parallel to the conception of the neighborhood at large and they follow a variety of planning concepts, as illustrated in Figure 5.8. The first decision involves the amount of land that will be devoted to green areas. A minimum public space requirement does not imply that the land be consolidated into one large park. It is better to evenly distribute green spaces throughout and create smaller, human-scaled ones. Since children may spend more play time outdoors, specific areas can be designed for them. Ideally all occupants will have direct access to these areas from their houses or reach them in a short walk (Russ 2002; Wei 2003).

Unit and Community Identity

According to Pfeifer and Brauneck (2008), homes are an expression of the occupants' identities. As a result, the façade must negotiate a compromise between the overall aesthetics of the neighborhood and the personal tastes of the homeowner. The balance between individual expression and architectural coherence is what has allowed many towns to become visually pleasing communities.

For ease of construction builders often rely on repetition of façades. The ensuing risk of bland environments resulting from the monotony of such repetition can be avoided if the designer conceives and provides identities for both the unit and the community at the initial design stage. If adequate provisions are made at the outset, the desired objectives can also be achieved economically. The high degree of repetition required for an economy of scale to be maintained at unit level, can be alleviated by ensuring that a fixed number of elements can be combined to create diversity, as illustrated in Figure 5.9. Varying the dormers, porches, or façade materials can give a home character that sets it apart from the rest yet fits in with the ensemble. There can also be exterior projection in the form of a front porch exposed to public view, which will also reinforce a house's distinct identity.

Although the façade represents the "public image" of a household, the composition of its key elements is based on interior functioning. The layout of the floors commonly influences the position and size of the openings in the elevations. Window dimensions depend on room requirements for sunlight and privacy. Varying the units' floor plans will ultimately vary the façades and change the street appearance as was the case in a housing development in Fredericton, Canada (Figure 5.10). Offering a selection of layouts has the added benefit of granting home buyers the opportunity to choose an interior configuration that suits their unique needs.

Community identity, on the other hand, is eventually established through evolution and a slow process of accretion, but the conditions for such a process to occur can be provided in the initial design. The location of trees and variations in communal outdoor areas are vital considerations, while the sequencing of views creates interest at the scale of the overall site

5.9 **While respecting an overall form and height, variation was included in the façades of these homes in Edam, the Netherlands**

5.10 **Entrance doors were reversed to offer variety in a project in Fredericton, Canada**

5.11 **City blocks of different sizes will foster a variety of dwelling types and urban appearances**

by punctuating the design to avoid dullness. Also, planning blocks of different sizes will contribute to having a variety of dwelling forms and configurations (Figure 5.11).

The principles listed above about form, mobility, open space, and identity ensure that small towns' neighborhoods will have a unique character and a sense of place while becoming sustainable.

Infill Housing

Constructing residences on vacant land in built areas, also known as infill housing, offers opportunities and challenges to municipalities and builders. Easy linking with nearby roads and utilities, and contribution to the rehabilitation of rundown neighborhoods are some valuable advantages. The likelihood of encountering contaminated soil and designing on odd-sized lots are some of the drawbacks. The need to curb urban sprawl, adopt sustainable growth strategies, and lower dwelling costs makes infill housing worth considering. This section elaborates on issues related to infill housing in small towns and lists strategies for their planning and integration.

An infill housing project is commonly found in urban areas. For a variety of reasons, when a single lot or a large area has been left vacant, interest can develop in filling the gap. An infill project may also include the building of residences on previously designated industrial lands, better known as brownfields, some of which may include existing industrial structures.

Infill housing developments can include single-family detached homes, attached dwellings, or apartment blocks as part of an existing fabric. The insertion process will include the careful consideration of physical and social attributes to create a seamless transition between the new project and the community around it.

Societal changes make the consideration of infill housing projects, primarily in the urban core, highly relevant. Perhaps the greatest consequence of building on vacant land is curbing rampant urban sprawl. While suburban developments may appear to offer a more attractive standard of living, this standard comes at a great cost that infill housing has a potential to reduce. Such projects can capitalize on already in-place public transportation routes, infra-structure, and green spaces. By building in existing communities, local commerce can serve the new residents, avoiding a need for new edge commerce.

Demographic changes offer another opportunity for initiators of infill housing. Traditional nuclear families no longer constitute the vast majority of households in small towns. Singles, single-parent families, and the elderly are more inclined to look for and afford smaller, lower cost dwellings built in higher density settings. Another potential benefit of infill housing is its effect on the surrounding area. Well-designed infill housing can help revitalize a rundown neighborhood and broaden the municipal tax base by drawing new business.

Despite the seemingly many advantages of infill housing and contribution to repairing social and urban fabrics, they are considered a challenge to build. When an entire area or a single plot of land has remained vacant, there is usually a good reason for it. Prior to acquiring such a lot and engaging in its design, the initiator needs to carefully assess these potential challenges.

Soil contamination is a barrier to infill developments. When the site was the location of a manufacturing plant or storage facility, poisonous materials could have found their way into the ground, and may pose a risk to the people who will inhabit the homes. The soil, therefore, needs to be tested and decisions made as to the clean-up method. When an industrial building is located on the site and cannot be converted, it must be demolished and cleared.

The size, shape, and location of the site may also make infill housing projects harder to design and costly to build. At times, such sites can be leftovers of a larger plot of land. Their odd shape may lead to substantial waste and cast doubts on the viability of the entire project. Also, zoning bylaws can further jeopardize the feasibility of infill projects. Whereas past zoning has served to separate incompatible land uses, today's zoning laws are more specific and prohibit the mixing of different activities (Duany et al. 2000). Working with local governments to ease zoning laws for an infill project can create opportunities for more diverse, innovative, and lively communities.

Selecting a Site

Since infill projects in small towns can vary greatly in size, from a single unit to many homes, a frequently asked question is what the size for such a project should be. Alexander, in *A Pattern*

Language, notes that attractive towns have organic structures that have grown gradually through a process based on a sequence of spatial relationships that is piecemeal and coherent (Alexander et al. 1977). By considering in existing urban context the spatial configuration and architectural vocabulary, designers of infill housing can succeed in continuing an area's organic growth.

Given the extremely varied and diverse nature of infill housing, no exact formula exists for determining an optimal density of a project. If public transportation is the leading criteria and for it to be practical, the general rule of thumb is a minimum of seven dwellings per acre (17 units per hectare) for a bus to run every 30 minutes (Duany et al. 2000). Studies have indicated that low-rise schemes below 80 bedrooms per acre (200 per hectare) are appreciated by residents (Goodchild 1997). Another strategy for maintaining high densities and resident satisfaction is to create a balanced mix of user age groups within a project. In exploring residents' satisfaction in central city areas, Howley (2010) concluded that it is not just a question of building more high-density housing, but of equal importance is creating attractive homes and neighborhoods, with small pockets of parking spots that are suitable throughout all stages of an individual's lifecycle (Figure 5.12).

5.12 **An infill housing project near historic York, UK**

Ultimately, however, notions of social acceptability are essentially local and density relative to a particular site often proves to be a better indicator of satisfaction in small towns. The density of a project in comparison to respectable and typical nearby housing will determine whether the new project will stand out as unusual or be easily stigmatized (Goodchild 1997). Therefore, the best way to increase the acceptability of an infill project is to design it with density similar to the area in which it is to be built.

Urban and Architectural Fit

An infill project will preferably fit in with the urban fabric and the architecture of neighboring buildings. This is especially important when avoiding repetitiveness takes on an added importance. Issues related to planning patterns, such as streets and sidewalks, as well as preserving adjoining properties' privacy, need to be accounted for. Architectural considerations range from respecting the overall scale and mass of a neighborhood to incorporating similar stylistic elements found on other homes along the street.

Continuing and enhancing the urban plan of a community is an important aspect in ensuring that a new infill development will complement its neighborhood. Streets can be regarded as the threads that tie the old and the new, and, therefore, their continuation ensures a fit. Similarly, sidewalks should be extended by utilizing the same surface materials. Trees, landscaping, decorative paving, pedestrian lighting, and street furniture on the new streets should all reflect those on the surrounding existing streets. Open or green space networks should be maintained and extended where possible to provide adequate access to nature, while preserving a site's mature trees, natural attributes, and topography.

Respecting adjoining properties is not enough to ensure a proper fit between an infill development and its neighborhood. The architectural patterns and character of an area need also to be considered. A designer should recognize the predominant style of a place keeping in mind the role that the new development forms as part of a street or a park. However, this does not mean mimicking or repeating existing architectural patterns but utilizing them as a basis for contemporary but visually related detail in new houses, as shown in Figure 5.13 (Kinnis 1997).

Most design guidelines suggest that the overall form of a new infill home should approximate that of its neighbors. Therefore, the overall height and roofline of a development should not exceed the average height of its neighbors, and the volume of the dwelling can also be similar to adjoining structures, as illustrated in Figure 5.14. Placing large, tall apartments in a community of predominantly small, single-family homes can visually dominate the neighborhood.

Furthermore, materials, windows, doors, roof slopes and shapes, and architectural details need to reflect the proportions and the character of the neighborhood. Designing dwellings with materials, finishes, and ornamentation similar to the adjacent detached dwellings can help those homes fit in with their surroundings. Ornamentation should be an integral part of the design rather than "stuck on" (Kinnis 1997). It is important to note that many historic or old neighborhoods do not meet today's safety requirements. While infill homes should reflect the character of these areas, safety codes such as those related to fire must be met.

To ensure that the architectural character of an infill neighborhood is respected, design guidelines are often specific in their recommendations. For example, they state that styles, materials, configurations, and proportions should be consistent with windows on surrounding existing structures. Further clarification stresses the particular importance of the proportion of the windows and the relationship between the amounts of window area with respect to the amount of non-window area of a particular façade (Moyes 1997). Although specific guidelines can be restrictive at times, more detailed guidelines help integrate new homes with any community.

5.13 **Proportions and vernacular style are respected in these contemporary infill dwellings in Den Burg, the Netherlands**

5.14 Planning patterns of existing urban settings need to be respected while inserting new buildings

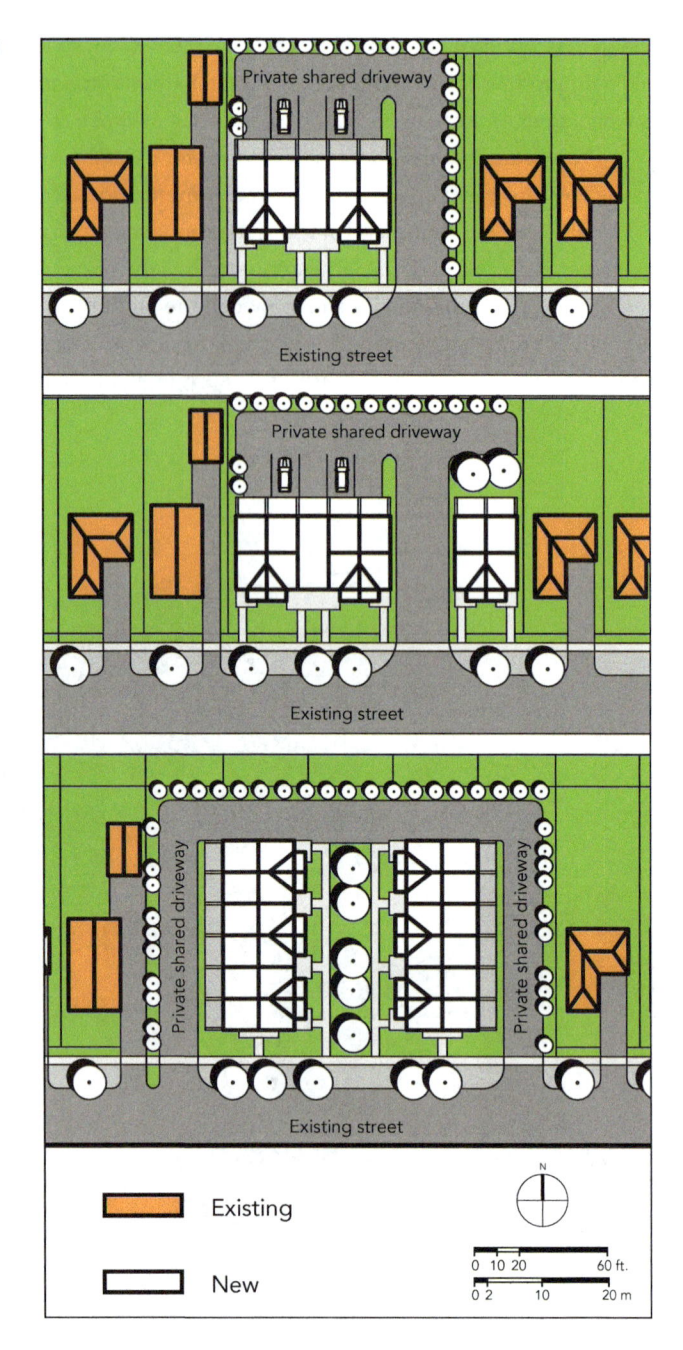

Dwelling Types

With an increase in household diversity in small towns, infill developments present a unique opportunity to provide non-traditional housing. An infill project, for example, can vary dwelling types and sizes to provide residences for the elderly, singles, and single-parent families. A mixture of housing types can contribute to neighborhood revitalization by attracting users who can support a greater variety of businesses and cultural activities. Furthermore, such projects can house people of different backgrounds, incomes, and ages to strengthen essential social webs (Jacobs 1961).

A dwelling type commonly used in high-density infill projects is the townhouse. It can be constructed in a variety of forms such as rows facing a street or clusters with individual open spaces. Another popular model for mixing residential and retail spaces that has proven successful in infill projects is shops on the ground floor with apartments above. When a separate entrance for the upper floor units is designed, the cost can be kept quite low and the model appeals to some user groups (Goodchild 1997).

Designing a Northern Neighborhood

I was foreign to the Canadian Arctic when I accepted an invitation to design a neighborhood in the City of Iqaluit, population 6,000, the territorial capital of Nunavut (Figure 5.15). My design and building knowledge above the 60th parallel and familiarity with the dwelling type and

5.15 **Images of Iqaluit, Nunavut, Canada**

culture of the Innu, the aboriginals who populate the place, was rudimentary. The barren landscape of Baffin Island and challenges faced by local architects were eye-opening. Cultural transformation and climate change are visible and introduce new issues that affect design.

History and Context

Canada's modern presence in the north is linked to trade, the military, and sovereignty over land. Until the nineteenth century, the north was the focus of early explorers and populated by few First Nations. In 1914, the Hudson's Bay Company began setting up trading posts throughout the Arctic. Growth came to Iqaluit, formerly Frobisher Bay, in World War II, when the Americans built an airbase in the area. During the 1950s the base was turned over to the Canadian government which populated the place and drew southerners who needed basic amenities. Additional expansion took place in the 1970s with the building of a hospital, school, homes, hotels, and other traits of a modern town. In 1999, with the creation of new Northern territories, Iqaluit became the capital of Nunavut, a region that occupies one-fifth of Canada's land mass and assumes its own governance and cultural identity.

Designing for extreme temperatures and a very short construction period poses awesome challenges. Perhaps the biggest of them all is a logistical one. Every building component needs to be ferried from the south by boat during the thawed season. It also means that most buildings need to be conceived as a well-designed kit of parts for rapid assembly.

Despite a vast land mass, finding terrain to build on is not easy in the north, since much of the ground under the topsoil is permanently frozen. Conventional southern foundation practices, deep or shallow, cannot be applied here and the rocky terrain does not make things easier once appropriate land is found. Steel piles need to be driven into the ground and beams, on which the superstructure sits, welded to their heads.

Climatic considerations affecting designs have extreme importance in northern climates. For one, energy costs, much higher due to transport, must be kept down and inhabitant comfort made a priority. Blowing snow in frigid arctic weather is an important aspect to consider. There is simply not much that can block wind and snow drift formation above the tree line but the structures themselves which need to be sited to shelter each other. The long axis of each building needs to be aligned with the wind and raised above grade to form an open crawlspace. A blocked underbelly will cause snow accumulation on the building's other side. The structure's silhouette also needs to be streamlined and the roof height shallow. Entrances cannot face the wind and deflectors to reduce zones of stagnating air need to be installed.

The importance of sunlight in northern climates cannot be overstated. At higher latitudes, the angle of incoming sunlight remains so low that it reaches its greatest intensity by reaching vertical surfaces such as walls, rather than the horizontal surfaces like flat roofs, roads, and parking lots, as occurs at lower latitudes. Therefore, it is important to ensure that sunlight is captured and focused by vertical surfaces to create thermally appropriate microclimates.

Planning a Community

The chosen site was located at the heart of an interesting and diverse part of Iqaluit, close to the waterfront and across from a visitor's center, library, museum, and school. It has a gently sloping terrain, a water stream that borders its eastern side, and a mountainous view at the rear (Figure 5.16).

Several cultural and lifestyle attributes invoked design ideas when I began contemplating an approach to site planning. First, the notion of demarcating property does not exist in the north. One will be hard-pressed to find a fence surrounding a yard. Residents freely walk or even drive through each other's lots.

Fishing and hunting is not a hobby here. It forms an essential part of a household economy and diet. Fishing gear, hunting equipment, skidoos, and a *kamotic*, the sled that is dragged behind, are part of a family's possessions which need to be safely stored. One is also struck by the inherent artistic talent of the Innu. Behind many homes you can hear the sound of power tools and see locals sculpting soapstone into magnificent works of art.

A lack of trees lends Northern communities a barren image. Yet, the beauty of the land, with its rock formations, flora and fauna, is captivating and can be made part of the landscaping and streetscaping. It is surprising to discover the large number of species that survive the harsh weather in the covering ground.

The site plan was conceived by exploring alternative site plans with the need to develop medium-density housing that safely accommodates pedestrians and snow machines alike (Figure 5.17). Communal spaces for children's play, soapstone carving, and socializing were identified. The introduction of common parking, reduced setbacks, and multi-unit buildings with private entrances were also included. Having individual entrances to homes rather than common ones was meant to foster personalization (Figure 5.18). Colors present in local art were chosen for the wood siding exterior façades. The design introduced individual storage units to accommodate land-based activities. Lastly, buildings were oriented to consider wind direction, solar exposure, and to shelter each other. The long axis of the houses was aligned with the prevailing winds, raised above grade to form an open crawl space, and their roofs were shallow in height.

At the unit level, flexibility applied to the three phases of the dwelling's lifecycle. Prior to occupancy, choice and adaptation were made part of community consultation ensuring that the units met the needs of the occupants (Figures 5.19 and 5.20). Flexibility also played an important role during occupancy and the interior was designed to be easily adaptable to changing household compositions. It was also an important factor in considering that at a later stage the dwellings will have to meet the needs of new tenants and be refurbished economically over time.

Paying attention to the natural features, the harsh climate, and the unique local culture were the main attributes in designing the neighborhood in Iqaluit. These principles also ensured that a sustainable community will be built and they need to be considered elsewhere when designing residences in small towns.

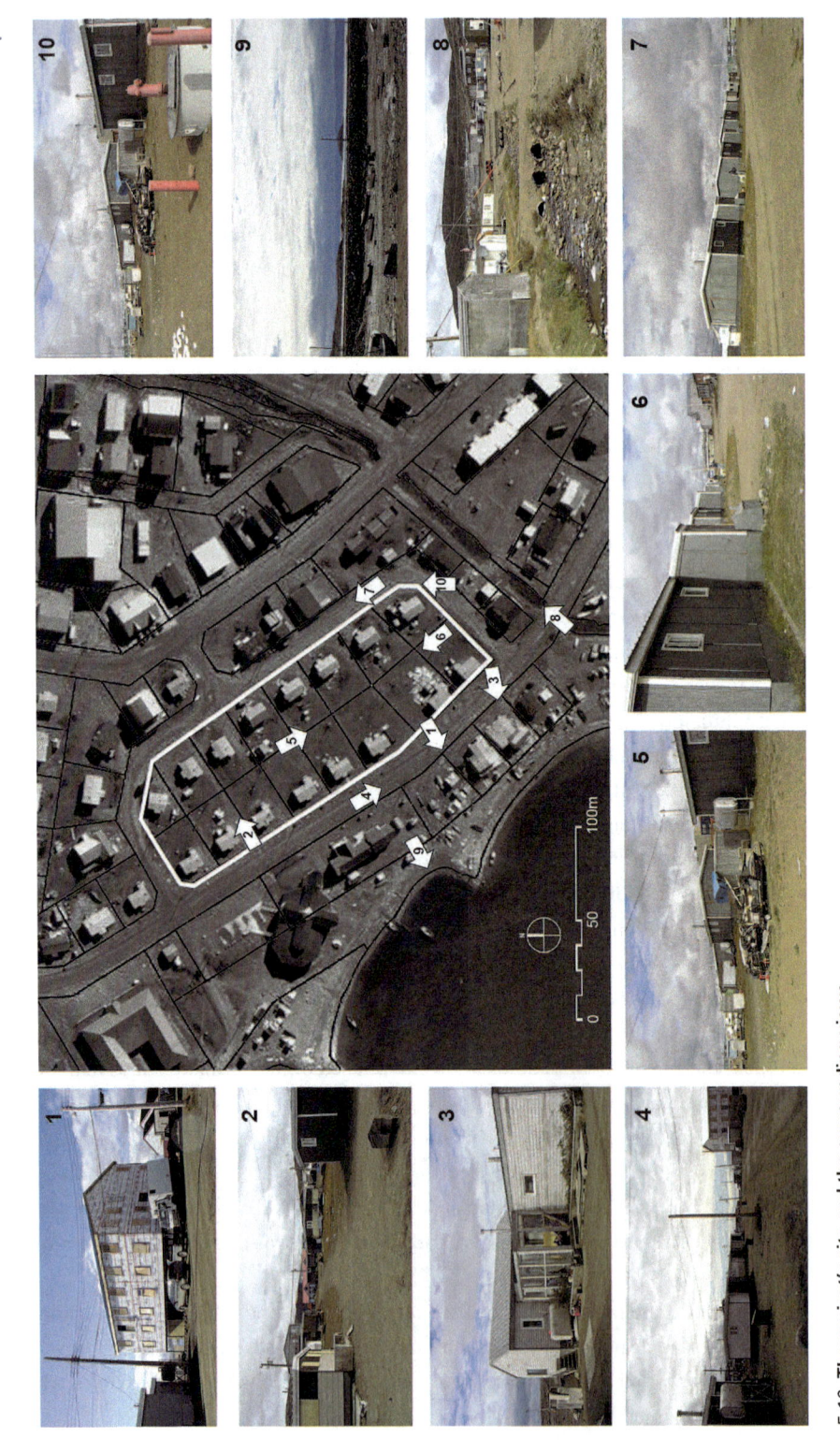

5.16 The project's site and the surrounding views

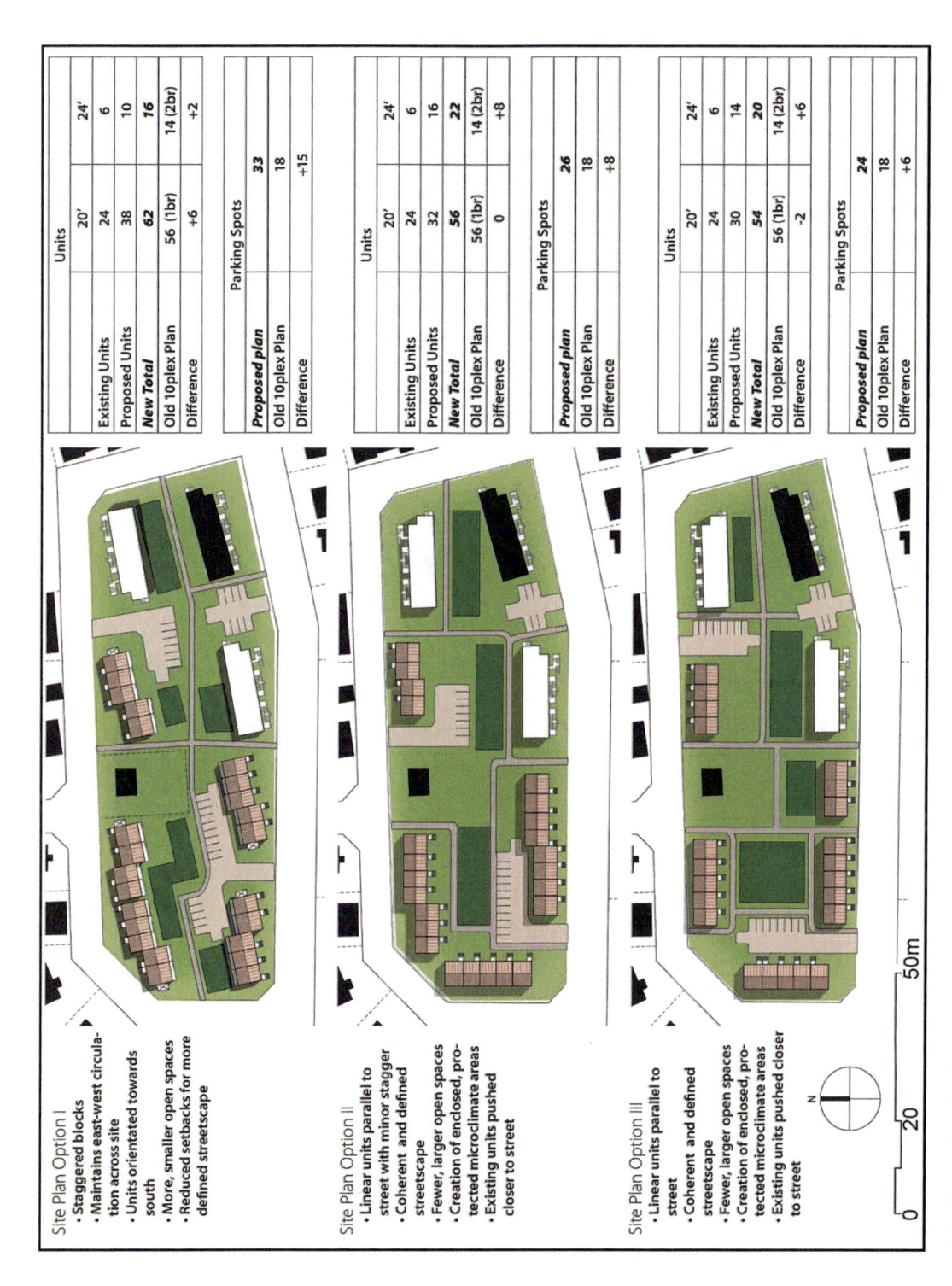

Site Plan Option I
- Staggered blocks
- Maintains east-west circulation across site
- Units orientated towards south
- More, smaller open spaces
- Reduced setbacks for more defined streetscape

Units	20'	24'
Existing Units	24	6
Proposed Units	38	10
New Total	62	16
Old 10plex Plan	56 (1br)	14 (2br)
Difference	+6	+2

Parking Spots	
Proposed plan	33
Old 10plex Plan	18
Difference	+15

Site Plan Option II
- Linear units parallel to street with minor stagger
- Coherent and defined streetscape
- Fewer, larger open spaces
- Creation of enclosed, protected microclimate areas
- Existing units pushed closer to street

Units	20'	24'
Existing Units	24	6
Proposed Units	32	16
New Total	56	22
Old 10plex Plan	56 (1br)	14 (2br)
Difference	0	+8

Parking Spots	
Proposed plan	26
Old 10plex Plan	18
Difference	+8

Site Plan Option III
- Linear units parallel to street
- Coherent and defined streetscape
- Fewer, larger open spaces
- Creation of enclosed, protected microclimate areas
- Existing units pushed closer to street

Units	20'	24'
Existing Units	24	6
Proposed Units	30	14
New Total	54	20
Old 10plex Plan	56 (1br)	14 (2br)
Difference	-2	+6

Parking Spots	
Proposed plan	24
Old 10plex Plan	18
Difference	+6

0 20 50m

5.17 **Alternative planning proposals and their qualifiable attributes**

4. Sculpting area

3. Gate feature

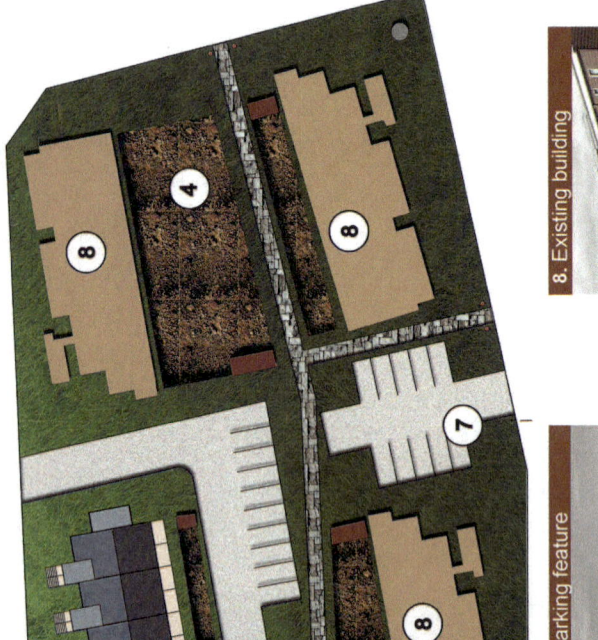

2. Arctic garden

1. Sculpture

8. Existing building

7. Parking feature

6. Centre square

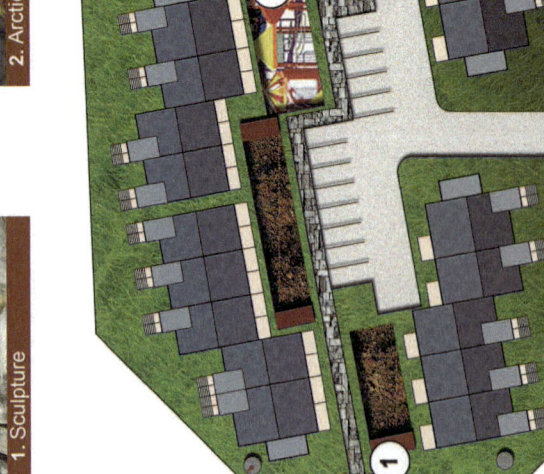

5. Kid's play area

5.18 **Key planning principles**

Design for passive solar gain

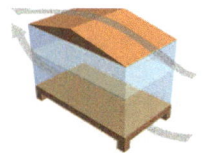
Wind consideration

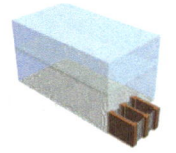
Airlock entrance

Rear storage room

Multi-purpose room

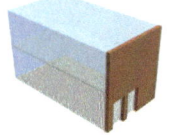
Individual entrances

Interior flexibility

Easy assembly

Colorful facades

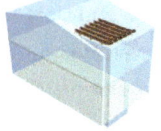
Roof top articulation

Choice of volumetric arrangements

Site related

5.19 **Key principles of the dwelling design**

5.20 **Rendering of a row**

6
Strengthening Core Areas

When one thinks about the horror and destruction of great wars, several cities that have sustained damage come to mind. Stalingrad, Hiroshima, and Dresden stand out immediately. But when you try to recall a small town impacted by war, Belgium's Ypres will likely top the list. The place's misfortune happened to be its location. During World War I the town was the center of shifting battle lines and intense artillery exchange between the German and Allied forces.

Ypres's origin dates back to the first century BC. During successive centuries the town grew to 40,000 inhabitants and became an important textile manufacturing post. The still standing Cloth Hall, built in the thirteenth century to serve as the main market and warehouse, is evidence of the town's wealthy past.

Standing in the Grote Market Square that faces the Cloth Hall and nearby St. Martin's Cathedral, it was hard to imagine that this place was once bombed to rubble. It looked vibrant and crowded with visitors when I stood in line waiting to visit the Flanders Field memorial museum (Figure 6.1). Most impressive was that the town, population now 35,000, looked as if it was never touched by war. Measures taken by the architect Jules Coomans, who was put in charge of the rebuilding effort, not only meticulously respected the buildings' original plans and façades, but also their uses. The area had a proper mix of stores and dwellings layered on top of each other. It did not feel like a restored monument but rather like an authentic place. The shops, restaurants, and the museum no doubt thrive on visitors who, much like me, want to know more about one of human history's greatest tragedies, but they cater mostly to locals.

As the day drew to a close I walked to the Menin Gate Memorial to the Missing, to attend the Last Post ceremony conducted here daily since the end of the war. I thought about the heart of towns and their leaders' ability to change their fortune when demise took place. I reflected on other places I had visited and the importance of the core to their distant past, recent history, and to their present social and economic fabrics. Recalling these values and ideas for maintaining active downtowns, their renewal and, if need be, preservation is the topic of this chapter.

6.1 **The reconstructed Grote Market Square in Ypres, Belgium**

The Importance of a Center

If one were to compare the districts of a small town to the rooms of a dwelling, the core, that is downtown, would be regarded as the living room or perhaps the dining room. The place affects most fabrics of a town's life, material and social among them. This section tells the importance of town centers, recalls their urban evolution, and lists the challenges that some of them face.

As noted in Chapter 2, small towns often grew organically from a core. Some places started and evolved spontaneously while others followed a formal plan. Regardless of their planning and evolution method, the town's center is where the old edifices would be. There, you will see the original town hall, fire house, school, and market square still bearing dates of construction on their façades, as shown in Figure 6.2. Burayidi (2010) notes that while many large cities have decimated their heritage through urban renewal projects, small city downtowns still have ample such sites and buildings that can provide the experiences heritage tourists seek in their travels. Old buildings hold meaningful connections to and a reminder of the past, which, as some towns have recognized, have an economic value and are a foundation upon which future development can be built.

The town center is where you will also find institutional buildings and amenities such as banks, medical clinics, food and hardware stores, and other essential community services

6.2 **Crests on the Plazzo Communale Wall in Crotona, Italy**

6.3 **Hardware store in Siana, Greece**

(Figure 6.3). In towns whose economies are tied to agriculture, this is where the annual fair may take place. Powe and Gunn (2008) maintain that these services are particularly important to those less mobile, often providing their only access to quality services. They are often local employment generators and help avoid commuting to a nearby city.

According to Robertson (1999) the enterprises of town centers are large contributors to the local tax base. Also, the type of commerce that one finds in small town main streets is also unique. Mom-and-pop stores, where familiarity and personal relations with customers are pivotal to the way business is conducted, are common. Although, economically vulnerable, these businesses offer a unique atmosphere and service that large retail outlets cannot provide.

The contribution that a town center makes to the local social vibrancy is also significant. It is where main streets, market squares, churches, parks, and notable monuments depicting the place's history are located. It is a gathering place where parades commemorating events in the town history and holidays are celebrated. In these events, those who contribute to the town's social fabric will meet, make their initial connections, and extend invitations to one another. Commonly, core areas also have a proper human scale, and treed streets that make them walkable and comfortable to be in.

Despite their many contributions, in some locations, particularly those in small metropolitan regions, downtowns have experienced a decline (Filion et al. 2004). The reasons for their demise are varied, but in general are rooted in the evolution of transportation, introduction of big box retail, e-commerce, and land-use planning, to name a few (Figure 6.4). Prior to

6.4 **Store closing on High Street, in Lancaster, UK**

offering strategies for strengthening core areas, it would be of value to consider the process of their downturn.

The 1950s federal investment in highway construction and the affordability of private automobiles, coupled with the proliferation of suburbia, marked the start of the downtown's decline in the US (Robertson 1999; Smith 2008). Having easy access to a vehicle and comfortable roads to drive on was also noticed by developers, who went on to build commercial and office parks away from old core areas (Figure 6.5). Shopping strips, malls, and later "big box" retail outlets offered plenty of parking spots, heated and air conditioned interiors, and lower cost products with which the owners of mom-and-pop stores could not compete (Smith 2008; Powe et al. 2009). Some towns, against the interest and action of small retailers, even invited and welcomed supersized outlets, which contributed to their tax base, created jobs, and sold low-cost products that the townspeople craved (Figure 6.6). Often, a single large retailer sold merchandise similar to several small downtown stores, which eventually had to close, as shown in Figure 6.7. Visually, the big outlets were "off the shelf" enormous buildings set in a sea of asphalt, with no windows, roofline, or attempt to respect a local architectural character (Beaumont and Tucker 2002).

6.5 **A big box retail store on the outskirts of the city of Rhodes, Greece**

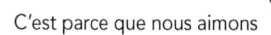

C'est parce que nous aimons

- *Notre ville*
- *Nos clients*
- *Notre métier*
- *Notre lien de proximité*
- *Nos collaborateurs*
- *Votre fidélité*

Que nous refusons le dictat qui
construit un centre-ville à
l'extérieur de la ville

*Pour que vous ayez encore le choix contre
l'hégémonie de le monopole qui pourrait
s'annoncer demain*

Soutenez vous commerçants de proximité
et la convivialité de votre ville

6.6 **A flyer from a campaign to stop the building of big box retail parks in Bergues, France**

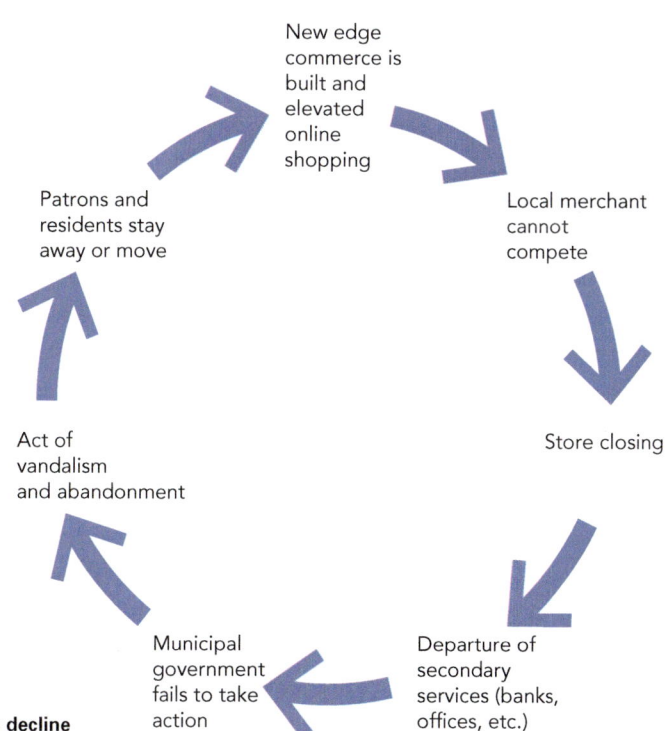

6.7 **The fly wheel of core area's decline**

On occasion attempts were made to attract large retailers to downtown locations, which proved unsuccessful due to the lack of large plots or high land cost thereby directing developers to the outskirts of towns. Attracting new investors to the core became more difficult. In addition, the malls often had a second story with leasable office space. Gradually, service amenities such as accounting offices, medical clinics, and law firms that drew people to downtown and employed others moved to the new locations, thereby contributing to the creation of additional vacant commercial areas (Robertson 1999).

Some small towns lacked the resources necessary to reverse the trend of a downward spiral. Others failed to alter old bylaws that limited mixed land use that layered residences over commerce. Gradually, the area became vacant after hours and on weekends since there was no local population to support commercial activities or animate the streets. On occasion, random acts of vandalism rendered those places unsafe, which further escalated their condition and mandated more policing.

Investments in creating welcoming environments have been attempted and they are ongoing in many small towns. The thrust of these efforts was to foster a walkable environment and ameliorate their appearance through façade and signage improvements, sidewalk enlargements, and better lighting installations. Drawing people in for a short time by staging events was another strategy used by other communities.

In some cases these efforts proved successful in reversing a decline, at least for a while. In other places they failed. The lure and the staying power of the well-financed large retail outlets on the edge of town was hard to compete with and win against, further leading to stores closing and enforcing the area's negative stigma. Strategies for strengthening the core and successful renewal cases will be outlined below.

Vision and Ideas

A look back to a core's old days would be a good beginning in a quest for an overarching approach for a downtown renewal. Then, those areas were populated by inhabitants and visitors. There were many good reasons to live and frequent the place and very few residential or commercial alternatives. These old patterns can also guide contemporary renewal efforts.

Robertson (2006) recommends the following guiding steps for an urban renewal process: craft a vision and a plan, identify local assets, forge public–private partnerships, and create a sense of place. Also, the retooling needs to respond to current challenges and make these areas resilient to emerging realities. Placing the process and the place on a sustainable economic, social, and environmental footing should be an underlying goal.

The draw of suburban living vacated small town core areas of their residents. Bringing them back needs to be a town's priority. Increased population will also support local businesses, enliven streets, and contribute to a sense of ownership. Housing constructed in downtowns

6.8 **Building infill housing on vacant lots in the heart of Cornwall, Ontario, Canada**

need not "suburbanize" the place. It has to house those whose needs and lifestyles suit robust urban places, as illustrated in Figure 6.8. Building apartments above commerce can attract a young cohort who would seek affordable accommodation. Some may even move to small towns from adjacent large cities in search of a lower cost residence. The units need to be innovatively designed and include smaller apartments, some with home offices that can become incubators for new enterprises. Another potential group of residents can be seniors who may trade a large home for an apartment in downtown. Such units need to be designed for people with reduced mobility and permit aging in place.

Crowhurst suggests that successful and livable urban spaces are commonly multifunctional, and "accommodate as many uses and activities as there are citizens" (Crowhurst and Lennard 2002). The place needs to have a proper mix of services and commerce to include pharmacy, hardware, and food stores essential for a thriving local community (Figure 6.9).

6.9 **A street with a mix of residences and commerce in Beuvron-en-Auge, France**

They would be supplemented by other amenities such as banks, medical clinics, cafés, and restaurants. When a young population is to be attracted, having nearby daycare provision and schools as well as public transit service to them will take on an added importance.

According to Robertson (1999), creating local activity generators is another worthwhile strategy to consider. These can include the town library, arena, museum, or performing art center. In small towns with limited funding some of these functions will be amalgamated in a single building. In addition, the town's main gathering square can be sited near such a building. Ensuring that these functions remain open after hours will also be of value to the core's vitality.

Considering the area's natural assets is another strengthening or renewal strategy. For example, unique rock formations, waterfalls and parks can be part of a strategy that would put landscapes in its center. Also, where a town was established near a waterfront, be it an ocean or a river, once developed this can become a regional draw further supporting local commerce. Waterfronts are popular places with tourists and many have played a pivotal role in turning the town's fortune around. Towns like Honfleur, France, are best known for making their water-fronts an international attraction (Figure 6.10).

6.10 **The waterfront in Honfleur, France**

Banking on the town's history and a well-preserved stock of old buildings will not only enhance a downtown's sense of place, but can become a draw. Towns that recognized the importance and value of their urban heritage have enacted bylaws to preserve them, and supported private building conversion initiatives that went on to create an urban museum of sorts like Lecce, Italy (Figure 6.11). Some towns put in place architectural guidelines to ensure that the original character of an old building will not be altered and that new adjacent buildings will fit in with the old. Establishing a historic society and affixing a plaque to the building's façade that describes the significance, style, or identity of the former occupants would support educational purpose as well. When funding permits, having a museum that recalls the place's history will be a worthwhile investment.

It is often assumed that it is hard, if not impossible, to attract large commercial anchors to the core. Having a mid-sized rather than a "superstore" with residences above or on its side would be a desired option (Figure 6.12). Beaumont and Tucker (2002) described measures taken by the town of Fort Collins, Colorado, for the architectural integration of such stores. They included prohibiting long blank walls that discourage pedestrian activity, mandating display windows, awnings, and other features to add visual interest, and requiring sidewalks linking stores to transit stops, street crossing, and suitable location of building entrances (Fort Collins 1995).

Creating around-the-clock attractions is also an important renewal feature. Places that are emptied after hours rarely succeed. An effort should be made to have evening activities and gathering places such as cafés and restaurants open late. At least on several weekdays,

6.11 **An old amphitheater was preserved in the heart of Lecce, Italy**

all commercial establishments can remain open to welcome locals or customers from afar. The town's traditional and newly introduced celebratory events or fairs can take place in the core (Figure 6.13). The events can be scheduled during evenings to further support late open local commerce.

When a decline in core areas begins and stores become vacant and streets emptied, a safety concern is likely to follow. The concerns can adversely affect the area's livability and

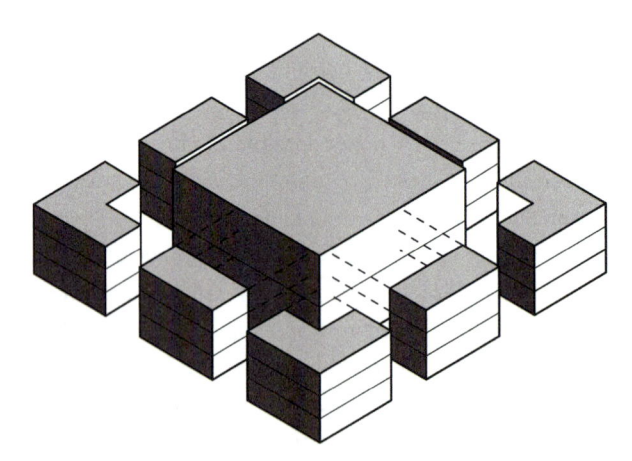

6.12 **A large downtown commercial establishment can be designed with residences along its exterior walls**

6.13 A charity fair in Perth, Scotland

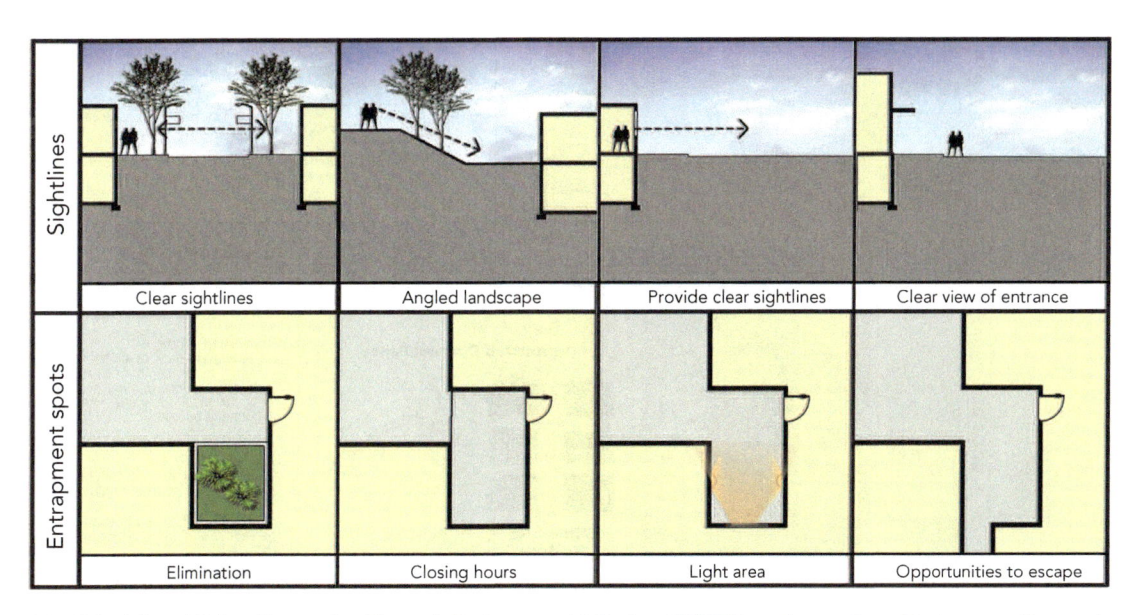

6.14 Principles of Crime Prevention Through Environmental Design (CPTED) can be employed to increase the core's safety

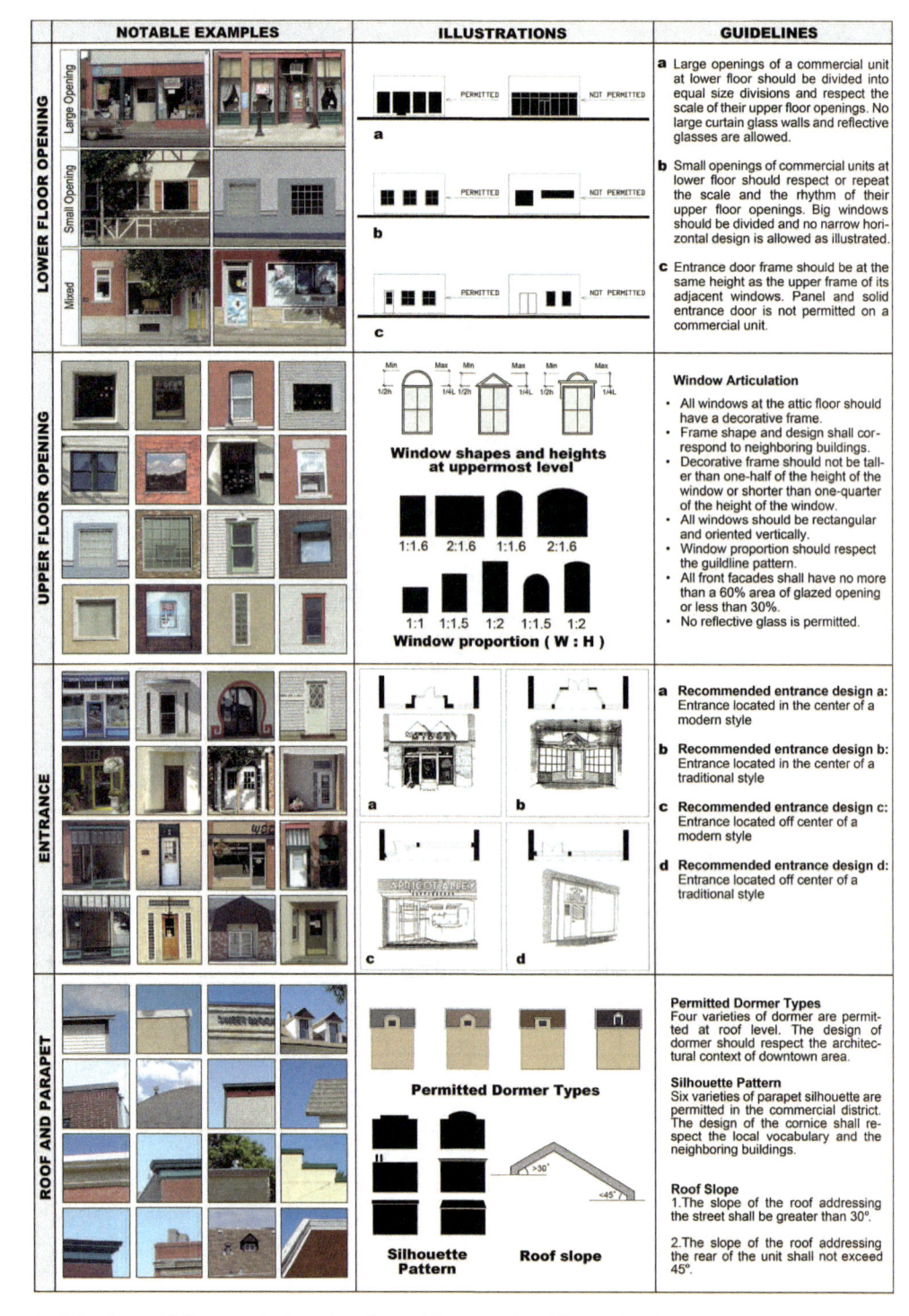

NOTABLE EXAMPLES	ILLUSTRATIONS	GUIDELINES

LOWER FLOOR OPENING

a Large openings of a commercial unit at lower floor should be divided into equal size divisions and respect the scale of their upper floor openings. No large curtain glass walls and reflective glasses are allowed.

b Small openings of commercial units at lower floor should respect or repeat the scale and the rhythm of their upper floor openings. Big windows should be divided and no narrow horizontal design is allowed as illustrated.

c Entrance door frame should be at the same height as the upper frame of its adjacent windows. Panel and solid entrance door is not permitted on a commercial unit.

UPPER FLOOR OPENING

Window shapes and heights at uppermost level

1:1.6 2:1.6 1:1.6 2:1.6

1:1 1:1.5 1:2 1:1.5 1:2

Window proportion (W : H)

Window Articulation

- All windows at the attic floor should have a decorative frame.
- Frame shape and design shall correspond to neighboring buildings.
- Decorative frame should not be taller than one-half of the height of the window or shorter than one-quarter of the height of the window.
- All windows should be rectangular and oriented vertically.
- Window proportion should respect the guildline pattern.
- All front facades shall have no more than a 60% area of glazed opening or less than 30%.
- No reflective glass is permitted.

ENTRANCE

a Recommended entrance design a: Entrance located in the center of a modern style

b Recommended entrance design b: Entrance located in the center of a traditional style

c Recommended entrance design c: Entrance located off center of a modern style

d Recommended entrance design d: Entrance located off center of a traditional style

ROOF AND PARAPET

Permitted Dormer Types

Silhouette Pattern **Roof slope**

Permitted Dormer Types
Four varieties of dormer are permitted at roof level. The design of dormer should respect the architectural context of downtown area.

Silhouette Pattern
Six varieties of parapet silhouette are permitted in the commercial district. The design of the cornice shall respect the local vocabulary and the neighboring buildings.

Roof Slope
1.The slope of the roof addressing the street shall be greater than 30°.

2.The slope of the roof addressing the rear of the unit shall not exceed 45°.

6.15 **Design guidelines can be introduced to guide renewal and future development of the core** reduce the number of patrons. Taking measures to increase safety would be worthwhile and will include strategies and principles based on Crime Prevention Through Environmental Design (CPTED) where installing better lighting, reducing entrapment spots, and having suitable signage would be implemented, as illustrated in Figure 6.14. In some instances increasing policing might be needed until safety is restored.

When planning an urban renewal, restoring or creating a sense of place that may have been lost by putting in place suitable guidelines is also critical (Figure 6.15). The aim is to create a welcoming environment for locals and visitors (Powe et al. 2009; Anders 2004). It involves improving street furnishing and landscaping, expanding sidewalks to improve walkability, replacing street lights, and installing bicycle racks, planters, and trash bins, which will send a positive message to merchants and patrons. Initiating façade improvement programs of private and public buildings as well as installing new store signs will also contribute to downtown commerce's ability to compete with large retail stores (Figure 6.16). In addition, the general

6.16 **Store signs can be innovative and eye-catching**

wayfinding needs to be unambiguous and direct visitors from afar to the core. If the design intention is to celebrate the town's past and at the same time soften the edges of existing structures, artists can be invited to depict scenes from the place's history on them. Public art can also be gradually introduced to create focal points and attract pedestrians.

Landscaping forms an important part of a place's appearance and comfort. Renewing the urban forest by planting trees and flowerbeds makes walking pleasant primarily in summertime. Trees, particularly in cold climate zones, need to be planted to block winds and create micro-climates. The landscaping can be integrated with sidewalk improvement and the introduction of outdoor cafés, and be part of the mobility and connectivity strategy for the area. Reaching downtown by foot, bike, or public transportation must be made a planning priority. Establishing networks of well-lit paths that connect all neighborhoods to the core will make walking attractive.

Implementing Renewal

Due to a lack of resources, implementing renewal strategies in small towns is not an easy task. Therefore, translating ideas into action ought to be done as carefully as the preparation of the plans themselves.

Ferguson (2005) suggests that the process of strengthening the core needs to begin by placing it on a list of important things that a town wishes to achieve. Municipalities also need to recognize that renewal processes last several years and appropriate planning stages accompanied by budget allocations need to be put in place. Those initiatives can be crafted to account for shifting trends and changes of governance so as not to bring a project to a halt, and are illustrated in Figure 6.17.

Another valuable objective is to foster a sense of ownership among key stakeholders. They may be galvanized around a common vision of how the place can look once the work is completed, which would foster a willingness to contribute to the process. It is also of value to form a steering committee aided by professional guidance if need be. The committee will meet regularly to review proposals, allocate funds, and monitor progress.

The planning and phasing of such processes also needs to be strategic. Since financial resources in small towns might be limited, it will be preferable to pay attention to one area, a single street, or even a street section (Robertson 2006). Parallel to the preparation of plans for a first section, guidelines for the remainder of the place can be introduced. It is hoped that when a section is constructed it will lead to additional private investment in building improvement and trigger further confidence among new investors.

The construction of residences needs to take on an added priority. Property owners with lots in strategic spots can be encouraged to build first. Having new infill structures on empty lots in the designated area will close gaping holes to create a continuous street appearance. Rear lanes can also be regarded as assets and be used as public spaces or covered (Figures 6.18 and 6.19). When buildings with no historic value have deteriorated beyond repair, they

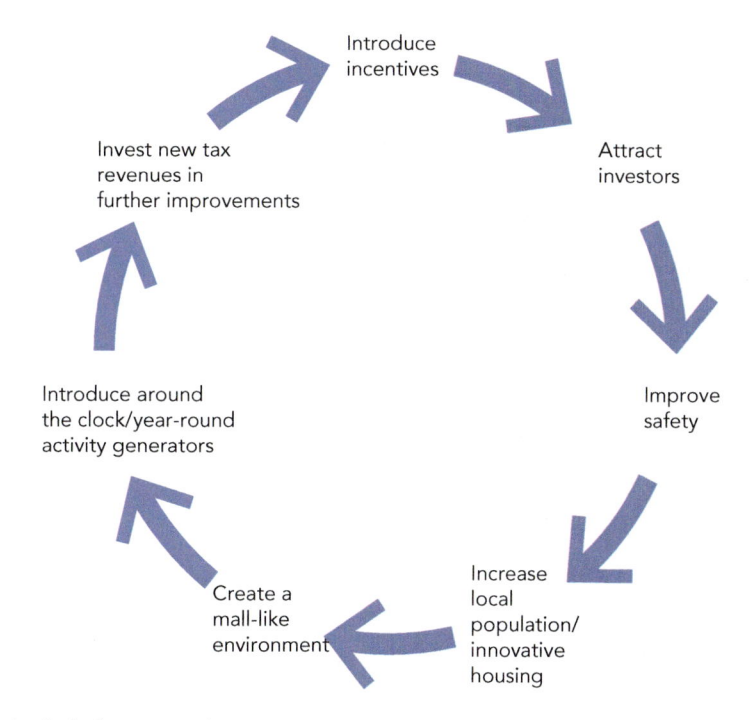

6.17 **A fly wheel of urban renewal**

6.18 **Turning a lane into a habitable social space in Fort Saskatchewan, Alberta**

6.19 **A covered lane turned into a pedestrian mall in Skipton, UK**

ought to be demolished rather than remain eyesores. Empty lots can be turned into temporary green public spaces maintained by the town or simply fenced.

An often-asked question is why should an investor open a store in the core rather than opt to locate it in a new mall on the edge of town? Enacting supporting policies are therefore necessary to demonstrate the town's intention to attract new merchants or residents. They may include a range of measures for different sectors. Residential developers may benefit from tax incentives, a reduction in connection fees to municipal utilities, and there can even be assistance given in the project promotion. Merchants may also benefit from professional assistance or interest-free loans or grants to improve their building façades or replace signage. Parking fees in the core can be reduced or waived altogether to encourage citizens to patronize the area.

Branding the core also needs to take place once the renewal process or a portion of it has been completed. When budget permits, professional marketing agencies may suggest a new name for the area, and distinguishing signage. Other contemporary means of mass communication such as websites and social media can let people know about events, new store openings, or offer a live webcam image of important spots.

Heritage Preservation

As noted above, heritage buildings in small towns should be regarded as assets and made an integral part of an urban renewal effort.

Several views have been introduced to reconcile modern development with heritage preservation. The *conservationist* view encourages the strict preservation of heritage structures, as shown in Figure 6.20. A *functionalist* optic, on the other hand, mediates heritage conflicts that arise between economic and cultural values. The *sense of place* perspective of heritage combines the two preceding principles of preservation. Instead of focusing on specific buildings, this view captures the uniqueness of the community as a whole. In other words, attractive communities are organic because they develop upon evolving social and built foundations (Feilden 1982).

When heritage preservation strategies are prepared for a large area, uniform rules cannot usually be applicable. The building of a community takes many years to complete; during this time, several building types are likely to be used in construction, following different styles and incorporating a range of details, materials, and technologies (Figure 6.21). Some "detective" work to decipher the architectural language of a place is necessary. This enables the identification of styles and determination of the zones in which they have been constructed.

The process begins by tracing the "building lifecycle." Familiarity with the date of construction leads to knowledge about style and construction techniques. It is also of value to know who designed and built them. Structures constructed by a speculative building firm often use a limited number of plans. On the other hand, when homeowners initiate construction, they engage different architects or building firms. Such data are commonly available via local

6.20 **Heritage preservation in Grasmere, UK**

6.21 **In proper urban restoration, attention can be paid to small details**

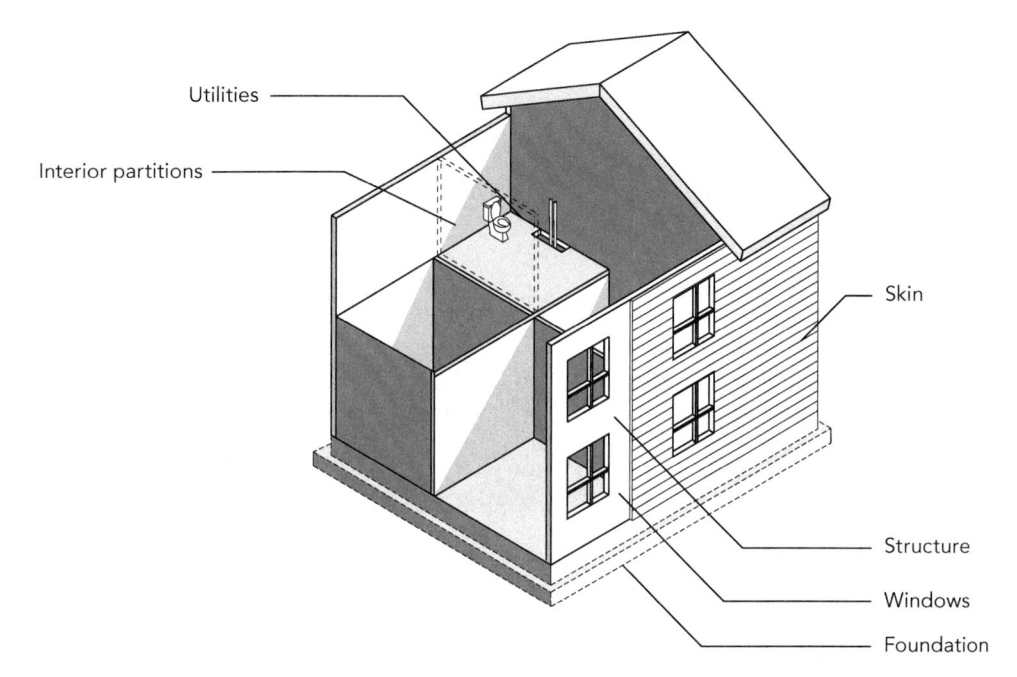

6.22 According to Brand (1994), structure needs to be seen and constructed as layers, each with its own lifecycle to accommodate transformation and preservation

planning offices and archives. Waves of economic upturn are often responsible for renovation cycles as well, as they provide the occupants with the means to renovate and can be traced.

Brand (1994) advocates studying buildings the way historians study the past: *diachronically*, with a view of changes over time, rather than *synchronically* with regard to a single point in time (Figure 6.22). Brand's observations of changes in buildings over time have led to a number of conclusions: buildings are layered by various rates of change, adaptation is easiest in cheaply made buildings that few people care for, and flux in the real estate market severs continuity in buildings. Brand's advice is to design and adapt with a sense of how a building originally looked and how it was adapted over time.

A study of the exterior features of buildings in small towns can offer advice as to a range and type of components that should be respected as the rehabilitation begins. In addition, it can provide a guide to the designers of new infill structures. The elements to be studied are cladding materials and colors, decorative wood and brickwork, porch design, and window and door types.

Retooling Downtown Westlock

Located north of Edmonton, the capital of the province of Alberta, in Canada, the town of Westlock, population 5,000, saw its downtown decline steadily. It still has a well-functioning core and is a

6.23 **Images of downtown Westlock, Alberta, Canada**

home to vibrant financial, professional, and commercial enterprises and services (Figure 6.23). Yet, it needed a makeover of sorts and alignment with revitalized downtowns of neighboring communities. As a result, I was asked to study the town's existing conditions, set renewal objectives, and draw a proposal that would put the area on a sustainable footing. The process involved fieldwork, interviews of key stakeholders, community consultation, and planning.

History and Context

The town's eventual site was mapped in 1912 and got its name from two of the original landowners: William Westgate and William Lockhart. Westlock was formally incorporated in 1916, three years after it was made part of the railroad network. A grain elevator and a bank were opened, making the town a grain exporting hub and service center to the area's farming communities.

Westlock's population has stagnated for a while, which posed a challenge to efforts to increase its tax base. Despite a relatively stable employment situation, the town does not have major employers and the citizens draw their income from small enterprises and services that are offered to the region and are located there.

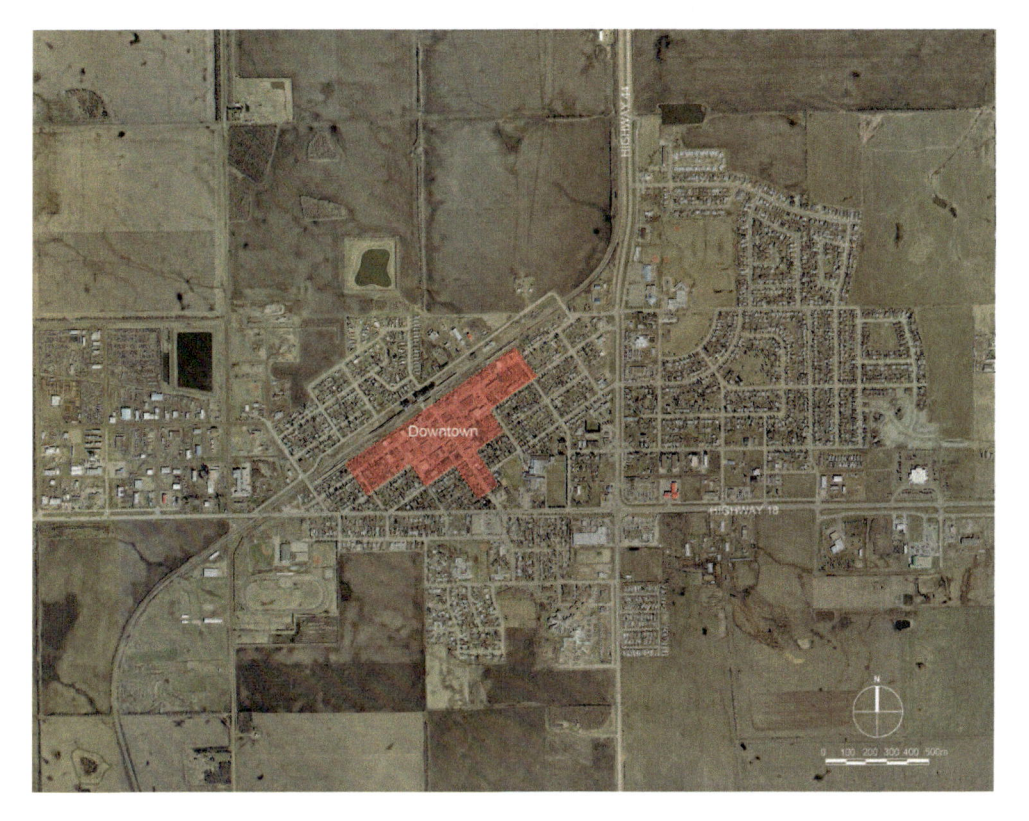

6.24 **Aerial photos of Westlock**

Geographically the town is split into two equal sections divided by a highway as illustrated in Figure 6.24. As a result downtown does not serve as a natural center for the entire town. Also, some commerce and light industrial enterprises are located along the highways, which weaken the core. The land in downtown has multi-purpose zoning designation, with a mix of service and commercial uses. The core borders the industrial area dominated by the highly visible grain elevators. Downtown is made up of a blend of low-rise turn-of-the-century styled structures and contemporary buildings. The old ones are cladded with brick and stucco, many of which are worth preservation. The residential areas that border the core are mostly post-World War II low-rise, single-family siding covered units.

The core is highly accessible from both the neighborhoods and the highways. Its road system is at a 45-degree angle to the highway. The streets are laid out in a gridiron form with lanes in between used mostly for parking.

Strengths and Weaknesses

As a prior step to developing a renewal plan for Westlock's downtown we listed the place's strengths and weaknesses. Having a proper mix of land uses and close proximity between residential and commercial areas was first recognized. Diversity of businesses makes the area attractive for both locals and regional visitors. Once people arrive, they find the place highly walkable with close proximity between the different amenities.

The core's empty lots offer opportunities for both residential and commercial developers. The rich urban and visual history acts as a suitable backdrop to those potential initiatives. The many mom-and-pop stores lend downtown a quaint sense of place that one hopes to find in small communities. The two museums—Pioneer and Tractor—have outstanding collections of material culture and farm equipment from the turn of the century. With proper promotion both museums can become regional and even national draws. One also notices the town's strong social fabric. It is a close-knit community in which people take pride and many are active in one of the social clubs.

Several barriers made it a challenge to launch an urban renewal plan in Westlock and needed to be addressed first. At present, there is no sufficient local population who call downtown home. Growing the town's overall population will also draw people, primarily young cohorts, to the core. The town also needs to broaden its narrow tax base by attracting large enterprises and turning assets such as the museums into a draw for regional and provincial visitors.

On a smaller scale, the area lacks definition and demarcation. An absence of clear way-finding was also noticed. As for current land uses, there are several enterprises of industrial nature that do not belong in the core. Garages and storage spaces give the place a poor image. Human scale can also be improved along landscaping and streetscaping interventions. Over the years, little attention was paid to tree planting, in particular in the main streets. The absence of a gathering place such as a public square was also noticed.

The Proposal

The main thrust of the proposed land use was to create suitable conditions for downtown population growth and retool the place to become welcoming and pleasant to live or be in, as illustrated in Figure 6.25. It was to be achieved by lending the place a unique identity grounded in its rich urban history and further increasing its walkability and unique commercial offering.

The proposal's key features were: the redesign of 100 Avenue, the core's main drag, the creation of a civic square, the introduction of elements that would visually designate the area, building on empty lots, and paying homage to heritage structures (Figure 6.26).

The plan's details called for the creation of a civic square at the end of 100 Avenue near an empty building to which the town hall can be relocated (Figure 6.27). A linear park will be

6.25 **A proposed land-use plan for downtown Westlock**

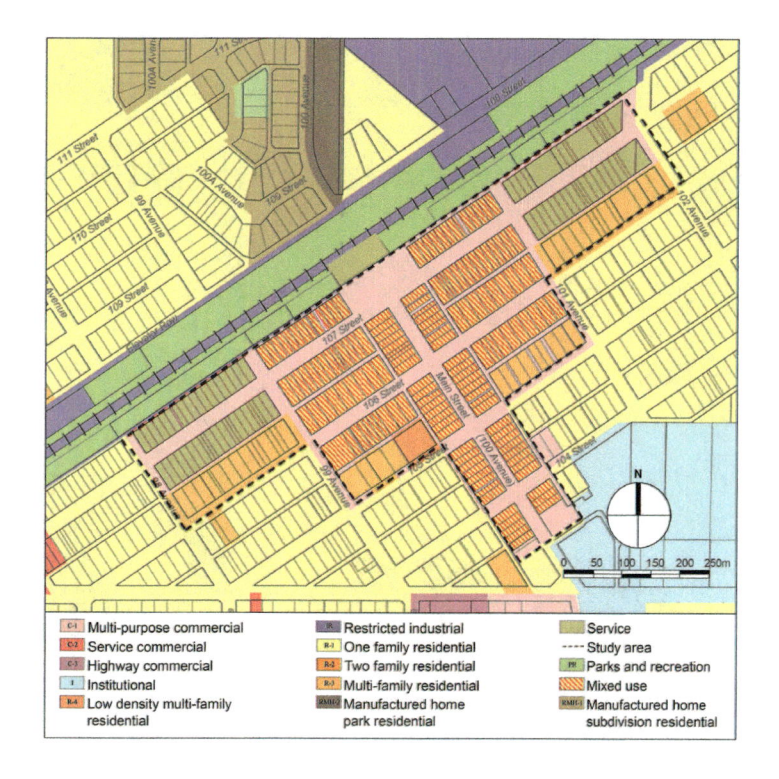

C-1 Multi-purpose commercial	R-1 Restricted industrial	Service
C-2 Service commercial	R-1 One family residential	---- Study area
C-3 Highway commercial	R-2 Two family residential	PR Parks and recreation
I Institutional	R-3 Multi-family residential	Mixed use
R-4 Low density multi-family residential	RMH1 Manufactured home park residential	RMH2 Manufactured home subdivision residential

6.26 **A proposed intervention plan for Westlock's downtown**

Industrial	Linear park
Existing building	Residential
Proposed building	Square
Parking	Rail line

1. New town hall
2. Civic square
3. Parking lot
4. Parallel parking
5. Linear park
6. Terminal
7. The mall

0 25 50 75 100 125m

6.27 **A proposed new civic square**

established along the train tracks parallel to the grain elevators area. The grain storage silos will be painted, lit creatively at night, and turned into artifacts. The area will also see its human scale and walkability improved with the addition of low-rise buildings, sidewalk expansion, tree planting programs, and new street furnishing. The core will also be supported by a façade improvement program—a joint undertaking by building owners and the town. To guide the renewal process, new urban and architectural guidelines have been introduced to regulate façade materials, scale of new additions, openings, and streetscaping, to name a few.

In addition, the following measures have been recommended: introduce an incentive program to attract apartment builders, implement a financial incentive package to entice new businesses to move to Westlock, encourage tourism through the construction of a new Pioneer museum, the introduction of summer movie and concerts in the park programs, and the initiation of a sound and light show projection on the grain elevators to celebrate the place's agricultural heritage (Figure 6.28). It was also suggested that after-hour activities will be encouraged by supporting local bars, cafés, and cinemas. In addition, a steering committee made of business owners, citizens, and other stakeholders will be established to monitor the renewal process.

Existing grain elevators

Proposed new city hall and painted grain elevators

6.28 **Existing and proposed painted grain elevator and a new city hall**

To align Westlock's downtown revitalization efforts with contemporary environmental challenges, it was suggested that the town dedicate a bike lane on all streets, install solar-powered light fixtures, explore the introduction of a community-wide shuttle bus, develop a recycling plan for downtown merchants, and insist on having all new street furniture made of recycled materials.

7
Wealth Generation

"There are very few small towns in China," a colleague told me half-jokingly when I asked him about a place whose economy is tied to its cultural and geographic heritage. He directed me to the Water Town of Zhouzhuang, population 138,000. After an hour-long drive from Shanghai, I arrived there on a rainy day.

Proudly referred to as the "Venice of China" and the "Number 1 Water Town," the place is a known tourist draw. Dating back to the year 1086 and the Ming Qing dynasty, the settlement was sited on a river delta where for generations the inhabitants fished. Homes cladded with stone and roofed with red tiles edged the canals and rows of small boats were tied to the banks (Figure 7.1).

Nowadays, the residents of Zhouzhuang are pursuing another source of income: tourism. People flock to the place to stroll on the narrow sidewalks that line the water, buy souvenirs in one of the many craft shops, be photographed on the stone bridges that arch over the canals, and eat fried pork, a local delicacy.

I disliked the place at first. I was hoping that there would be fewer shops and on-site craft production staged for tourists like me. But then, walking in the place's side streets and back alleys and seeing the impoverished homes, I realized that more than a tourist draw, it is a ladder. It is a way for craftmakers, boat rowers, waitresses, and shopkeepers to improve their lives. The people of Zhouzhuang realized that their place of living is of interest to others and a source of wealth. They invested in making their town welcoming and publicized it to draw international visitors like me.

Many small towns were caught in a global economic transition that saw their traditional sources of revenues drain out. This chapter looks into the economy of small towns. Recalling historical evolution, their uniqueness, the potential for tourism, cultural industries, and economic retooling strategies are some of the topics discussed. The chapter ends with a case study that describes an economic renewal in a small community.

7.1 **One of the canals that runs through the water town of Zhouzhuang, China**

The Economy of Small Towns

A scan through the history of human settlements demonstrates that communities were founded where opportunities for survival existed. The ability to defend against enemy attack and gather or produce food are rudimentary manifestations of ancient locational choice. The need to exceed survival and prosper was also an inherent aspect of settlements. Jane Jacobs (1969) referred to cities as "places that produce wealth." Indeed, many communities are engaged in activities whose aim is to improve their economic standing through additional development either by individuals or as a communal effort. Lapping et al. (1989) defined economic development as a process of change whose goal is to increase the wealth of a community by raising incomes, increasing access to services, and reducing unemployment. The accent here is on proactive attitudes that see cities and towns chart their own future.

Historically, the economy of many small and rural towns was tied to basic resources. They have traditionally functioned as retail and service centers to surrounding farmers and as a processing and shipment point for farm commodities, timber, and minerals (Daniels 1991). The type of economic activity was largely dependent on the town's location, the resources in the surrounding area, and the local hierarchical economic organization (Weber and Rahe 2010). Some heavily relied on a big city nearby, while others were more independent. Such towns had vital transportation links with main manufacturing hubs, primarily via water or rail.

This economic structure saw its major transformation during the Industrial Revolution. The swelling of large urban hubs also contributed to the evolution of some smaller hubs. For example, locations near waterways and the development of machine-based production saw the fortunes of some small towns rise and others decline. The mid-sized city of Cornwall, in the Province of Ontario, Canada, was such a place. Its proximity to the St. Lawrence River made it possible to obtain raw cotton from afar, and private investment led to the development of cotton mills to weave fabric, which was then sent elsewhere (McCullough 1992) (Figure 7.2). Across the ocean, a similar development history can be attributed to Scotland's New Lanark, where Robert Owen introduced his far-reaching social reforms (New Lanark Trust n.d.).

The next evolutionary stage can be traced to the aftermath of World War II. Further transformation of industrial production methods, the amalgamation of several small family farms into a large single entity, and the evolution of the interstate highways system and air travel dealt a blow to the economy of some places and allowed others to thrive. Towns which forged long-standing partnerships with one large employer saw their industries close when their products were no longer in demand or when companies were offered tempting incentives

7.2 **Former cotton weaving sheds were converted into residences and offices in Cornwall, Ontario, Canada**

by other municipalities. More critically, the challenge for economic developers of small rural towns was adapting a nineteenth century economic, political, and small town urban pattern to the shopping culture and public service requirements of larger firms and a mobile population (Fox 1962).

Under these circumstances and to a large extent as a result of the entrepreneurial skills and the place's governance structure, some communities were able to retool their economy and others became stagnant or shrank further. Their small size was clearly a disadvantage. They lacked the means to diversify economically, take preemptive measures, or act swiftly when downturns occurred (Hibbard and Davis 1986).

Bedroom communities to large cities that did not have industry and whose economy was based on property taxes were affected marginally. In fact, many saw their wealth increase when a building boom occurred. Small edge towns altered their zoning to increase their revenue and accommodate land developers. Wide roads were introduced, large lots mandated, and big homes constructed in the interest of securing continuous revenue streams based on property values.

The 1980s marked the start of another economic transformation with effects on small town economies: globalization. The interconnectedness of the world's economies and the proliferation of trade agreements increased competition between nations and cities several-fold. It also made it easier and more convenient for companies, primarily those producing labor-intensive products, to manufacture offshore in low-wage countries. Industries that for very

7.3 **A typical scenario of economic decline**

long were the core of their town's economy and wealth generation either shut their doors or moved to other cities or countries, leaving a gaping hole in the local economy and a frantic effort to find a replacement (Figure 7.3). Firms, capital, and labor moved to places that offered lucrative incentives to ensure higher profitability with little sentiments or attachment to a previous place.

A change which benefited some small edge towns was the relocation to them of head offices or manufacturing facilities that were formerly in big cities. Cheap land, lower taxes, proximity to highways, availability of a trained labor force and affordable housing for employees led to the construction of office parks and distribution centers. The era also brought to the forefront the tension between *global* and *local*. The need to create or keep jobs by supporting locally based enterprises and consume local products made economic sustainability a bold goal for all communities (Figure 7.4). Although some still relied heavily on a single employer, many towns attempted to diversify their economies and expand their tax base by seeking other sources of revenue. Some mounted campaigns to encourage consumption of locally

7.4 **Cheeses and sausages are promoted as "local products" in Alberobello, Italy**

manufactured products or food. In addition, those whose economies relied heavily on natural resources saw their fortunes fluctuate along with the price of these commodities (Daniels and Lapping 1987). For example, when a demand for housing declined, lumber mills in small towns had to lay off employees, which led to a negative chain effect that hurt other businesses.

The dawn of the information age marked an additional phase in business development with potential ramifications on the economy of small towns. The World Wide Web offered a tool to broadcast the existence of a product, service, or a place to many. It has become easier to reach and order a product and find out about an event online, for example. Dillman (1983) suggests that the transition to the information age could benefit small towns. The use of information appliances means that workers do not need to commute physically to a distant office. Some small towns that offered an attractive lifestyle, lower taxes, and affordable housing attracted firms and individuals whose businesses did not rely on face-to-face interaction with customers, like call centers.

The after-effect of the 2008 economic downturn, along with new global trends, is bound to affect the economies of small towns once more. Economic fluctuation, the expected retirement of the "baby boom" generation, the need to address environmental issues such as climate change, and reduce high emission levels will leave some imprint on the economies of all communities. It may require a review of current strategies and the adoption of new ones.

Strategies for Sustainable Economies

Prior to offering concrete strategies for economic development in small towns, it would be of value to set the stage for their introduction. Daniels (1989) argues that theorists who write on economic development are split into two main camps: those who believe that local efforts can generate sustainable growth and those who feel that outside forces are the arbiters of whether or not a small town will grow. It is clear that some see the process as fatalistic in nature, a product of unavoidable global forces. Tweeten and Brinkman (1976) divide the economic activities of communities into two: they call the first type of place "locations with internal combustion," where activities are primarily the outcome of local initiatives be they entrepreneurial or government-driven. The second is referred to as "external combustion" and regards places whose economic livelihood is managed by outside forces such as national or multinational corporations. Strategies for wealth generation in both will naturally be different.

Local traditional patterns also play an important role when it comes to economic development. Blakely (1983) identifies five types of communities, each with its own development attitude, as listed in Figure 7.5. He calls the first "entrepreneurial communities" and characterizes them as pro-growth with strong local leadership and ample financial resources which seek out employers and investors in order to further their goals. "Analytical communities" are very cautious about change and suffer, according to Blakely, from "paralysis by analysis" as they fail to take action. Similarly, "defender communities" strongly guard what they have, block

Type	Definition	Characteristics
Entrepreneurial	• Culture of initiation and implementation	• Pro-growth • Steady leadership • Ample resources • Capable implementers • Broad population support
Analytical	• Overly studied communities	• Each process begins with a study • Take long time to decide • Weak implementers
Defender	• Rejects new ideas and initiatives	• Content with the status quo • Avoid decision-making • Lack of vision • Population rejects initiatives
Destroyer	• Action results in negative consequences	• Poor consultation process • No understanding of cause and effect • Poor reading of global trends • Do not resist external pressure
Desperate	• Action is driven by desperation ("loss of major employer")	• Poor strategic thinking • Hasty decision-making • Under pressure by population • Willing to offer incentive

7.5 **Five types of communities and their development characteristics**

any initiative and outreach, and rarely display active attitudes. "Destroyer communities" adopt decisions that end up harming the community prosperity or reputation such as allowing the type of commerce that lowers the ability of existing mom-and-pop stores to compete (Figure 7.6). The last community on Blakely's list is a "desperate community" whose actions are a result of misfortune. The departure of a large employer that has resulted in major job losses will guide their action that, often times, would be to "sell out for a quick economic fix." Therefore, it is clear that the adoption of any recommended economic strategy for a small town will largely depend on the "culture of the place" and generalization cannot be used.

In regard to development, Daniels (1991) sees four pillars anchoring the structure of any economic proposal: the type of economic base desired; the pace of economic change; the distribution of wealth and income; and how to go about encouraging economic growth. Levy (2009) suggests that prior to charting an economic path, communities should conduct needs assessments, market evaluations, study the potential consequences of their actions, and only then formulate their plan.

So, what would it take to put a small town's economy on a sustainable footing? To begin with, based on the aspects noted above and global economic fluctuations, communities need

7.6 Supermarket chain stores in small towns lower the ability of locally run mom-and-pop grocery stores to compete

- Visionary, good long- and short-term planners

- Know what they can be best at

- Act on economic opportunities with no delay

- No internal political feuds

- Know how to gain and use wide population support

- Strategic thinkers

- Work toward achieving a goal with tenacity

- Know how to match tasks and people

- Good communicators and successful in social marketing

- Good caretakers/managers

- Ability to prioritize and use resources wisely

- Good stewards of the environment

- Give voice to everyone/put interest of the citizens first

7.7 Characteristics of good municipal leadership teams

capable leadership. It is both a personal and strategic issue. Analysis and knowledge must drive entrepreneurial undertakings of communities. It seems that the era of waiting for things to occur on their own without initiatives or interventions or knowledge has passed. Leaders need, therefore, to set the stage for opportunities to occur by revisiting the relevance of old policies and introducing new ones. It is a more dynamic, responsive style of governance rather than one that acts as a "caretaker." The competitiveness between communities both globally and locally requires a fast response to and action following inquiries. The governing council and the senior administration must also possess the knowledge and skills needed for decision-making when economic matters are discussed and proposals evaluated (Figure 7.7).

The economies of a small town can be categorized in several ways that are illustrated in Figure 7.8. Yet, establishing an overall sustainable economic footing is paramount to a place's prosperity and another key pillar to consider. Reliance on a single employer or industry has proven to be harmful to many small towns. When demand for that industry's product declines or the company is lured away with a better incentive package, alternative sources of revenue need to fill the gap. Therefore, diversification is seen as a necessary approach to the meeting of the current economic challenges. In choosing new areas of activities, the town's existing assets are likely to be the prime source for opportunities to exploit. A charming downtown can

Service	Offer amenities and material support to neighboring communities	Fairly stable economy
Administration	Serve as a government and/or educational hub	Fairly stable economy
Single industry	Most jobs are generated by a single employer (e.g. mining, forestry)	Prone to economic downturns
Diverse	Employment is generated by several employers	Diversified economy
Tourist	Most jobs are generated by tourist-related industries	Seasonal employment
Resource	Economic vitality is related to nearby natural resources	Prone to economic downturn

7.8 **Types of common economies of small towns. At times, several aspects may join to form the place's economy**

7.9 The *1001 Pots* pottery fair in Val-David, Quebec, Canada

become the backdrop to an annual fair that draws local and regional tourists (Figure 7.9). A town's location near a major highway in proximity to several large cities may be a desirable site for an enterprise that may wish to locate a large distribution center. The aim is to find a niche in which a town can become a local or even regional leader and which can be carried on passionately over time.

Places, to a large measure, are shaped by the people who reside in them and, as noted above, by their leaders. Enriching the town's population and attracting those who can initiate enterprises or work in them is a valuable step to sustainability. Florida's (2002) recognition of a "creative class" contribution to the triumph and prosperity of cities has recast the way policymakers regard their population. It is therefore not only the age distribution of the town's population that counts, but their interests and occupations.

Two groups are seen as vital to the economic prosperity of small towns. Young cohorts are often known to contribute to, and possess the drive needed to start, new enterprises. They are likely to be attracted by the availability of affordable housing and a unique lifestyle that offers alternatives to the fast rhythm of the big city. On the other end, an elderly population can also contribute to a town's economy. Daniels (1989) argues that seniors are an important source of internal and external combustion in small towns. Often, they contribute a steady stream of cash transfers in the form of purchasing goods and services. Several small towns made attracting seniors the prime target of their economic prosperity.

Located in Northern Ontario, Canada, halfway between the cities of Sudbury and Sault Ste. Marie, Elliot Lake, population 12,000, is surrounded by more than 4,000 pristine lakes and rivers, magnificent old-growth forests, and dramatic rock escarpments. In 1990, the two uranium-mining companies that operated near the town announced they were terminating their operations. From 1990 to 1991 the town lost its entire industry and employment and experienced the most rapid decline in population of any small Canadian municipality.

As a first course of action, the municipality established a "mayor's action committee." This committee consisted of mine managers, labor representatives, educators, business leaders, and city councilors who decided that the town had to be balanced and diversified, independent of mining, and avoid the boom-and-bust cycle it had experienced.

One recommended strategy for the City of Elliot Lake was to aggressively pursue the "retirement business" as a key future industry. In 1992, Elliot Lake Retirement Living was established and then the corporation negotiated the acquisition of 1,400 housing units from the mining companies. The challenge for Retirement Living was that the mining companies wanted to demolish the rest of their housing stock, some of which were brand new homes in recently constructed subdivisions. The city enacted bylaws and land-use planning regulations to prevent the demolition of these homes. In the end, the mining companies relinquished the homes and the new corporation acquired the remaining units.

Currently, the town has successfully positioned itself as Canada's senior citizen capital. Effective marketing attracted 3,600 retirees to Elliot Lake and it is estimated that each senior accounts for 0.6 full-time jobs for a younger resident.

Initiating suitable policies and creating the right regulatory environment contributes significantly to a town's economy. It begins by evaluating and putting into place a mechanism that guards existing community economic assets. It is often hard to prevent a firm from moving away but "keeping an eye on" and supporting companies already in town may prevent the negative consequences of abrupt departure and becoming desperate.

Firms will be drawn to a place due to its human and natural assets. Yet, in a highly competitive business environment, incentives count. They can play a role and become the tipping point in selecting one site over another. The incentives need to be based on the expected return of the anticipated investment and economic opportunity. Number of future jobs, anticipated tax revenue, or contribution to the town's overall image would be some of the criteria that would determine the type of incentives given. The incentives may include tax holidays, as well as exemption from some fees and levies, to name a few.

Policies can also include amending zoning and bylaws to create suitable locations for potential investors. Increasing densities and allocating land for industrial uses are some zoning-related interventions. In some cases, the retooling of downtown can also become a vehicle for increased economic activity. Simplifying applications for building permits will also be of value. Some towns have reviewed and simplified their protocols in order to convey an "open for business" attitude.

Promotion and branding are also vital instruments. Having a clear and accessible website, partaking in promotional fairs, and creating well-articulated literature are some of the tools. Branding is a way for a town to address and cast its local and global image (Winfield-Pfefferkorn 2005). The concepts of brand strategy are increasingly being adopted from the world of commerce and applied to cities that are seeking growth, regeneration, and a good quality of life for their residents. To some extent, places are no different than companies: those with a strong brand find it much easier to sell their products and services as well as attract people and investment. A strong brand can shift the perception of a place that may be suffering from a poor image among external and internal constituents; create a common vision for the future of the community and its potential; provide a consistent representation of the place; enhance its local or regional awareness and position; shed unfavorable stereotypes associated with place; and make it more appealing (Dinnie 2011).

Developing Tourism and Cultural Industries

In response to the economic challenges that forced communities to diversify their economies, some towns began to explore other sources of wealth generation. Tourism is commonly brought up when questions about new economic strategies are discussed. This section looks at the potential of establishing tourism and cultural industries in small towns.

Tourism involves activities by people who travel to and lodge away from their home for business or pleasure. Some definitions also regard the length of stay, which is commonly over one day. According to the Commission on Sustainable Development (1999), travel and tourism are some of the world's largest industries and creators of jobs across national and regional economies. The report goes on to suggest that in 1998, tourism directly and indirectly generated 11.7 percent of the gross domestic product (GDP) and nearly 200 million jobs worldwide. It is indeed an industry with significant economic potential for large and small places alike. It can also be referred to as an "added value" industry due to its contribution to a number of related activities. A traveler will spend time in a hotel, dine in restaurants, patronize shops, and visit cultural venues such as theaters or museums.

Travel has become easier in recent decades. The building of interstate highways, the proliferation of and competition among airline companies, and the digital age has made business or leisure tourism simpler and more accessible. Yet, it seems that the golden age of tourism is still to come. When surveyed, members of the "baby boom" generation placed travel at the top of a list of desired retirement activities. Therefore, it is no wonder that small towns are taking a closer look at their suitability for this industry.

A good place to begin contemplating tourism for a small town is to ask what the place has to offer. Every town will welcome a visitor, and to a great extend many already have

7.10 **The Village of Gerberoy, in the Picardie Region, France, attracts tourists, who come to see the roses and take part in the Rose Festival**

fragments of tourism. Yet "industry" refers to a coordinated and focused effort to align the town's "brand" with a segment in which investments are made, infrastructure constructed, and name recognition cultivated (Figure 7.10).

There are reasons that make one visit a spot for leisure or for an association to choose a town for their annual meeting. They all wish to travel to a place with a unique advantage or take part in a special activity. Types of tourism include agritourism (staying or working in a farm), culinary tourism (dining in unique places or taking cooking lessons), educational tourism (attending courses), cultural tourism (visiting museums and other events), ecotourism (enjoying nature), religious tourism, wildlife tourism, and heritage tourism (travel to ancestral sites), to name a few (Figure 7.11). Each of these activities will have its own characteristics and support services.

Tourism is also categorized by the length of time that a visitor may stay in a place. There are day trips, limited stay, or people who stay in a place for a prolonged period of time. The spending of tourists will also be diverse. "Budget tourists" will camp or stay in a low-cost lodging establishment, whereas business travelers are likely to choose a more luxurious place of stay. Another aspect of note is the method of travel people use to reach their destination. There are easy-to-reach locales nearby airports or train stations, and others that can only be reached by car (Figure 7.12).

7.11 **The town of Grasmere, UK, where poet William Wordsworth lived and is buried, draws many visitors**

Types of tourism	Types of tourists	Length of stay	Accommodation	Mode of travel	Draws
• Business	• Business	• Pass through	• Camp ground	• Air	• Sporting event
• Eco/wild life	• Personal travel	• Day trip	• Hostel	• Ground/public	• Cultural event
• Cultural	• Group	• Several days	• B&B	• Recreational vehicle	• Natural beauty
• Sports		• Prolonged stay	• Budget hotel	• Own car	• Shopping
• Culinary			• Luxury hotel		• Heritage buildings
• Heritage/religion					

7.12 **Key determinants of a tourist industry**

Not every town can cultivate and launch a tourist industry. It takes many years to turn existing assets, be they natural or cultural, into worthwhile places to visit. The first step is therefore to identify a niche in which steady investment can be made. For example, natural assets will require the clearing of a riverbank and private investment in waterfront restaurants (Figure 7.13). Cultural industry will require building a museum and assembling a suitable display. Funding, either public or private, will be essential.

Despite the direct and indirect positive contributions that tourism can make to a small town's economies, researchers also warn of some negative consequences. Davis and Morais (2004) suggest that acceptance of tourism activity drops sharply when the negative consequences of tourism development—such as crime, parking problems, traffic, and loss of local

7.13 **Peggy's Cove, Nova Scotia, Canada, attracts tourists to its natural beauty**

"sense of place"—engulf a community overwhelmed with tourists. Also, the authors note that in some cases, when municipal investment in tourism fails to benefit a town in the short run, it may trigger animosity in the town's people towards tourism enterprises. The authors go on to suggest that it would be wise to critically evaluate the promised advantages of tourism before investment is made.

Several steps and actions can be recommended in the process of establishing tourism in a small town that already has a budding industry or wishes to start a new enterprise (Figure 7.14). The process may begin by taking a close look at the town's assets and evaluating whether they can constitute a foundation upon which a tourist industry can be established. A second step would be to establish the amount of public and private funds that will have to be invested and find out whether the town is able to sustain such resources of both time and money. Such inquiries are commonly made by engaging specialized consultants.

Once a decision to move ahead has been made, the initial step will be to get key stakeholders on board. The town's leadership, administrative staff, and major contributing private enterprises need to take part in setting short- and long-term strategies and tasks. The plan also needs to be brought to the attention of the general public via consultation, particularly when funds are to be spent. In addition, a mechanism can be put in place to oversee the process. Hiring a trained coordinator to steer the long process would be of great value.

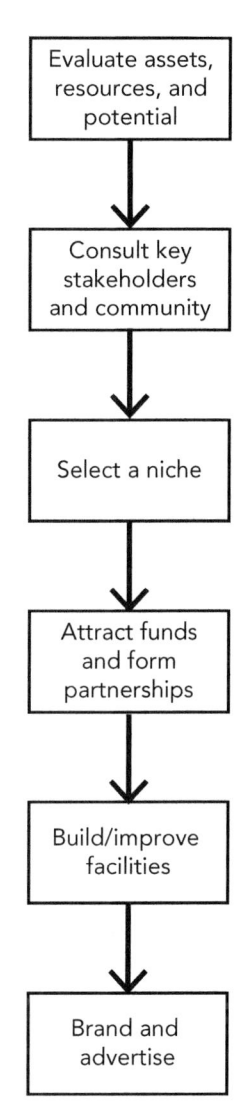

Evaluate assets, resources, and potential

↓

Consult key stakeholders and community

↓

Select a niche

↓

Attract funds and form partnerships

↓

Build/improve facilities

↓

Brand and advertise

7.14 **Steps in initiating a tourist industry**

When looking for assets that can constitute the anchors of a tourist industry, decisions will likely depend on budget. When resources are limited, the town can bank on assets already in place. A ski hill or a golf course operated by the municipality can be improved and promoted to become the core of a seasonal draw. Small-scale music or theater festivals or even a horse race can be expanded and brought to the attention of regional and national audiences (Figure 7.15). A local nature reserve can be further developed and house a camping ground.

Beechworth, population 3,500, located in the northeast of Victoria, Australia, can serve as a model for such an approach. In 1984, the town began a transformation from a stagnant community based on government services employment to one built on its architectural heritage and tourism. In 1984, Tom O'Toole, a native of Beechworth, returned to the community and purchased a struggling bakery, and began a journey that has not only revitalized the town of Beechworth, but has instigated a national business icon. The Beechworth Bakery has been an outstanding enterprise and has become synonymous with the town's success. The most remarkable part of this story is that Beechworth is located three hours from a capital city and is not accessed by a major highway. The impact of the bakery on the community and its business and employment sectors is equally impressive. The founder's vision inspired others in the community and today the town is a major tourism center, and despite the closure of a major hospital and the associated job cuts, Beechworth is growing.

The natural assets of the Dutch town of De Koog, population 1,300, on Texel Island, made it a draw to an international bird-watching tourist industry. When it realized that it was located on a bird migration path, and noted a growing interest in bird watching, the town went on to establish bird sanctuaries. A shop selling gear and equipment to bird watchers and the building of camp grounds, hotels, and restaurants in the town center followed.

When a foundation upon which a tourism industry can be established does not exist, one can be created. The type of industries will largely depend on the resources that the town wishes to invest. Several small towns have undertaken such initiatives.

The Kaap Skil museum in the town of Oudeschild, also on the Dutch island of Texel, is another example of a core initiative that stimulated a local tourist industry. The beautifully designed museum opened its doors in 2012. The museum pays homage to the town's maritime history and archeology, as well as having an assembly of local heritage buildings. A center-piece of the museum is a collection of beachcombing artifacts assembled by several of the

7.15 **The Palio horse race draws regional tourists to Casole d'Elsa, Italy**

townspeople, shown in Figure 7.16. Bottles, ropes, and countless personal items that drifted ashore are on display. The museum's façade was apparently constructed of driftwood.

Two North American towns have selected extraterrestrial fictional activities as a theme to develop a tourist industry around. The town of Vulcan, population 2,000, in the Province of Alberta, Canada, capitalized on its name, made famous by the *Star Trek* television and feature film series. A tourist station that displays Star Trek memorabilia, a replica of a starship, and hosts an annual convention are some of its initiatives (Mair 2009). A similar initiative took place in Roswell, which over the years claimed national and international name recognition with no monetary investment. The town is associated with mysterious crash landings of UFOs and was used in feature movies, such as *Independence Day*. There, too, a theme for downtown retail businesses, and an international UFO museum and research center became a tourist draw (Paradis 2002).

Other places have banked on their historic heritage. The Scottish town of New Lanark, home to Robert Owen's revolutionary social ideas, took on the refurbishment of old cotton mills to turn them into a museum, hotel, and a visitors' center (Figure 7.17). Similarly, the UK town of Hay-on-Wye, population 1,900, on the east bank of the river Wye, also known as the "Town of Books," has become a sought-after location of some 30 bookstores, many of which

7.16 Beachcombing artifacts are on display in the Kaap Skil museum in the town of Oudeschild, the Netherlands

7.17 The cotton mills in New Lanark, Scotland, were converted into a museum, hotel, and a visitors' center

sell specialist and second-hand titles. However, what propelled the town into international stardom was an annual literary festival that was initiated in 1988 and draws some 80,000 visitors for ten days at the beginning of June.

Another vital aspect related to tourism in small towns is lodging. If the town is to mount an event and draw a large number of visitors, it needs to have a place to house them. Attracting hotel investors is not an easy task, since their guiding criteria for choosing a location are based on number of travelers, location, and size of community. There are, however, small hotel chains that would welcome the opportunity to be among the first to come to a community. In addition, hotels may choose to locate near clusters of towns for convenience and draw visitors from them all.

Other solutions can be the establishment of bed and breakfast (B&B) accommodation. In some cases, bylaws permitting residents to convert their homes into B&B need to be introduced and, at times, opposition from neighboring residents will have to be overcome (Figure 7.18). Agritourism, attracting visitors to farming establishments, is also common and popular in a number of European countries. Farmers are permitted to convert an existing building or build a new structure for hospitality purposes.

Weaving the development of a tourist industry in with other undertakings by the town can also be considered. Main street improvements and downtown renewal can be initiated

7.18 **Stately homes have been restored and converted into B&B in Stratford, Ontario, Canada**

7.19 **A public tourist information structure in Montpelier, Vermont, USA**

in parallel with the start of the active pursuit of tourism. Several towns that have invested in improving their sports facilities capitalize on a regional need for a location for play space by amateur junior teams. It has created a thriving tourism for the players and their families.

During the urban renewal process, an effort should be made to make the place amiable to visitors. Wayfinding is an important part of this effort. Installing information booths, direction signs, and having volunteers welcome tourists during key large gatherings should also be considered (Figure 7.19).

Finally, no tourist industry in a town can succeed without letting others know about it. The various media networks are instrumental to the dissemination of news about an event or a town. Setting up a website, associating a place with a food product, taking part in a tourism convention and fairs, and placing ads in newspapers and travel magazines are bound to draw a crowd (Figure 7.20).

7.20 **The branding of some towns and regions is associated with food products, such as Calvados, the liquor from France (top left), Edam cheese from the Netherlands (top right), Greek honey from Rhodes (bottom left), and Limonchello from Sorrento, Italy (bottom right)**

Building an Economy from the Ground Up in Langford

If one is looking for a municipality that turned its fortunes around and built a sustainable economy, the city of Langford in the Province of British Columbia, Canada, is a place to visit. The city, population 27,000, is located on the southern end of Vancouver Island. It is one of the West Shore municipalities in the Capital Regional District with an area of 10,245 acres (4,146 hectares). Langford is linked by highways, rail, and bus service to Victoria, the capital, to the rest of Vancouver Island by ferries, and by air to the City of Vancouver and the US.

The land on which Langford exists had been used by various First Nations' bands as hunting and gathering grounds. In 1851 Captain Edward Langford established one of four Hudson's Bay Company farms in the area. The place was incorporated as a Municipal District in 1992, and gained City status in 2003 (Figure 7.21).

7.21 **Images of Langford, British Columbia, Canada**

Charting a Path

When following Langford's economic development, one soon recognizes that both the rapid growth and the way the city "does business" is unique among Canadian municipalities. Until its incorporation, the city's economy was mainly agriculture-based. After incorporation and with a population of 16,000 people, the community's land use consisted mainly of single-family dwellings on large lots without sanitary sewers, small commercial areas, and farms. There were few paved roads with curbs, sidewalks, or street lighting. It had a poor regional reputation as a city where unemployment, at a rate of 25 percent, was common and vandalism rampant (Wicks 2008). In addition, due to the absence of local commerce, most people drove to shop in the City of Victoria.

One can argue that at the core of Langford's transformation and success are its location and uncommon initiatives by its leaders. The Council's strategy was threefold: increase the tax base by attracting and allocating more land for commercial and industrial enterprises, invest the additional revenues into improving the place's appearance and image, and finally undertake selected large-scale community improvement projects, such as new parks and trails (Buchan 2005).

Bisecting Langford are the Trans Canada Highway and Sooke Road, both of which have helped make the city a prime commercial spot. The search for an attractive location and the emergence of large format retail outlets as a leading shopping trend in the 1990s made Langford the target of large retailers such as Costco, Wal-Mart, and the Home Depot. An initiative by Langford's leaders to reduce taxes and create a pro-development environment also assisted those enterprises to locate in the city. As a result, Langford's tax revenue from commercial land use was increased from 9.8 percent in 1997 to 15.9 percent in 2004. Of that revenue, the large retail stores accounted for about two-thirds (Buchan 2005).

The same attitude was also vital in the attraction of both the developers of the Bear Mountain residential project and other new large-scale housing developments. Bear Mountain, a high-end community and resort featuring a hotel and two world-class golf courses, added residents, attracted tourists, and generated an estimated 1,000 jobs, as shown in Figure 7.22.

Through strategic investment, innovative thinking, and responsible management, the money was directed to further enhancing Langford's appearance. What was once considered a visually unfavorable place had now become an attractive location. Sidewalk expansion and repaving and the establishment of a pedestrian mall have created a "village" atmosphere downtown. These initiatives diversified the city's economy and placed Langford on a sustainable economic footing and reduced the number of residents who traveled to Victoria to shop, which contributed to reduction of the city's overall carbon footprint.

A population increase in Langford also established the critical pool of clientele from which both small and large enterprises prospered (Figures 7.23 and 7.24). The strategic instruments that included the redevelopment of old neighborhoods and the introduction of two free-of-charge trolley lines were not only unique in their scope but also in the rapidity of their execution. They created the economic cycle that most communities wish to have, whereby an ongoing, stable stream of revenue is established and investment in further improving lifestyles,

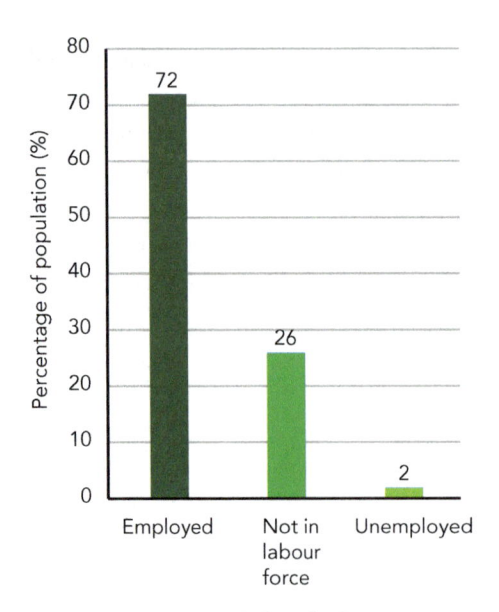

7.22 **Employment rate in Langford**

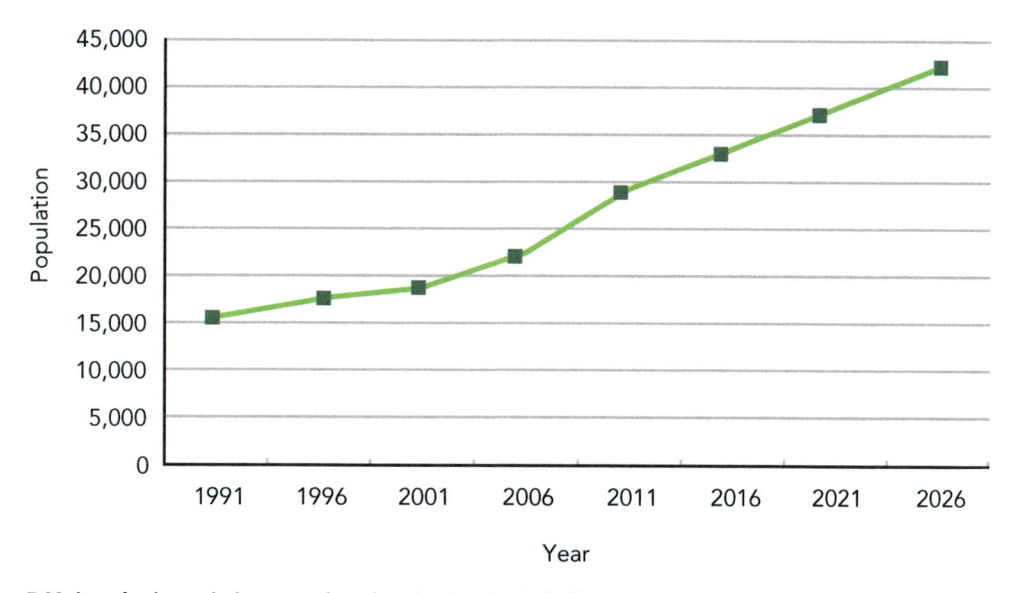

7.23 **Langford population growth and projection, 1991–2026**

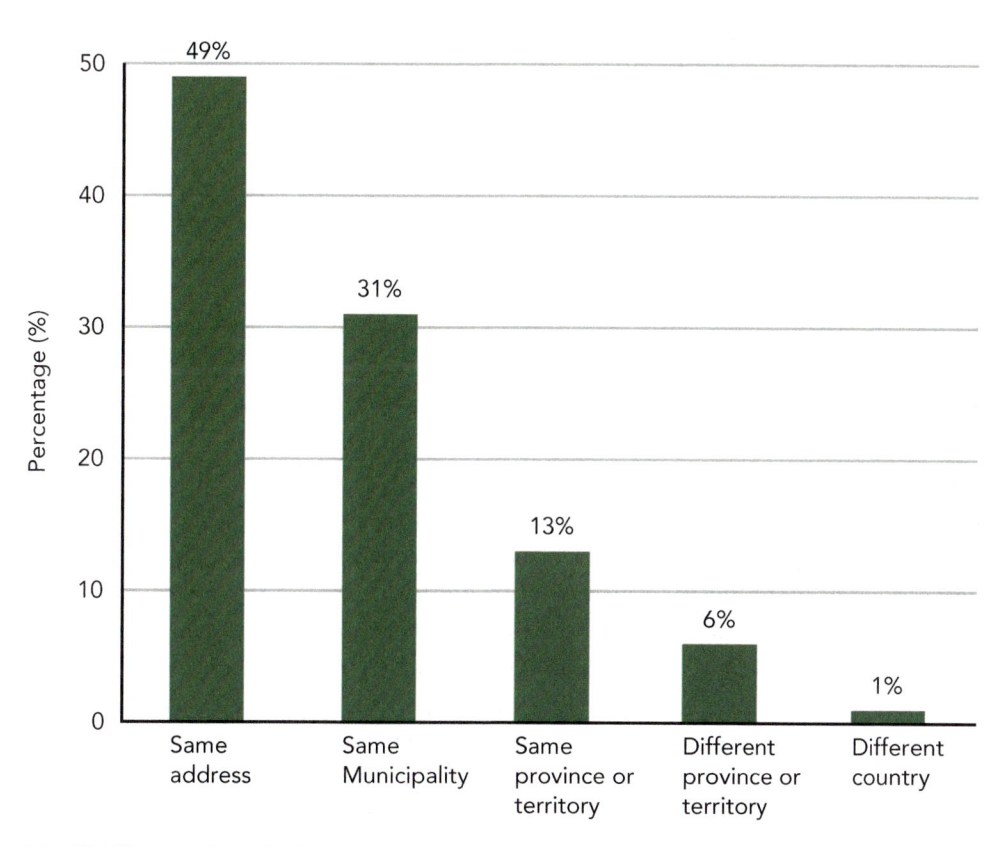

7.24 **Mobility rate of Langford's citizens**

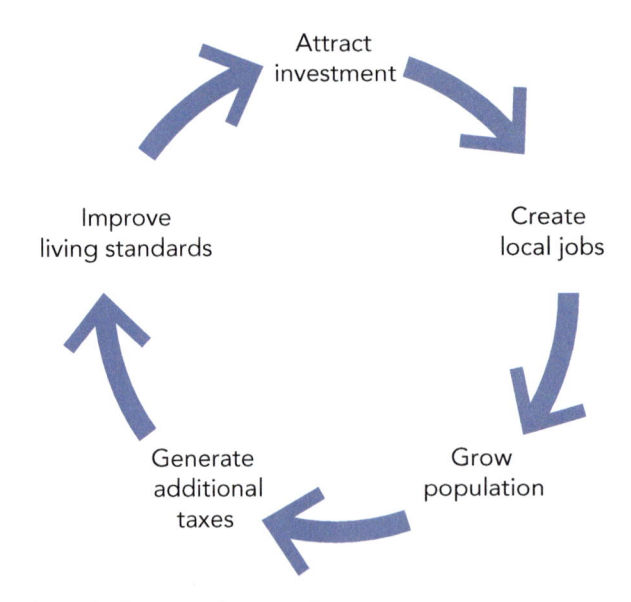

7.25 **The fly wheel of Langford's economic prosperity**

amenities, and urban conditions are made (Figure 7.25). It is perhaps even more unique that in the past two decades Langford has only had to raise taxes minimally, allowing the city to remain competitive.

In its Official Community Plan (OCP), the city set smart growth standards as its key objective. The intention was to designate development areas near or in neighborhoods and avoid long commutes by residents to their places of employment. These centers will complement several existing business parks (Figure 7.26).

Affordable Housing

One of the integral aspects of Langford's economy, which contributed to its success, is residential construction. Thoughtful initiatives and policies allowed the city to have a broad range of dwelling types and costs. Intense activity in this area has also contributed to the overall prosperity by increasing the population, which in turn drew to the city employers who created jobs. It is of value to review these initiatives and their effects on the city (Figure 7.27).

Densification, primarily in the downtown area, led to the replacement of single-family homes with low- to mid-rise apartment buildings, many of which have commercial uses on the ground floor. By accommodating some of the 19 percent population increase between 2001 and 2006, expanding the stock of affordable rental units, attracting young households, and avoiding sprawl, the city benefited. It also brought to the core the clientele needed to support local commerce.

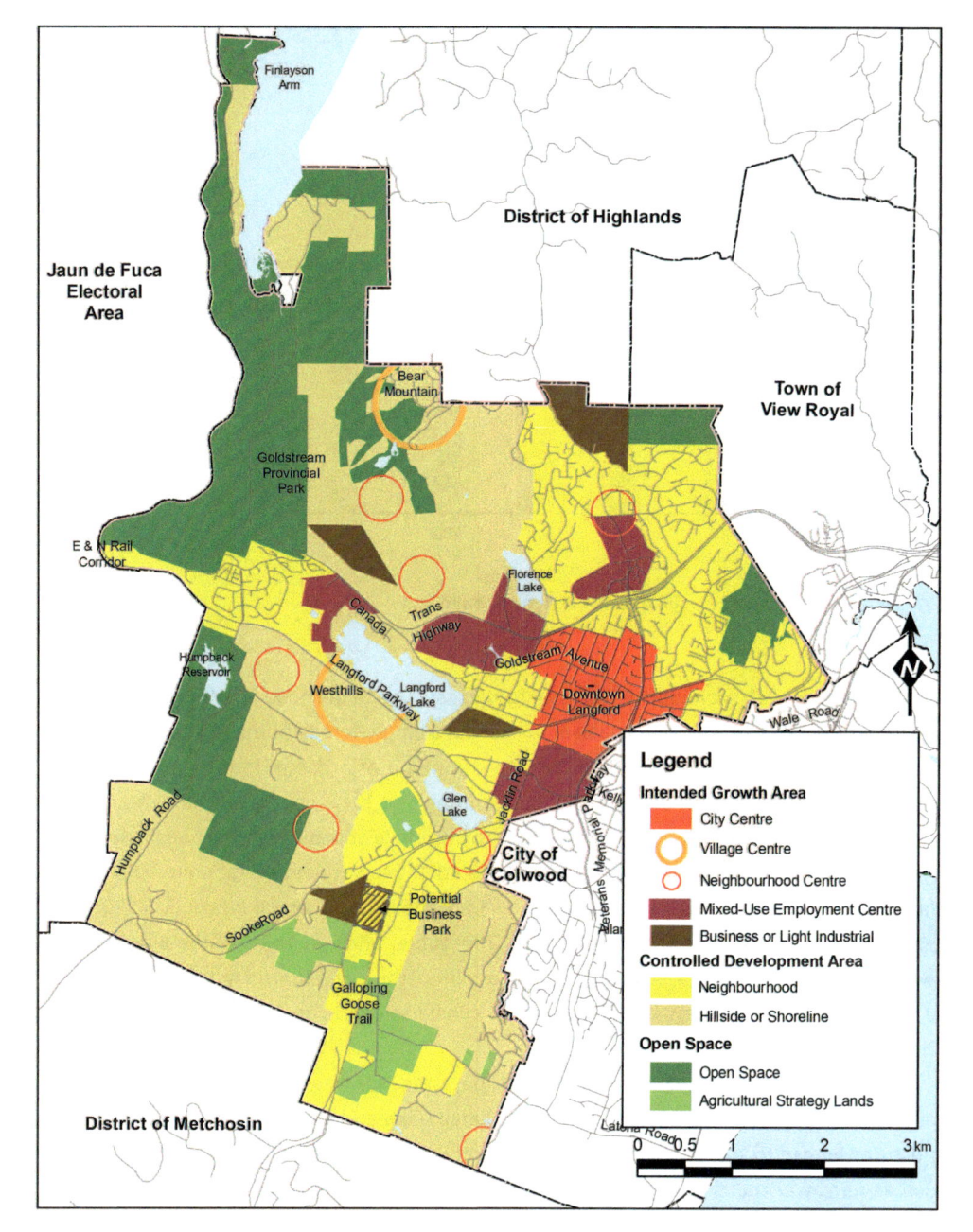

7.26 **Langford's municipal boundaries and its intended growth area**

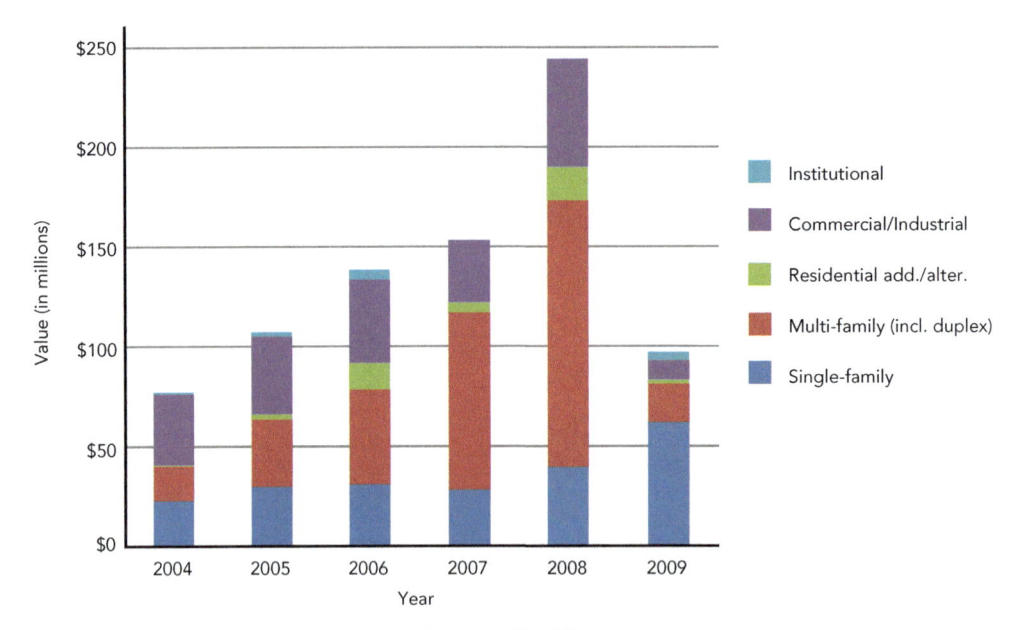

7.27 Langford's annual construction value by type of buildings

Another significant initiative was Langford's response to the need for affordable housing. According to a city report, the increase in the cost of a single-family home is a strong example of this issue (City of Langford 2010). In its award-winning Affordable Housing policy, the city addressed its need for lower cost housing by requiring that 10 percent of new units be rezoned as small lot/small units. The city also took steps to introduce affordable rental housing policies. The Westhills Master Plan, for example, designated 150 lower cost rental units. The Master Plan also requires secondary suites, known as Carriage Houses, on all lots over 5,920 sq. ft. (550 sq. m); and 5 percent of all housing is affordable, and one-third of the single-family dwellings are built on less costly small lots. In addition, the city required that one out of every 10 single-family units in new developments be subsidized and constructed by the developer (City of Langford 2010).

By collaborating closely with local developers, the City was also able to introduce innovative housing types. Prototypes such as very small units and secondary suites or accessory structures helped to keep costs down. Other initiatives included reducing planning standards such as narrower roads and smaller setbacks, which contributed to densification and, as a result, cost reduction (Figure 7.28).

Having a continuous revenue stream, keeping taxes down, and supporting affordable housing initiatives resulted in increased population and ongoing improvement in the standards of living. Many amenities have been added, including a sports complex, park, and an extensive trail system which help make Langford's economy prosperous and sustainable.

7.28 **Housing starts in Langford, 1994–2010**

8
People, Places, and Well-Being

I arrived in Courseulles-sur-Mer, population 4,000, on a market day. The coastal town in the Basse-Normandie region of northern France was the landing site of the Canadian troops who stormed Juno Beach on World War II's D-Day.

The place, it felt, marched to a slower rhythm. Stalls full of fresh produce and household goods, some under tents, lined Rue de la Mer. Merchants recognized their patrons and greeted them in a joyful voice. A meat vendor asked an old woman: "même chose [same thing]?" and went on to slice for her what he had probably served her for a long time (Figure 8.1).

Walking further I arrived at the port where small fishing trawlers were tied to the quay. Their owners were tending to their gear, stopping from time to time to exchange a word with one another.

8.1 **Market day at Courseulles-sur-Mer, France**

It was lunchtime when I headed back to the main square. Merchants locked their front doors for the afternoon break, and went home or to local eateries. Looking around, I noticed a restaurant called Brasserie du Marche. When I entered, a man gestured to a corner table. The place had few formalities. There were no tablecloths and the walls were made bright by three large windows that faced the square. Bottles of house wine and bread were brought to each table. It was obvious that the patrons knew each other. There were conversations across tables, exchanges of anecdotes and laughter. Four men wearing blue overalls occupied an adjacent table. It sounded as if they debated the performance of their favorite sports team while the meal was served and eaten. An old man noticed me, a foreigner, and brought me into the conversation. His eyes lit up when he found out that I was Canadian, claiming that our army saved his town.

You could not help but be part of the moment and the place. It felt more like a social hangout than a dining place. I kept wondering if the physical and social attributes of small towns such as Courseulles-sur-Mer had something to do with it. I also questioned whether such spots can be choreographed to become what they are or if good places are a result of local cultural traditions that have matured over many years.

This chapter examines general human attributes of small towns and relates them to places. The manifestations of the term "social capital" are explored, the notions of places and place-making are studied, and selected gathering places and their contribution to the communal fabric described. The chapter ends with a case study about a town that went on to restructure its urban makeup by introducing unique meeting spots.

Social Capital

It can be argued that their reduced population size can also affect social attributes in small towns and potentially lead to greater familiarity with and closeness between residents. Having fewer places to meet will result in more frequent chance encounters, for example. Close-knit relations can be of great value in times of need. For example, in farming communities, farmers are known to extend a helping hand to one another in busy seasons. There might also be resentment of the closeness by some who may dislike the lack of privacy or anonymity.

Communal behavioral attributes are referred to by scientists as *social capital* or *human capital*. Putnam (in Svendsen 2010) described social capital as outward-looking open networks that encompass people across diverse "social cleavages." In contrast, Putnam defines "bonding" social capital as consisting of inward-looking networks that tend to reinforce exclusive identities and homogeneous groups. Svendsen (2010) suggests that social capital is about people who meet, get to know one another, and help each other in various ways. The *Slow Cities* movement, for example, attempted to put a name and draw some social characteristics of these unique places (Figure 8.2). Another all-encompassing term, which includes economic,

8.2 **The Slow Cities movement includes communities with populations smaller than 50,000 inhabitants that accept certain principles that enhance their sense of well-being**

social, spiritual, and health-related aspects by a group, is *well-being*. It is a holistic term that looks at how well groups are doing using various scales and criteria.

Known as *socio-spatial* attributes, meeting places provide the spots in which human interaction takes place. Without them, there would be fewer opportunities for communal encounters vital for societal proper functioning. American sociologist James Coleman (1988) argues that human capital presupposes social capital much like among family members. If people do not spend time together, there would be fewer opportunities for transfer of knowledge, material, learning, cooperation, and trust (Figure 8.3).

Some researchers also draw a link between well-developed social capital and a place's creativity, urban growth, and economic performance. In their article "Rethinking Human Capital, Creativity and Urban Growth," Storper and Scott (2009) asked "Do jobs follow people or do people follow jobs?" They suggest that current approaches to urbanization, most notably Florida's (2002) "Creative Class" notion, privilege the role of individual locations as engines of urban growth. The mark of successful small towns is that their leaders saw community development as economic development by encouraging leadership and youth entrepreneurial activity for example. They balanced short-term economic gain with longer term community goals and as a result people learned from each other (*Small Towns Big Ideas* n.d.; Feldman 1994).

8.3 **Restaurant as a social meeting place in Deauville, France**

What draws people to a place will be, among other factors, the amenities it has to offer. These include cultural attractions such as museums, orchestras, attractive architecture, and innovative urban planning, to name a few (Figure 8.4). Therefore, creating a suitable place for information exchange has been regarded as a direct contributor to a place's economic prosperity (Figure 8.5). Svendsen (2010) argues that regular face-to-face meetings also involve increased formation of human capital and ultimately contribute to economic and social sustainability.

Williams (2006) suggests that opportunities for meetings between people diminished with the invention of information and communication tools and rise of social media. Indeed, the power of the Internet and "Skype conversations" cannot be discounted. On the other hand, the digital age has offered people and communities effective tools to connect across a wide range of geographical spectrums. For example, a visit to a local café demonstrates that those places are often the sites where digital devices are used. Patrons enjoy the company of others while attending to their information appliances.

Public health is another aspect of a town's well-being. It includes physical and mental health, which are affected by, among other factors, the way a place was planned. Gidlow et al. (2010) and Baum et al. (2009) argue that people's mental health would be better when they are socially active, feel supported, safe, and trust their neighbors. These studies often regard key indicators of social capital, such as trust and participation, as predictors of physical health as well. For example, residing in a walkable neighborhood will improve people's chances of being active.

8.4 **A beach library in Saint-Aubin-sur-Mer, France**

8.5 **Street theaters are used to educate citizens about the dangers of unsafe sex in Langa, South Africa**

Evans (2003) suggests that characteristics such as type of housing, crowding, noise, indoor air quality, and natural light will have a direct effect on mental health (Figure 8.6). For example, crowdedness and higher density will diminish supportive relations within a household. Among the positive social attributes that are associated with the built environment, Evans (2003) includes natural areas, visual prospects, and inclusion of activity generators such as markets and streetscaping.

Two cohorts to which researchers pay special attention are younger and older populations. Abbott-Chapman and Robertson (2009) found that adolescent preferences for having their own bedroom and a secluded place in the natural environment express a way to define personal sought-after privacy. It is part of a young person's self-discovery and socialization that leads to their emerging identity. Having access to congregation and open spaces is highly valued as an aspect that fosters a sense of freedom through playing and experimenting. Towns that lack such places or those that locate them away from residences deprive these populations of various opportunities.

Children hold different perceptions of spaces. Generally, small towns offer more natural outdoor play areas that are liked by children and are not common in big cities. Several researchers have found that younger people value locations where they can engage in sports or physical activities, due to objects or meeting spots that the place has. On the other hand, they dislike places with features that they perceive to pose social or physical threats to their safety (Castonguay and Jutras 2009).

On the other end of the age spectrum, studies have been conducted on the relationships between older people and their social space. Andrews and Phillips (2005) suggested that attachment to a place enables seniors to draw meaning, security, and a sense of identity that facilitates lifecycle adjustment. Therefore, residences that were designed for Aging in Place can be seen not only as cost-effective for individuals and governments, but beneficial from a communal point of view. Wiles et al. (2009) coined the term *social space* when studying places preferred by seniors (Figure 8.7). The authors suggest that these places are multilayered, connected,

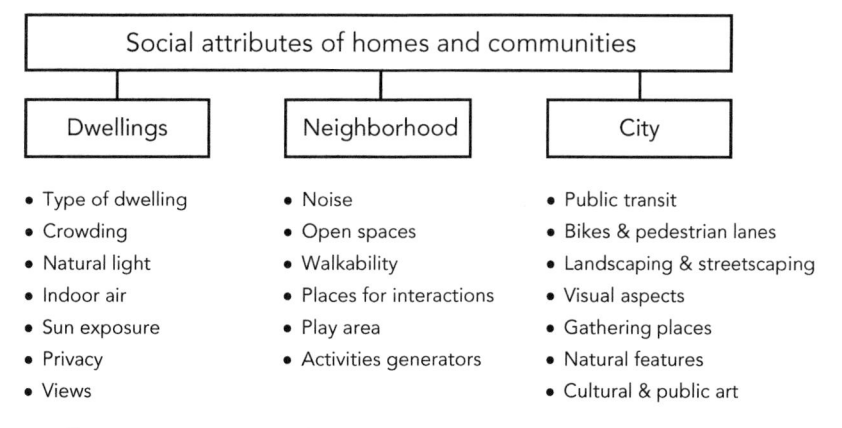

8.6 **Aspects affecting social attributes of homes and communities**

8.7 Seniors occupying a small neighborhood square in Salerno, Italy imaginative, emotional, and symbolic. As people age and their mobility becomes reduced, their ability to reach some destinations will also be diminished. Seniors who do not drive will not endeavor to reach places that are not served by public transit for example.

The prevalence of overweight and obese populations among all ages, particularly children, has become a global concern of public health officials. Joens-Matre et al. (2008) found that the rate of overweight people was higher among rural children at 25 percent compared to urban areas at 19 percent and small cities at 17 percent. A 2010 *New York Times* article suggests that in the US, despite attempts by some states and cities to tax and limit the size of soda pop servings, promote farm stands, require healthier school lunches, or mandate calorie information in chain restaurants, obesity rates are still growing. The article goes on to report that, according to recent data published by the United States Center for Disease Control and Prevention, an estimated 72.5 million adults are obese (Singer 2010).

Only recently has attention been given to the fact that the built environment has over time been altered to curtail physical activity. Low residential density, the mark of many small, suburban edge towns, implies that basic services and amenities, which can potentially get people active, are not economically viable. For example, there are not sufficient riders to justify the introduction of a public transit service and not enough shoppers to support a corner grocery store to which people can walk. In fact, things have gone from bad to worse when it comes to public health implications of town planning decisions.

In the name of efficiency, schools have been relocated from their traditional spots in the heart of neighborhoods to the outskirts where they can easily be accessed from major roads by car. That has meant that a pupil's short walk or easy bike ride to school has been rendered impossible. Another feature that found its way into the municipal wastebasket was small play areas near homes which have been replaced by a huge play field, to which children have to be driven. The play itself has been morphed into regimented leagues and strict schedules. Spontaneity, unfortunately, has been taken out of kids' play. It is no wonder that TV watching and computer games have replaced outdoor play. Studies suggest that TV viewing is North American youth's primary activity, with 1.5 to 2.5 hours on average per day. Some of this time includes watching advertising for high-caloric foods (Larson 2001).

Another casualty of contemporary suburban planning in many small towns was the sidewalk. Since no one walks, some argued, why are they needed at all? Seniors, parents pushing a stroller, and children had to share the road with motorists, often putting their lives at risk. When the sidewalk vanished, benches followed, leaving no places to sit on, or trees to stand under and talk with a neighbor on a sunny day.

How should active lifestyle be introduced in small towns? Recasting the features of the built environment that, over the past half-century, have been taken out would be a good beginning (Figure 8.8). Homes and cities must be regarded as exercise machines for all ages (Figure 8.9). Along with the reintroduction of physical changes, public health officials need to continue to warn citizens about the grim consequences of inactive lifestyles.

The importance of some unique spots to a community's social capital and their proper planning will be outlined below.

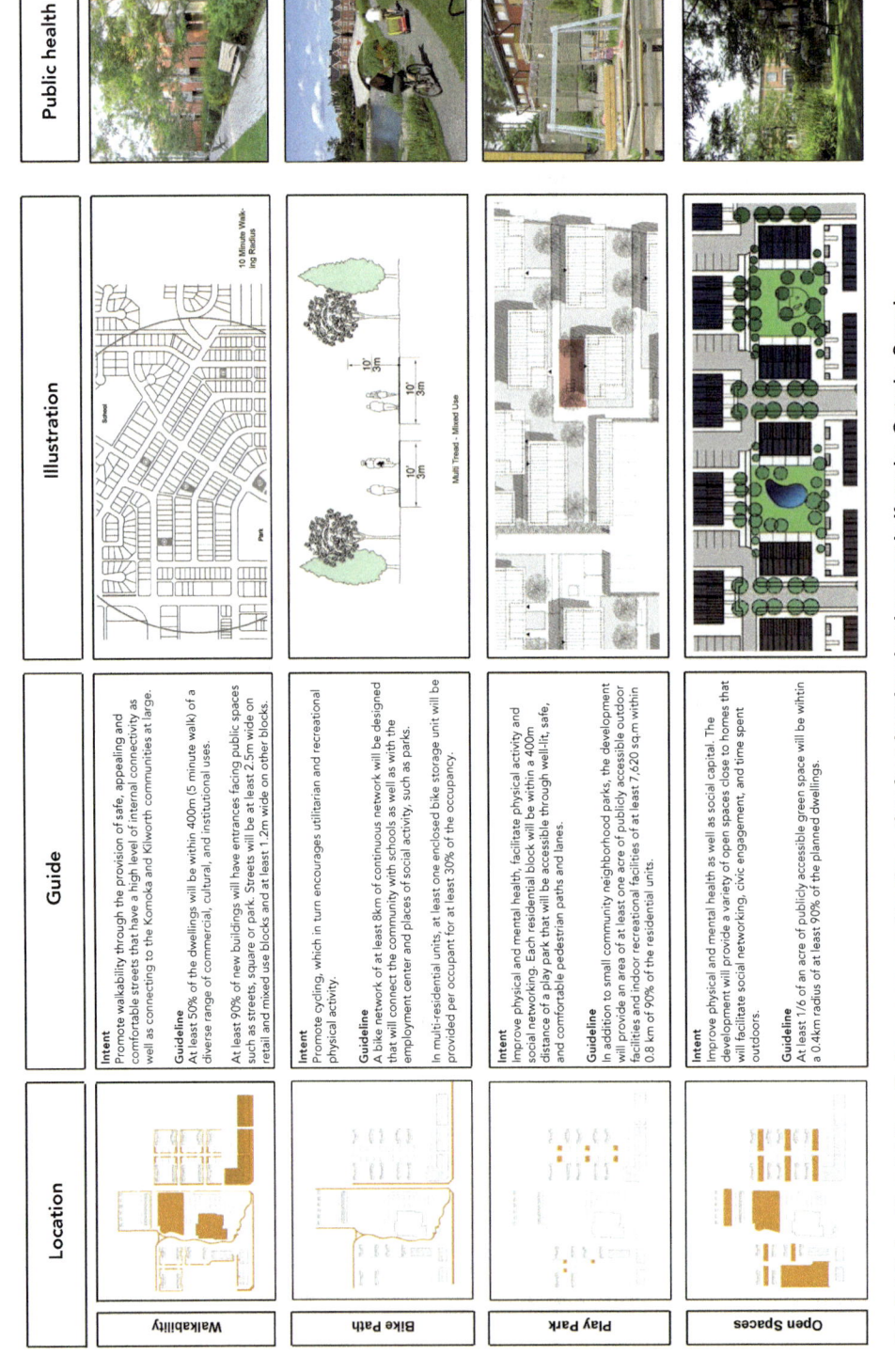

Location	Guide	Illustration	Public health
Walkability	**Intent** Promote walkability through the provision of safe, appealing and comfortable streets that have a high level of internal connectivity as well as connecting to the Komoka and Kilworth communities at large. **Guideline** At least 50% of the dwellings will be within 400m (5 minute walk) of a diverse range of commercial, cultural, and institutional uses. At least 90% of new buildings will have entrances facing public spaces such as streets, square or park. Streets will be at least 2.5m wide on retail and mixed use blocks and at least 1.2m wide on other blocks.		
Bike Path	**Intent** Promote cycling, which in turn encourages utilitarian and recreational physical activity. **Guideline** A bike network of at least 8km of continuous network will be designed that will connect the community with schools as well as with the employment center and places of social activity, such as parks. In multi-residential units, at least one enclosed bike storage unit will be provided per occupant for at least 30% of the occupancy.		
Play Park	**Intent** Improve physical and mental health, facilitate physical activity and social networking. Each residential block will be within a 400m distance of a play park that will be accessible through well-lit, safe, and comfortable pedestrian paths and lanes. **Guideline** In addition to small community neighborhood parks, the development will provide an area of at least one acre of publicly accessible outdoor facilities and indoor recreational facilities of at least 7,620 sq.m within 0.8 km of 90% of the residential units.		
Open Spaces	**Intent** Improve physical and mental health as well as social capital. The development will provide a variety of open spaces close to homes that will facilitate social networking, civic engagement, and time spent outdoors. **Guideline** At least 1/6 of an acre of publicly accessible green space will be within a 0.4km radius of at least 90% of the planned dwellings.		

8.8 Public health guidelines that were prepared by the author for a housing development in Komoka, Ontario, Canada

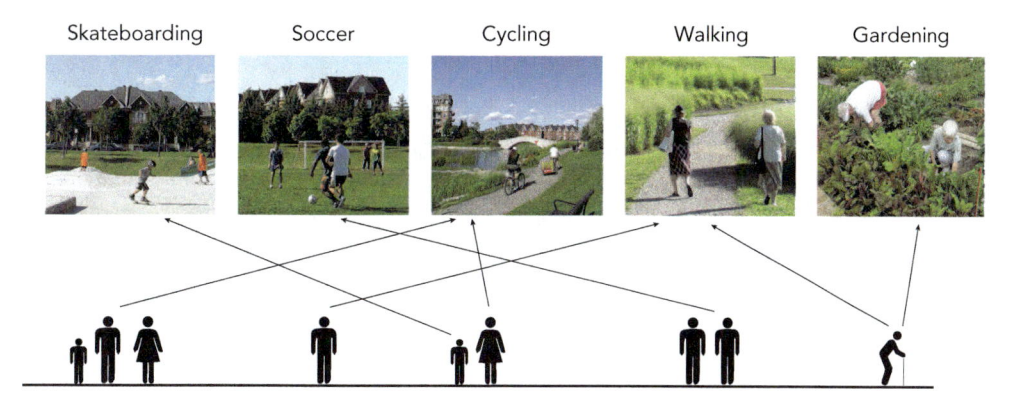

Skateboarding   Soccer   Cycling   Walking   Gardening

8.9 **Well-designed towns offer a wide range of recreational opportunities to citizens of all ages**

Places and Place-Making

This section focuses on places. In particular, attention has been paid to spots that draw large numbers of people and are vital to communal life. Here, too, what sets towns apart from cities are size and opportunities; there are often few locations, such as civic squares and main streets, to congregate. When they are introduced or retooled, they have to be designed properly to become a functional draw and, according to Clark et al. (2002), also contribute to local economic development.

In recent years, some communities saw the disappearance of good social spots. The newly introduced places are part of what Zukin (1998) calls a "landscape of consumption." Small towns have become dependent on property developers to create "destination retail" which unfortunately has replaced good old-fashioned meeting places.

What are the general characteristics of good places? Engaging spots do not function as containers of social activities but often generate them. For example, a treed square streetscaped with benches will offer people a place to be in, initiate a conversation, and watch others. The Project for Public Spaces (PPS) (2011) identified four elements to help communities evaluate places: sociability, uses and activities, access and linkages, as well as comfort and images. Among the principles that describe a proper approach to place-making, adaptability, inclusive-ness, inspiring, and community-driven are listed. Processes that are imposed from above, reactive, use one-size-fits-all methods, and offer a quick fix are all likely to end up poor-looking. Gehl (2010) suggests that cities need to be regarded as "meeting places" and designed to the human scale and senses. According to Gehl successful public spaces offer protection, comfort, and enjoyment. A good scale to begin articulating good spots is the large one—the public square.

Open spaces devoted to public gatherings have formed an integral part of the urban and cultural heritage of many societies and towns throughout history and played a critical role in the genesis of commerce, the emergence of democracy, and the vitality of civic life. Bearing different names, the square is known as *agora* in ancient Greek towns, the *plaza* in cities of Spanish origins, *piazza* in Italy, *village green* in settlements with feudal pasts, and *market*

8.10 **The *agora* was a public gathering urban space as seen here in Kamiros, Greece**

squares in others (Figure 8.10). The names all mean a physical clearance in the heart of a city which can be of any shape—including square.

In the *Wisdom of Cities*, Crowhurst and Lennard (2002) argue that squares have provided a school for social learning, exercise of responsibility, development of a sense of community, and democracy (Figure 8.11). Creating an outdoor "living room" for citizens to meet was instrumental in fostering a strong web of relationships and communal security.

The advantages of traditional squares were not possible to achieve in contemporary small town settings. Their planning rarely called for such places, as the low population density could not support much commerce under apartments, and a configuration of detached low-rise dwellings was inadequate to lend suitable urban scale to begin with. Golf courses, public parks, and shopping malls were meant to be the new village green. Unfortunately, none of these amenities could replace face-to-face encounters, the mixing of age groups, and the symbolic value of squares.

What are the physical attributes of a good public square? Several features have been noted by some designers. The Renaissance architect Alberti Batista looked at scale and suggested a proportion of one to six, since the viewing distance from the center easily permits

8.11 **Public squares in Mexican towns are often used by seniors for weekend dancing**

enjoyment of all the surrounding buildings (Moughtin 1992). Using this ratio, he suggested that each side of a square surrounded by three-story buildings would be 180–230 feet (54–68 meters) long, and each side of a place with four-story buildings would measure 240–300 feet (72–90 meters). Such proportions foster a proper human scale which contributes to "sense of place" and comfort. They are sufficient to house large crowds, yet create intimacy. A valuable contributor to a square's good design is the type of surrounding buildings. The preferred choice would see properly scaled buildings with commerce on ground floors and residences above. Patrons of the lower floor stores, cafés with outdoor seating, and upper floor dwellers will animate the place. If a choice of location is given in the early planning stage, a square should have a central location accessible by foot or bike from the town's edges (Figure 8.12). The roads leading to it should also be pleasantly articulated to walk in with less vehicular traffic.

Well thought-out streetscaping is also necessary for a successful square design. Having a central feature such as a statue or a fountain will give the place a focal point. When a square is designed with pedestrians in mind and car traffic is minimized or prohibited altogether, it will make the place people-friendly. Parking spots can be provided on side streets and alleys. In small towns, however, one needs to bear in mind that proper scale has to guide all planning decisions since there are fewer people.

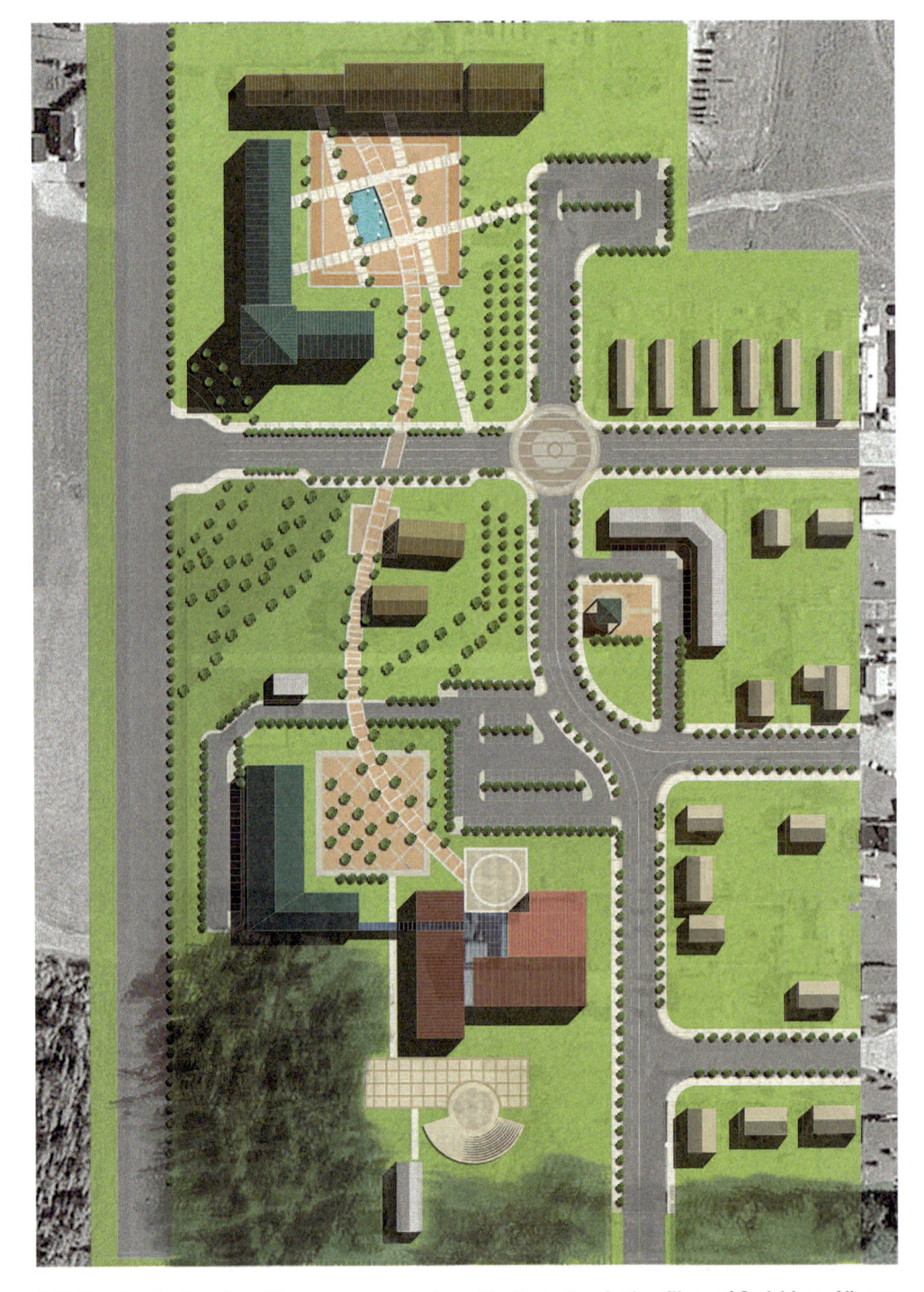

8.12 **Small gatherings in public spaces were designed by the author in the village of St. Isidore, Alberta, Canada**

Public art is another valued feature of squares and other civic places (Figure 8.13). Florida (in Riddle 2008) suggests that public art that is tied to a place can "highlight a community's soul, history and uniqueness." Also, in a talk about his work, German public artist Bonifatius Stirnberg expressed his conviction that public art can stimulate play, creativity, and imagination among children. It promotes contact, communication, and, at times, debate and dialogue among citizens. It accommodates people by incorporating steps, ledges, and benches on which people can sit or lean to appreciate, admire, and reflect. It can also bring the various factions of a society together by stimulating curiosity and interest in heritage (Stirnberg 1985).

Markets, be they in closed public structures or open air, can also be regarded as "social magnets" (Figure 8.14). Recently, the gradual disappearance of formal markets from small towns has occurred. For the most part, they have become parts of large food stores where produce is arranged to create a market-like setting.

Yet, it seems that the natural instincts of the buying public have served it well when it has come to saving vital commercial and social institutions, such as old-style markets, from complete extinction. The quest for freshness, lower prices, and direct exchange with the grower have led to a resurgence of farmers' markets in small towns, which generally recur at fixed locations where products are sold by the farmers themselves (Brown 2001).

Studies show that growers are inclined to sell in farmers' markets of small towns because they often see them as the best, or the most profitable, venue for selling their produce.

8.13 Public art can play a role in promoting creativity and dialogue among citizens

8.14 **Market day in Lancaster, UK**

Consumers visit them because they provide high quality produce at a reasonable price (Summer and Wing 1980). Market gardeners and other small-scale farmers, many of whom farm part-time, drive, on average, 19 miles (30 kilometers) to their place of trade. Their customers come primarily from adjacent neighborhoods to create a social meeting point. The contribution of these markets to local economies is also of high value, as they lead to spending in nearby shops, which generates further tax revenue. Some analysts suggest that farmers' markets create jobs, build new businesses, strengthen and diversify regional agriculture, and elevate farm profitability (Curry and Oland 1998).

On the other scale of places that contribute to the creation of human capital and reinforcement of social bonds among citizens, one can find small gathering places. In his ook *The Great Good Place*, Ray Oldenburg (1989) calls such spots *third places*. Whereas our homes and work—first and second places—are sites of routine events and, at times, regimented schedules, third places are spots where we can shed our usual being and relax. A third place can be a pub, coffee shop, diner, or a bookstore (Figure 8.15). People who patronize a third place are not tied to a particular schedule and they are welcome to come and leave as they please. Third places are levelers. Patrons' wealth, social status, or even educational

8.15 A local diner and gathering place in Montpelier, Vermont, US

backgrounds are of secondary importance. Oldenburg states that the charm and flavor of the patrons' personality, irrespective of their station in life, is what counts.

Conversations in third places are lively, colorful, and engaging. Being attentive to others, considering each other's feelings, talking about topics of interest to all will make for a lively exchange. The noise level and the choice of background music must allow everyone to listen and talk in a normal tone of voice. They are places to which one can go alone at any time of the day or evening and be pretty sure that an acquaintance will be present. The regulars set a tone of conviviality that makes a stranger feel welcome.

Good third places need to be around long enough to age gracefully. They have special odors or beaten-up furnishings. Neatness is not the primary concern of those who run the place, but the comfort and the happiness of the patrons. Food, when the spot is an eatery, is not masterfully designed on the plate, but is tastefully cooked and cheerfully served. In a bookstore, you are welcome to sink into a sofa, undo your shoelaces, and sip from a tea that was offered to you by the owner, with whom you will later have a discussion about the book. You will also probably not mind when a total stranger asks you how your meal was or whether you enjoyed the book (Figure 8.16).

Not surprisingly, Tolbert et al. (2002) found that third places were a vehicle of civic welfare in both metropolitan and non-metropolitan small towns. Coffee shops are cited by Jeffres

8.16 **A sign in a bookstore in Trani, Italy reads: "We open when we wake up, we close when the dreams wake up"**

et al. (2009) to be the most frequent places. Pubs, senior centers, parks, and malls also appear on the list. One wonders whether the use of social media stands to erode the appeal of "third places." It no doubt has had an effect on encounters, but cannot replace face-to-face interactions.

Place-Making in Peace River

Peace River was named after the river that runs through it. The town, population 6,000, is located in the northern part of the Province of Alberta, Canada, and is also the meeting point of the Smoky and the Heart rivers (Figure 8.17). Some 302 miles (486 km) separate the town from the capital Edmonton and 123 miles (198 km) from the City of Grande Prairie.

Whereas in its early beginnings at the turn of the century, the town was somewhat isolated and less accessible, it is now linked via highways to distant urban hubs. It has an airport used primarily by chartered flights and private airplanes.

With the building of a new commercial center on its edge, Peace River's core experienced a decline. Several businesses closed and others moved to the new commercial section. Another

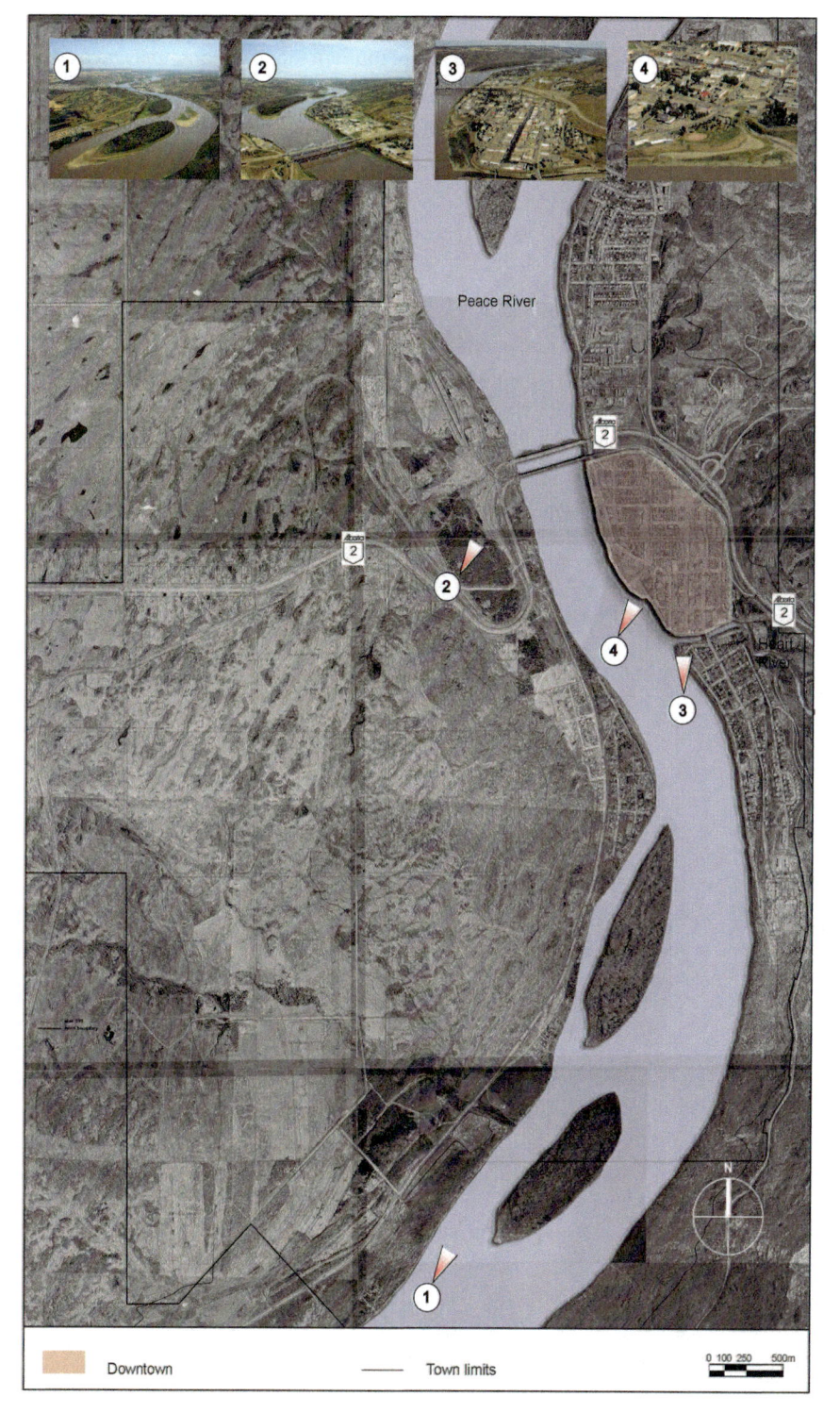

Peace River

Downtown
Town limits
0 100 250 500m

8.17 **Aerial view of Peace River**

aspect of concern was the town's economic dependence on a few key industries. The need to broaden its economic base led to the exploration of tourism that can potentially take advantage of the area's natural beauty. There was also a strong desire to enhance the town's "sense of place" and to create meeting spots for its people. It is with this background that I was asked to offer ideas and prepare a plan for the town's future that would consider these emerging realities.

Urban Evolution

The urban evolution of Peace River is similar in nature to other mid-western towns of its size (Figure 8.18). The place was established to service traders, missionaries, and, in later years, the surrounding farming communities. The town adopted a gridiron street layout and roads were oriented parallel and perpendicular to the river. Despite its scenic view, the river was not always kind to the town and flooding was common (Figure 8.19).

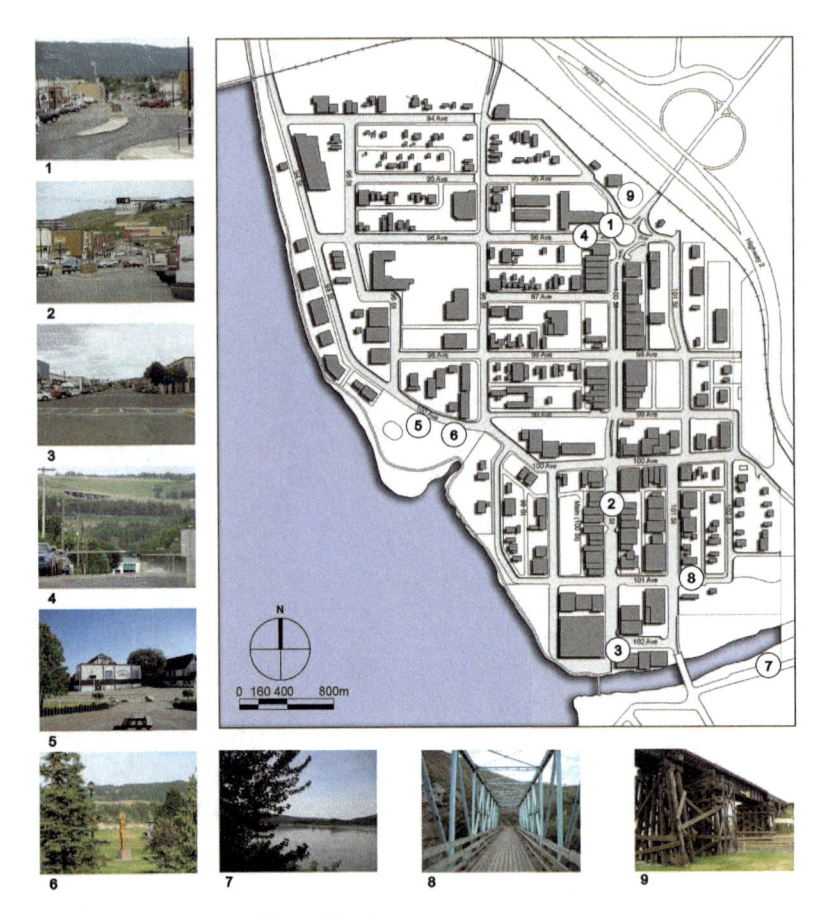

8.18 **Plan and images of Peace River's core area**

8.19 **Flooding in Peace River in 1935. The white building in the center is the town's old fire hall**

Peace River grew outwards from Main Street, which over the years has retained prominence as the chief commercial artery. Despite the harsh winter winds and floods, the town did not adopt a compact urban form and continued to evolve northward along the valley, where land was available. Subsequent flooding led to the construction of a protective berm along the river, which did not help create a riverside pedestrian experience.

Downtown Peace River had a healthy mix of businesses and residences in close proximity, as shown in Figure 8.20. During successive periods of growth, homes were built around downtown and, in particular, south of the Heart River. The building on the western bank of the Peace River took place with waves of immigration and subsequent growth spurts after World War II. Single-family detached dwellings were the common housing type and, in later years, some townhouses and low-rise apartment buildings were added. Lumber was a common façade material in the early years, yet with the town's population and economic expansion, masonry buildings were constructed to offer a sense of permanence.

The construction of a new commercial area with "big box" retail along with the move of the hospital to the river's west side marked a decline of the downtown, which our intervention attempted to address.

Opportunities and Barriers

Prior to offering retooling ideas we looked at the opportunities and the barrier that Peace River poses. At the outset we recognized that currently the town acts as a well-established regional service draw to the surrounding communities. Due to its location and easy access, it is an excellent geographic focal point with natural beauty as its greatest asset. A location in a valley, a meeting place of rivers, and a breathtaking view of the surrounding forested mountaintops make it unique.

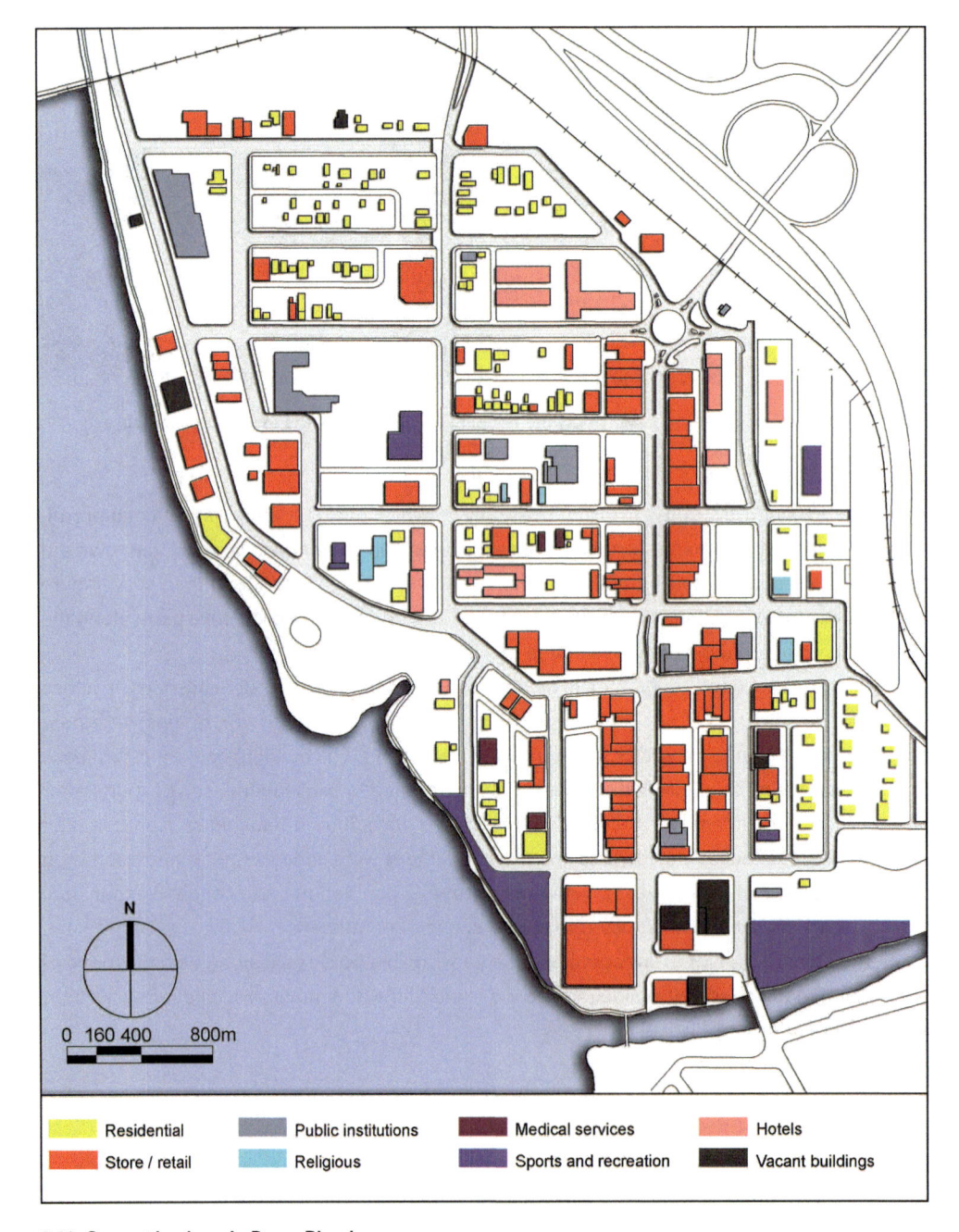

Residential	Public institutions	Medical services	Hotels
Store / retail	Religious	Sports and recreation	Vacant buildings

8.20 **Current land use in Peace River's core**

Downtown Peace River, a home to hotels, restaurants, government buildings, banks and offices, still acts as a draw. In addition, although not many residents call downtown home, the area is surrounded by several neighborhoods, which offers a patronage base to the businesses. Also, it has a pedestrian-friendly character with wide sidewalks facing storefronts.

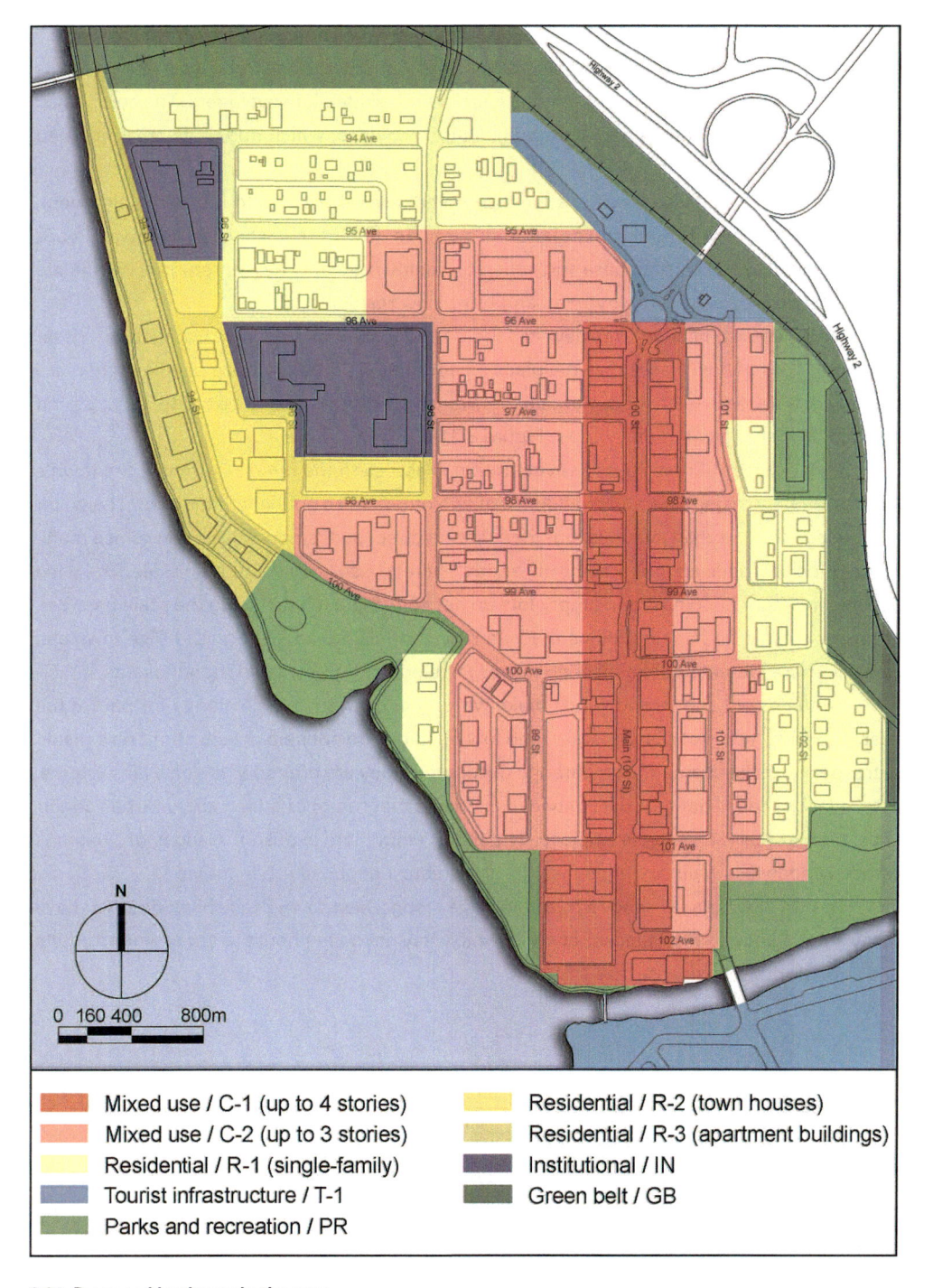

Legend

Color	Category
	Mixed use / C-1 (up to 4 stories)
	Mixed use / C-2 (up to 3 stories)
	Residential / R-1 (single-family)
	Tourist infrastructure / T-1
	Parks and recreation / PR
	Residential / R-2 (town houses)
	Residential / R-3 (apartment buildings)
	Institutional / IN
	Green belt / GB

8.21 **Proposed land uses in the core**

Main Street is the area's natural center with short walking distances from the place's edges and plenty of parking nearby. Downtown has a number of centrally located empty lots that offer investment opportunities for commercial and residential developers. The core is also the location of many annual and sessional cultural activities, which add to its attraction and help turn it into a tourist draw.

In mapping existing conditions we also noted several barriers to future development, first among them are stagnant population growth. To cover the costs of its renewal, Peace River needed to expand its tax base and generate wealth. Attracting new enterprises will initiate a prosperity cycle, create employment, and bring new residents.

The town also needed to review its land-use allocation and bylaws. Garages and other industrial types of businesses give the place a poor image, primarily those buildings that face the river. If the area is to be made attractive, current regulations need to be tightened to permit only residential and commercial uses (Figure 8.21).

A vital facet of Peace River's revitalization is access to the rivers. Currently, the town's location along a major river and confluence of two others does not benefit the core. The water can be seen from several avenues, but there are no direct pedestrian connections since many of the principal roads are oriented north–south. There is also a lack of human scale. The wide streets, one-story buildings, and empty lots do not contribute to narrowing the scale gap. Yet, there are notable heritage buildings that can be distinguished and recognized. The town can also use more intimate public meeting places to celebrate holidays and mount events.

Winter's cold and strong winds make walking in downtown a challenge for part of the year. The many open lots, lack of trees, and low buildings do not help the situation. As a result, patrons have a disadvantage compared to the comfort they are offered at the new large stores. Also, a lack of coordination exists between elements that can offer a measure of urban coherence, human scale, and sense of place. The many empty lots expose the edges of buildings whose windowless walls are highly visible and create a negative urban image.

To be a draw, places need to be active all day long. Downtown Peace River does not have many social venues, "third places" of sorts, which stay open after hours to attract young adults and support other businesses.

A Proposal

When we contemplated renewal strategies and began the planning process, a pivotal question was how the town of Peace River, and in particular its core, could be made more welcoming to local residents and out-of-town visitors. We went on to establish several design anchors that are illustrated in Figure 8.22.

There needs to be a population increase in downtown by encouraging, through a system of grants and incentives, residential construction, which will target primarily young families. The new housing projects, three- and four-stories tall, will have on-site parking, either on or

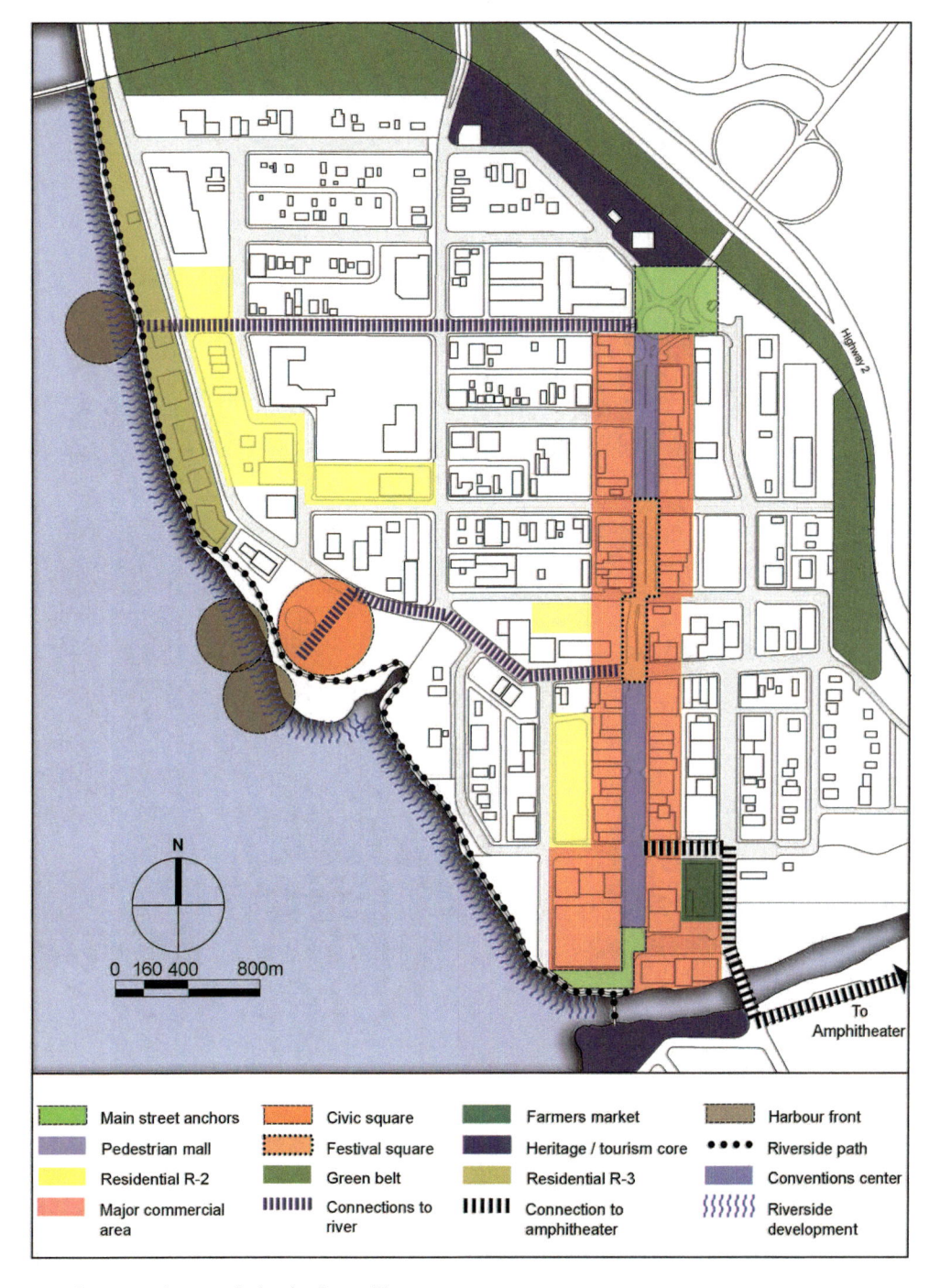

Main street anchors — Civic square — **Farmers market** — Harbour front
Pedestrian mall — Festival square — **Heritage / tourism core** — •••• Riverside path
Residential R-2 — Green belt — **Residential R-3** — Conventions center
Major commercial area — Connections to river — **Connection to amphitheater** — §§§§§ Riverside development

8.22 **Conceptual renewal plan for Peace River**

Existing buildings

Proposed commercial/residential building on main street (11 units)

Proposed new infill housing and services building (20 units)

Proposed town houses (175 units)

Proposed apartment buildings (148 units)

New festival square on main street

8.23 **A detailed development plan**

underground. Also, since downtown is surrounded by neighborhoods, it makes sense to connect them to the core by a safe network of bike paths.

Connecting the town to the river was another key feature of developing a new harbor front area in which water-related activities will include a marina. A land strip from the Heart River in the south to the railway bridge in the north along the water will be developed for this purpose. To create a better link with the river, two avenues will become prime corridors facilitating pedestrian and vehicular access. The area facing the river will be designated mixed-use, where four- to six-story apartment buildings will be constructed above businesses (Figure 8.23).

To enliven Main Street and turn it into a meeting place and a draw, a segment will be redesigned to include large-scale awnings and street furniture. To offer a "counterpoint" to the roundabout at the northern edge of the street, a direct access and opening to the Heart River will be made in the south. Public art can also be placed at that point as well as other spots in downtown.

To encourage tourism, the area north of the roundabout, one of the main entrances to the core, would be developed as a welcome and heritage site to include a public display of the town's visual history. In addition, the 12 Foot Davis Ball Park will be turned into the new festival grounds and fitted with seating and a stage. A week-long festival will be initiated and advertised regionally and provincially (Figure 8.24).

8.24 **Close-ups of the area's design: the welcome area (top left); festival square on Main Street (top right); a civic square (bottom left); the opening to the river at the bottom of Main Street (bottom right)**

Project Teams

I would like to thank those who contributed to the design of the projects mentioned in the book. I have attempted to recall them all. If I have omitted someone, my sincere apologies and I will do my best to correct it in future editions.

Considering Urban Form in Ponoka

Avi Friedman, Architect

Fa Xivong Wu

Placing Nature in the Center of Komoka

Avi Friedman, Architect

Josie White

Nyd Garavito-Bruhn

Retooling for Sustainability in Stony Plain

Avi Friedman, Architect

Juan Mesa

Fa Xivong Wu

Designing a Northern Neighborhood

Avi Friedman, Architect

Jeff Jerome

Fa Xivong Wu

Retooling Downtown Westlock

Avi Friedman, Architect

Jie Liu

Basem M. Eid

Building an Economy from the Ground Up in Langford

Avi Friedman, Architect

Emily Yates

Place-Making in Peace River

Avi Friedman, Architect

Renier Silva

Cynthia Nei

Illustration Credits

Figures not listed here are in the public domain or have been conceived, drawn, or photographed by the author and members of his research and design teams, whose names are listed in the acknowledgments. Every effort has been made to list all contributors and sources. In case of omission, the author and the publisher will include appropriate acknowledgment or correction of any subsequent edition of this book. The full citations of the sources indicated below are noted in the References.

Chapter 1: Affixing a Lens

Figure 1.1: Based on United States Census Bureau 2009
Figure 1.2: Based on Statistics Canada 2006a
Figure 1.4: Based on Statistics Canada 2006b
Figure 1.5: Based on Statistics Canada 2006a
Figure 1.6: After United Nations Department of Economics and Social Affairs 2009
Figure 1.7: After Alter 2009
Figure 1.9: After Hodges 2010

Chapter 2: Form and Function

Figure 2.10: After Gehl 2010

Chapter 3: Green Small Towns

Figure 3.14: After Utility Savers, http://savewaterus.com/conserving.jpg

Chapter 4: Moving Around

Figure 4.2: After Hodges 2010
Figure 4.6: After Center for Transit-Oriented Development 2010
Figure 4.9: After Litman 1999

Chapter 5: Dwelling in Small Towns

Figure 5.5: After Diamond 1976

Chapter 6: Strengthening Core Areas

Figure 6.8: After a proposal by Xu Yang and Jian Zhang for urban renewal of downtown Cornwall, Ontario, Canada. Avi Friedman, Instructor.

Chapter 7: Wealth Generation

Figure 7.5: After Blakely 1983
Figure 7.22: After Statistics Canada 2006a
Figure 7.23: After City of Langford 2010
Figure 7.24: After Statistics Canada 2006a
Figure 7.27: After City of Langford 2010
Figure 7.28: After BC Stats 2011

Chapter 8: People, Places, and Well-Being

Figure 8.12: Drawn by Basem Eid for Avi Friedman Consultants Inc.

References

Abbott-Chapman, J. and M. Robertson (2009) "Adolescents' favourite places: redefining the boundaries between private and public space." *Space and Culture*, 12(4), 419–434.

Adams, R. M. (1960) "The origins of cities." *Scientific American*, 203, 153–168.

Alessa, L., A. Kliskey, and G. Brown (2008) "Social-ecological hotspots mapping: a spatial approach for identifying coupled social–ecological space." *Landscape and Urban Planning*, 85, 27–39.

Alexander, C., S. Ishikawa, and M. Silverstein. (1977) *A Pattern Language: Towns, Buildings, Construction*. New York: Oxford University Press.

Alter, L. (2009) "Graph of the day: driving vs. residential density." http://www.treehugger.com/files/2009/04/driving-vs-density.php (Accessed May 2009).

Anders, M. (2004) "Understanding and balancing mixed-use schemes: the key to creating successful communities." *Journal of Retail and Leisure Property*, 3(4), 353–364.

Andrews, G. J. and D. R. Phillips (2005) *Aging and Place: Perspectives, Policy, Practice*. London: Routledge.

Badland, H. M. and G. M. Schofield (2006) "Understanding the relationship between town size and physical activity levels: a population study." *Health and Place*, 12, 538–546.

Badland, H. M., G. M. Schofield, and N. Garrett (2008) "Travel behaviour and objectively measured urban design variables: associations for adults traveling to work." *Health & Place*, 14, 85–95.

Batty, M. (2008) "The size, scale and shape of cities." *Science*, 319, 769–771.

Baum, F. E., A. M. Ziersch, G. Zhang, and K. Osborne (2009) "Do perceived neighbourhood cohesion and safety contribute to neighbourhood differences in health?" *Journal of Epidemiology and Community Health*, 15, 925–934.

BC Stats (2011) *British Columbia Housing Starts for Urban Areas and Communities*. http://www.bcstats.gov.bc.ca/Files/ 3ed931fc-b3c2-4aaa-bda8-4c2611afe9e4/HousingStarts.pdf (Accessed January 2011).

Beaumont, C. and L. Tucker (2002) "Big-box sprawl (and how to control it)." *Municipal Lawyer*, March/April.

Ben-Joseph, E. and D. Gordon (2000) "Hexagonal planning in theory and practice." *Journal of Urban Design*, 5(3), 237–265.

Besser, L. M. and A. L. Dannenberg (2005) "Walking to public transit: steps to help meet physical activity recommendations." *American Journal of Preventive Medicine*, 29(4), 273–280.

Blakely, E. J. (1983) "Community attitudes toward change." Paper presented at the American Collegiate Schools of Planning Conference, San Francisco, CA, October.

Bowler, D. E., L. Buyung-Ali, T. M. Knight, and A. S. Pullin (2010) "Urban greening to cool towns and cities: a systematic review of the empirical evidence." *Landscape and Urban Planning*, 97: 147–155.

Bramley, G., N. Dempsey, S. Power, C. Brown, and D. Watkins (2009) "Social sustainability and urban form: evidence from five British cities." *Environment and Planning A*, 41(9), 2125–2142.

Brand, S. (1994) *How Buildings Learn: What Happens After They're Built.* New York: Viking.

Brennan, C. K. and C. Hoene (2007) "Demographic changes in America's small cities, 1990–2000." In B. Ofori-Amoah (Ed.), *Beyond the Metropolis: Urban Geography as if Small Cities Mattered* (pp. 69–86). New York: University Press of America.

Bressi, T. W. (2002) *The Seaside Debates.* New York: Rizzoli.

Brown, A. (2001) "Counting farmer's markets." *Geographical Review*, 91(4), 655–674.

Brown, G. Z. (1985) *Sun, Wind and Light.* New York: John Wiley.

Buchan, R. (2005) "Using land development to finance community development." Paper presented at the Planning Institute of British Columbia (PIBC) Conference, Victoria, BC, April 19–22.

Burayidi, M. (2010) "A new four-point strategy for downtown renewal." *Downtown Idea Exchange*, November.

Burton, E. (2000) "The compact city: just or just compact? A preliminary analysis." *Urban Studies*, 37(11), 1969–2001.

Calthorpe, P. (1993) *The Next American Metropolis.* New York: Princeton Architectural Press.

Canada Mortgage and Housing Corporation (CMHC) (2000) *Practice for Sustainable Communities.* Ottawa, Ontario: CMHC.

Canadian Centre for Justice Statistics (2006) *Victimization and Offending among the Aboriginal Population in Canada.* Statistics Canada Catalogue no. 85-002-XPE, Vol. 26, no. 3. Ottawa.

Canadian Heart and Stroke Foundation (2005) *Heart and Stroke Foundation 2005 Report Card on Canadians' Health: Has the Suburban Dream Gone Sour?.* Montreal: Canadian Heart and Stroke Foundation.

Cao, X., P. L. Mokhtarian, and S. L. Handy (2007) "Do changes in neighbourhood characteristics lead to changes in travel behaviour? A structural equations modeling approach." *Transportation*, 34, 535–556.

Carson, R. (1962) *Silent Sprint,* Boston, MA: Houghton Mifflin.

Castonguay, G. and S. Jutras (2009) "Children's appreciation of outdoor places in a poor neighbourhood." *Journal of Environmental Psychology*, 29, 101–109.

Center for Transit-Oriented Development (2010) *TOD: 203 Transit Corridors and TOD.* Retrieved May 2011 from: http://www.reconnectingamerica.org/resource-center/books-and-reports/2010/tod-203-transit-corridors-and-tod/

Center for Transit-Oriented Development (2011) *Metro TOD Development Strategic Plan.* Retrieved May 2011 from: http://reconnectingamerica.org/assets/Uploads/2011-portland-tod-final-web.pdf

Cervero, R. (2008a) "Public transport and sustainable urbanism: global lessons." In C. Curtis, J. Renne, and L. Bertolini (Eds.), *Transit Oriented Development: Making it Happen.* Farnham: Ashgate.

Cervero, R. (2008b) "Transit-oriented development in America: strategies, issues, policy directions." In T. Haas (Ed.), *New Urbanism and Beyond: Designing Cities for the Future*. New York: Rizzoli.

Chambers, N., C. Simmons, and M. Wackernagel (2000) *Sharing Nature's Interest: Ecological Footprints as an Indicator of Sustainability*. London: Earthscan.

Cirillo, C. and L. Podolsky (n.d.) *Health, Prosperity and Sustainability: The Case for Green Infrastructure in Ontario*. Ontario: Green Infrastructure Ontario Coalition.

City of Langford (2010) "Affordable housing, park & amenity contribution policy." City of Langford, BC, December 20.

Clark, T. N., R. Lloyd, K. K. Wong, and P. Jain (2002) "Amenities drive urban growth." *Journal of Urban Affairs*, 24(5), 493–515.

Coleman, J. S. (1988) "Social capital in the creation of human capital." *American Journal of Sociology*, 94, 95–121.

Commission on Sustainable Development (1999) *Tourism and Sustainable Development: The Global Importance of Tourism*. Seventh Session, April 19–30. New York: UN DESA.

Croci, S., A. Butet, A. Georges, R. Aguejdad, and P. Clergeau (2008) "Small urban woodlands as biodiversity conservation hot-spot: a multi-taxon approach." *Landscape Ecology*, 23, 1171–1186.

Crowhurst, S. H. and H. L. Lennard (2002) *The Wisdom of Cities*. Carmel, CA: International Making Cities Livable.

Curry, J. and H. Oland (1998) *Prince George and Region Public Market Study*. Prince George, BC: University of Northern British Columbia Environmental Studies Program.

Dale, A., C. Ling, and L. Newman (2008) "Does place matter? Sustainable community development in three Canadian communities." *Ethics, Place and Environment*, 11(3), 267–281.

Daniels, T. (1989) "Small town economic development: growth or survival?" *Journal of Planning Literature*, 4(4), 413–429.

Daniels, T. L. (1991) "The goal and values of local economic development strategies in rural America." *Agriculture and Human Values*, Summer.

Daniels, T. L. and M. B. Lapping (1987) "Small town triage: a rural settlement policy for the American Midwest." *Journal of Rural Studies*, 3(3), 273–280.

Davis, J. S. and D. B. Morais (2004) "Factions and enclaves: small towns and socially unsustainable tourism development." *Journal of Travel Research*, 43, 3–10.

DeBruyn, J. and D. Hilborn (2010) *Anaerobic Digestion Basics*. Ontario Ministry of Agriculture, Food and Rural Affairs (OMAFRA). http://www.omafra.gov.on.ca/english/engineer/facts/07-057.htm

De la Salle, J. and M. Holland (2010) *Agricultural Urbanism: Handbook for Building Sustainable Food and Agriculture Systems in 21st Century Cities*. Winnipeg, Manitoba: Green Frigate Books.

Deng, T. and J. D. Nelson (2011) "Recent developments in bus rapid transit: a review of the literature." *Transport Reviews*, 31(1), 69–96.

Diamond, J. (1976) "Residential density and housing form." *Journal of Architectural Education*, 3, February.

Dillman, D. (1983) "Rural North America in the information society." *Rural Sociologist*, 3(5), 345–357.

Dinnie, K. (2011) *City Branding: Theory and Cases*. New York: Palgrave Macmillan.

Dittmar, H. and G. Ohland (2004) "The new transit town: best practices." In H. Dittmar and G. Ohland (Eds.), *The New Transit Town.* Washington, DC: Island Press.

Duany, A. and E. Plater-Zyberk (1991) *Towns and Town-Making Principles.* Ed. Alex Krieger with William Lennertz. New York: Rizzoli.

Duany, A., E. Plater-Zyberk, and J. Speck. (2000) *Suburban Nation: The Rise of Sprawl and the Decline of the American Dream.* New York: North Point Press.

Dumbaugh, E. and Li, W. (2011) "Designing for the safety of pedestrians, cyclists, and motorists in urban environments." *Journal of the American Planning Association,* 77(1), 69–88.

Ecoworld (2007) *Landfills vs. Recycling.* http://www.ecoworld.com/technology/landfills-vs-recycling.html

Edwards, M. M. and A. Haines (2007) "Evaluating smart growth: implications for small communities." *Journal of Planning Education and Research,* 27, 49–64.

England, J. (1980) "Residential land and prices in the city." *Habitat,* 23(3).

Ercoskun, O. Y. and S. Karaaslan (2011) "Guidelines for ecological and technological built environment: a case study on Gudul-Ankara, Turkey." *Gazi University Journal of Science,* 24(3), 617–636.

European Union (2011) *Cities of Tomorrow: Challenges, Visions, Ways Forward.* http://ec.europa.eu/regional_policy/sources/docgener/studies/pdf/citiesoftomorrow/citiesoftomorrow_final.pdf (Accessed February 2013).

Evans, G. W. (2003) "The built environment and mental health." *Journal of Urban Health,* 80(4), 536–555.

Evans-Cowley, J. (2006) "Sidewalk planning and policies in small cities." *Journal of Urban Planning and Development,* 132(2), 71–75.

Ewing, R., T. Schmid, R. Killingsworth, A. Zlot, and S. Raudenbush (2003) "Relationship between urban sprawl and physical activities, obesity, and morbidity." *American Journal of Health Promotion,* 18(1), 47–57.

Farr, D. (2008) *Sustainable Urbanism: Urban Design with Nature.* Hoboken, NJ: John Wiley.

Feilden, B. (1982) *Conservation of Historic Buildings.* Boston, MA: Butterworth Scientific.

Feldman, M. (1994) *The Geography of Innovation.* Boston, MA: Kluwer.

Ferguson, B. K. (1987) "Water conservation methods in urban landscape irrigation: an exploratory overview." *Water Resources Bulletin,* 23(1), 147–152.

Ferguson, G. (2005) *Characteristics of Successful Downtowns: Shared Attributes of Outstanding Small and Mid-Sized Downtowns.* Ithaca, NY: Cornell University.

Filion, P. (2010) "Growth and decline in the Canadian urban system: the impact of emerging economic, policy and demographic trends." *GeoJournal,* 75(6), 517–538.

Filion, P., H. Hoernig, T. Bunting, and G. Sands (2004) "The successful few: healthy downtowns of small metropolitan regions." *Journal of the American Planning Association,* 70(3), 328–343.

Fischer, C. S. (1982) *To Dwell Among Friends: Personal Networks in Town and City.* Chicago, IL: University of Chicago Press.

Florida, R. (2002) *The Rise of the Creative Class.* New York: Basic Books.

Fort Collins, CO (1995) *Design Standards and Guidelines for Large Retail Establishments,* City of Fort Collins Community Planning and Environmental Services.

Fox, K. A. (1962) "Area economic interaction models." *Journal of Farm Economics,* 44(1), 1–34.

Freeman, C. and R. Quigg (2008) "Commuting lives: children's mobility and energy use." *Journal of Environmental Planning and Management*, 52(3), 393–412.

French, P. E. (2005) "Policy, management and political activities: 'A current evaluation of mayors and managers in small cities and towns.'" *Social Science Journal*, 42(4), 499–510.

Garmendia, M., J. M. Urena, C. Riablaygua, J. Leal, and J. M. Coronado (2008) "Urban residential development in isolated small cities that are partially integrated in metropolitan areas by high speed train." *European Urban and Regional Studies*, 15, 249–264.

Garreau, J. (1988) *Edge City: Life on the New Frontier*. New York: Doubleday.

Gehl, J. (2010) *Cities for People*. Washington, DC: Island Press.

Gidlow, C., T. Cochrane, R. C. Davey, G. Smith, and J. Fairburn (2010) "Relative importance of physical and social aspects of perceived neighbourhood environment for self-reported health." *Preventive Medicine*, 51, 157–163.

Goldsteen, J. B. and C. D. Elliot (1994) *Designing America: Creating Urban Identity*. New York: Van Nostrand Reinhold.

Goodchild, B. (1997) *Housing and the Urban Environment: A Guide to Housing Design, Renewal and Urban Planning*. Oxford: Blackwell Sciences.

Grant, J. (2002) "Mixed use in theory and practice: Canadian experience with implementing a planning principle." *Journal of the American Planning Association*, 68(1), 71–84.

Green Living Tips (2009) http://www.greenlivingtips.com/articles/185/1/Consumption-statistics.html

Handy, S. L. and Y. Xing (2011) "Factors correlated with bicycle commuting: a study in six small U.S. cities." *International Journal of Sustainable Transportation*, 5(2), 91–110.

Hanna, K., A. Dale, and C. Ling (2009) "Social capital and quality of place: reflections on growth and change in a small town." *Local Environment,* 14(1), 31–44.

Hansen, M. and Y. Huang (1997) "Road supply and traffic in California urban areas." *Transport Research,* 31(3), 205–218.

Hibbard, M. and L. Davis (1986) "When the going gets tough: economic reality in the cultural myths of small town America." *Journal of the American Planning Association*, 52, 419–428.

Higgins, P. (2005) "Exercise-based transportation reduces oil dependence, carbon emissions and obesity." *Environmental Conservation,* 32(3), 197–202.

Hodges, T. (2010) "Public transportation's role in responding to climate change." Federal Transit Administration, US Department of Transportation. Retrieved May 2011 from: http://www.fta.dot.gov/documents/PublicTransportationsRoleInRespondingToClimateChange.pdf

Holden, E. (2004) "Ecological footprints and sustainable urban form." *Journal of Housing and the Built Environment*, 19, 91–109.

Hopkins, R. (2008) *The Transition Handbook*, Totnes: Green Books.

Howard, E. (1898) *Garden Cities of Tomorrow: A Peaceful Path to Real Reform*. London: Swan Sonnenschein & Co.

Howley, P. (2010) "'Sustainability versus liveability': an exploration of central city housing satisfaction." *International Journal of Housing Policy*, 10(2), 173–189.

Howley, P., M. Scott, and D. Redmond (2009) "Sustainability versus liveability: an investigation of neighbourhood satisfaction." *Journal of Environmental Planning and Management*, 52(6), 847–864.

Hyndman, J., N. Schuurman, and R. Fiedler (2006) "Size matters: attracting new immigrants to Canadian cities." *Journal of International Migration and Integration*, 7, 1–25.

ICF Consulting (2005) *Determination of the Impact of Waste Management Activities on Greenhouse Gas Emissions: 2005 Update*. Toronto, Ontario: Environment Canada and Natural Resources Canada.

ICF Marbek (2012) "Low impact development discussion paper." Ottawa, Ontario. March.

Institute of Transport Engineers (ITE) (2005) *Improving the Pedestrian Environment Through Innovative Transportation Design: An Informational Report of the Institute of Transportation Engineers*. Washington, DC: Institute of Transportation Engineers.

Jabareen, Y. R. (2006) "Sustainable urban forms: their typologies, models, and concepts." *Journal of Planning Education and Research*, 26(1), 38–52.

Jackson, F. (1985) *Sir Raymond Unwin: Architect, Planner and Visionary*. London: Zwemmer.

Jacobs, J. (1961) *The Death and Life of Great American Cities*. New York: Random House.

Jacobs, J. (1969) *The Economy of Cities*. New York: Random House.

Jacobsen, P. L., F. Racioppi, and H. Rutter (2009) "Who owns the roads? How motorised traffic discourages walking and bicycling." *Injury Prevention*, 15, 369–373.

James, S. and T. Lahti (2004) *The Natural Step for Communities: How Cities and Towns can Change to Sustainable Practices*. Gabriola Island, BC: New Society Publishers.

Jeffres, L. W., C. C. Bracken, G. Jian, and M. F. Casey (2009) "The impact of third places on community quality of life." *Applied Research Quality Life*, 4, 333–345.

Joens-Matre, R. R., G. J. Welk, M. A. Calabro, D. W. Russell, E. Nicklay, and L. D. Hensley (2008) "Rural–urban differences in physical activity, physical fitness, and overweight prevalence of children." *Journal of Rural Health*, 24(1), 49–54.

Kinnis, R. (1997) *Small-lot Single Family Infill Housing, City of Victoria*, Prepared for the Federation of Canadian Municipalities, Canadian Home Builders' Association, Canadian Housing and Renewal Association and Canada Mortgage and Housing Corporation. Ottawa: Federation of Canadian Municipalities.

Kostof, S. (1991) *The City Shaped*. New York: Bulfinch Press.

Kuby, M., A. Barranda, and C. Upchurch (2004) "Factors influencing light-rail station boardings in the United States." *Transportation Research Part A*, 38, 223–247.

Lampard, E. E. (1965) "Historical aspects of urbanization." In P. M. Hauser and L. F. Schnore (Eds.), *The Study of Urbanization* (pp. 519–554). London: John Wiley.

Lapping, M., T. Daniels, and J. Keller (1989) *Rural Planning and Development in the United States*. New York: Guilford Publications.

Larson, R. W. (2001) "How U.S. children and adolescents spend time: what it does (and doesn't) tell us about their development." *Current Directions in Psychological Science*, 10(5), October.

Levy, J. M. (2009) *Contemporary Urban Planning*. Upper Saddle River, NJ: Pearson Prentice Hall.

Lindsay, M., K. Williams, and C. Dair (2010) "Is there room for privacy in the compact city?" *Built Environment*, 36(1), 28–47.

Litman, T. (1999) *Parking Requirement Impacts on Housing Affordability*. Victoria Transport Policy Institute, November.

Litman, T. (2009) *Economic Value of Walkability*. Retrieved May 2011 from: www.vtpi.org

Liu, S., Y. Dong, M. Wen, and B. Chen (2009) "Quantify the landscape effect and environmental sustainability of rural region planning at town scale near metropolis." *Frontiers of Earth Science in China*, 3(1): 112–117.

Lovejoy, K., S. Handy, and P. Mokhtarian (2010) "Neighborhood satisfaction in suburban versus traditional evaluation of contributing characteristics in eight Californian neighborhoods." *Landscape and Urban Planning*, 97, 37–48.

Lund, H. and P. A. Østergaard (2010) "Sustainable towns: the case of Frederikshavn—100% sustainable energy." In W. W. Clark II (Ed.), *Sustainable Communities*. New York: Springer Science+ Business Media.

McCullough, A. B. (1992) *The Primary Textile Industry in Canada, History and Heritage*. Ottawa: Minister of Supply and Services, Canada.

McDonald, R. I. (2008) "Global urbanization: can ecologists identify a sustainable way forward?" *Frontiers in Ecology and the Environment*, 6(2), 99–104.

McPherson, E. G., J. R. Simpson, and M. Livingston (1989) "Effects of three landscape treatments on residential energy and water use in Tucson, Arizona." *Energy and Buildings*, 13: 127–138.

Mair, H. (2009) "Searching for a new enterprise: themed tourism and the re-making of one small Canadian community." *Tourism Geographies*, 11(4), 462–483.

Marshall, W. E. and N. W. Garrick (2006) "Parking at mixed-use centers in small cities." *Transportation Research Record: Journal of the Transportation Research Board*, 1997, 164–171.

Meier, R. I. (1962) *A Communication Theory of Urban Growth*. Cambridge, MA: MIT Press.

Meijers, E. (2008) "Summing small cities does not make a large city: polycentric urban regions and the provision of cultural, leisure and sports amenities." *Urban Studies*, 45(11), 2323–2342.

Meisel, A. (2010) *LEED Materials: A Resource Guide to Green Building*. New York: Princeton Architectural Press.

Minster, C. (2010) "Urban design, mobility, and obesity: a study of obesity in Germany." *Transport Studies Unit School of Geography and the Environment*, 1051, 1–10.

Moughtin, C. (1992) *Urban Design: Street and Square*. Oxford: Butterworth-Heinemann.

Moyes, R. E. (1997) *Zoning Standards and Design Guidelines for Infill Housing and Redevelopment, City of Saint John*. Prepared for the Federation of Canadian Municipalities, Canadian Home Builders' Association, Canadian Housing and Renewal Association and Canada Mortgage and Housing Corporation. Ottawa: Federation of Canadian Municipalities.

Mumford, L. (1961) *The City in History: Its Origins, Its Transformations, and Its Prospects*. New York: Harcourt.

New Lanark Trust (n.d.) *The Story of New Lanark*. Scotland: Tartan.

Newman, D. (2008) "Large district energy systems." In D. Farr, *Sustainable Urbanism: Urban Design with Nature*. Hoboken, NJ: John Wiley.

Ofori-Amoah, B. (2007) "Small city studies and geographic perspectives." In B. Ofori-Amoah (Ed.), *Beyond the Metropolis: Urban Geography as if Small Cities Mattered* (pp. 3–16). New York: University Press of America.

Oktay, D. (2002) "Design with the climate in housing environments: an analysis in Northern Cyprus." *Building and Environment*, 37, 1003–1012.

Oldenburg, R. (1989) *The Great Good Place*. New York: Marlowe.

Paradis, T. W. (2002) "The political economy of theme development in small urban places: the case of Roswell, New Mexico." *Tourism Geographies*, 4(1), 22–43.

Partridge, M. D., D. S. Rickman, K. Ali, and M. R. Olfert (2008) "Lost in space: population growth in the American hinterlands and small cities." *Journal of Economic Geography*, 8(6), 727–757.

Pfeifer, G. and P. Brauneck (2008) *Row Houses: A Housing Typology*, trans. Usch Engelmann, Basel, Switzerland: Birkhauser.

Powe, N. and S. Gunn (2008) "Housing development in market towns: making a success of 'local service centres'?" *Town Planning Review*, 79(1), 125–148.

Powe, N. and T. Hart (2011) "Housing development and small town residential desirability." *Town Planning Review*, 82(3), 317–340.

Powe, D., T. Hart, and D. Bek (2009) "Market town centres in England: meeting the challenge of maintaining their contemporary relevance." *Planning Practice and Research*, 24(3), 301–319.

Project for Public Spaces (PPS) (2011) http://www.pps.org/reference/benefits_public_spaces/

Pucher, J. and R. Buehler (2008) "Making cycling irresistible: lessons from the Netherlands, Denmark and Germany." *Transport Reviews*, 28(4), 495–528.

Pucher, J., R. Buehler, and M. Seinen (2011) "Bicycling renaissance in North America? An update and reappraisal of cycling transit and policies." *Transportation Research Part A*, 45, 451–475.

Quiney, A. (2003) *Town Houses of Medieval Britain*, New Haven, CT: published for the Paul Mellon Centre for Studies in British Art by Yale University Press.

Ramage, J. (1997) *Energy: A Guidebook*. Oxford: Oxford University Press.

Raman, S. (2010) "Designing a liveable compact city: physical forms of city and social life in urban neighbourhoods." *Built Environment*, 36(1), 63–80.

Regional Municipality of Waterloo (1990) *Healthy Lawns and Gardens with Less Water*. Waterloo, Ontario.

Riddle, M. (2008) "Interview with Richard Florida." *Public Art Review*, 20(1), 52.

Robertson, K. (1999) "Can small-city downtowns remain viable? A national study of development issues and strategies." *Journal of the American Planning Association*, 65(3), 270–284.

Robertson, K. (2006) "Rural downtown development: guiding principles for small cities." *Rural Research Report*, 17(3), Spring.

Rohrer, J., J. R. Pierce Jr, and A. Denison (2004) "Walkability and self-rated health in primary care patients." *BMC Family Practice*, 5, 29–35.

Russ, T. H. (Ed.) (2002) *Planning and Design Handbook*. New York: McGraw-Hill.

Saelens, B. E., J. F. Sallis, J. B. Black, and D. Chen (2003) "Neighbourhood-based differences in physical activity: an environment scale evaluation." *American Journal of Public Health*, 93(9), 1552–1558.

Schoenauer, N. (2000) *6,000 Years of Housing*. New York: W.W. Norton.

Schwela, D. and O. Zali (1999) *Urban Traffic Pollution*. London: E & FN Spon.

Shepperson, M. (2009) "Planning for the sun: urban forms as a Mesopotamian response to the sun." *World Archaeology*, 41(3): 363–378.

Shibu, R. (2010) "Designing a liveable compact city: physical forms of city and social life in urban neighbourhoods." *Built Environment*, 36(1), 63–80.

Singer, N. (2010) "Fixing a world that fosters fat." *New York Times*, Sunday edition, August 22, p. 3, business section.

Small Towns Big Ideas: Case Studies in Small Town Community Economic Development. (n.d.) UNC School of Government, N.C. Rural Economic Development Center.

Smith, K. (2008) "You say you want a devolution? Lessons from the Main Street Program." *Local Economy*, 23(1), 86–93.

Smith, M. E. (2007) "Form and meaning in the earliest cities: a new approach to ancient urban planning." *Journal of Planning History*, 6(1), 3–47.

Statistics Canada (2005) *Human Activity and the Environment, Annual Statistics 2005, Solid Waste in Canada*. Ottawa: Ministry of Industry.

Statistics Canada (2006a) *From Urban Areas to Population Centres*. http://www.statcan.gc.ca/subjects-sujets/standard-norme/sgc-cgt/notice-avis/sgc-cgt-06-eng.htm (Accessed July 2013).

Statistics Canada (2006b) *CYB Overview 2006: Population and Demography*. Retrieved 11 August 2009, from: http:// www41.statcan.gc.ca/2006/3867/ceb3867_000-eng.htm

Stirnberg, B. (1985) Excerpts from a presentation of his work by the sculptor, at the First International Making Cities Livable Conference, Venice, Italy.

Storper, M. and A. J. Scott (2009) "Rethinking human capital, creativity and urban growth." *Journal of Economic Geography*, 9, 147–167.

Summer R. and M. Wing (1980) "Farmer's markets please their customers." *California Agriculture*, April, p. 10.

Svendsen, G. L. H. (2010) "Socio-spatial planning in the creation of bridging social capital: the importance of multifunctional centers for intergroup networks and integration." *International Journal of Social Inquiry*, 3(2), 45–73.

Tabuchi, T., J. F. Thiesse, and D. Z. Zeng (2005) "On the number and size of cities." *Journal of Economic Geography*, 5(4), 423–448.

Talen, E. (2006) "Connecting new urbanism and American planning: an historical interpretation." *Urban Design International*, 11(2), 83–98.

Tasker-Brown, J. and S. Pogharian (2000) *Learning from Suburbia: Residential Street Pattern Design*, Prepared for Canada Mortgage and Housing Corporation. Ottawa, Ontario: CMHC.

The Why Factory (2010) *Green Dream*. Rotterdam: NAi Publishers in association with MVRDV, The Why Factory, and Delft University of Technology.

Thomas, R. (2005) *Sustainable Urban Design: An Environmental Approach*. New York: Spon Press.

Tolbert, C. M., M. D. Irwin, T. A. Lyson, and A. R. Nucci (2002) "Civic community in small-town America: how civic welfare is influenced by local capitalism and civic engagement." *Rural Sociology*, 67, 90–113.

Torres, J. (2009) "Children and cities: planning to grow together." Vanier Institute for the Family. Retrieved May 2011 from: http://reconnectingamerica.org/assets/Uploads/childrencities2009.pdf

Turcotte, M. (2008) *Dependence on Cars in Urban Neighbourhoods*. Retrieved June 5, 2011, from: http://www.statcan.gc. ca/pub/11-008-x/2008001/article/10503-eng.htm#4

Turner, S. (2011) "The farms are not all right." *The Walrus*, 8(8), 34–44.

Tweeten, L. and G. L. Brinkman (1976) *Micropolitan Development*. Ames: Iowa State University Press.

UNEP/GRID-Arendal (2002) *Municipal Solid Waste Composition*. United Nations Environment Programme (UNEP)/ GRID-Arendal. http://maps.grida.no/go/graphic/municpal_solid_waste_composition_for_7_oecd_countries_ and_7_asian_cities

UN Population Division (UNPD) (2005) *World Urbanization Prospects: The 2005 Revision*. New York: UN Population Division.

United Nations, Department of Economic and Social Affairs, Population Division (2009) *Trends in International Migrant Stock: The 2008 Revision* (United Nations database, POP/DB/MIG/Stock/ Rev.2008). http://esa.un.org/ migration/p2k0data.asp

United States Census Bureau (2009) "Americans spend more than 100 hours commuting to work each year, Census Bureau Reports." http://www.census.gov/prod/2011pubs/acs-15.pdf (Accessed May 1).

United States Census Bureau (2011) *Commuting in the United States: 2009.* American Community Survey Reports, ACS-15, by B. McKenzie and M. Rapino. Washington, DC: US Census Bureau.

Urban Design Tools (2012) "Introduction to LID." http://www.lid-stormwater.net/background.htm

Van der Ryn, S. and P. Calthorpe (1986) *Sustainable Communities: A New Design Synthesis for Cities, Suburbs and Towns,* San Francisco, CA: Sierra Club Books.

Van Rensburg, J. and M. Campbell (2012) "The management of urban sprawl by applying an urban edge strategy." *Urban Forum*, 23, 61–72.

Van Timmeren, A., D. Sidler, and M. Kapitein (2007) "Sustainable decentralized energy generation and sanitation: Case EVA Lanxmeer, Culemborg, the Netherlands." *Journal of Green Building*, 2(4), 137–150.

Weber, B. and M. Rahe (2010) "Wealth creation and rural–urban linkages: an exploratory study of economic flows in two natural resource-rich regions." *Wealth Creation in Rural Communities*. Ford Foundation.

Wei, J. (2003) "Open spaces in high-density affordable housing communities in Montreal: pattern site, design and use." M. Arch Report, McGill University, School of Architecture.

Wicks, M. (2008) "Dispatches Langford." *Westshore: The Art of Island Living*, Winter.

Wiles, J. L, R. E. S. Allen, A. J. Palmer, K. J. Hayman, S. Keeling, and N. Kerse (2009) "Older people and their social spaces: a study of well-being and attachment to place in Aotearoa New Zealand." *Social Science & Medicine*, 68, 664–671.

Williams, D. (2006) "Why game studies now? Gamers don't bowl alone." *Games and Culture*, 1, 13–16.

Winfield-Pfefferkorn, J. (2005) *The Branding of Cities: Exploring City Branding and the Importance of Brand Image*. Retrieved from: http://www.brandchannel.com/images/papers/245_Branding_of_ Cities.pdf

Winters, M., M. Brauer, E. M. Setton, and K. Teschke (2010) "Built environment influences on healthy transportation choices: bicycling versus driving." *Journal of Urban Health*, 87(6), 969–993.

Wolf, K. L. (2007) "The environmental psychology of shopping: assessing the value of trees." *Research Review*, 14(3), 36–43.

World Commission on Environment and Development (WCED) (1987) *Our Common Future*. Oxford: Oxford University Press.

WWF (2002) *Living Planet Report 2002*, Gland, Switzerland: World Wide Fund for Nature.

Zukin, S. (1998) "Urban lifestyles: diversity and standardisation in spaces of consumption." *Urban Studies*, 35, 825.

Index

Note: Page numbers followed by 'f' refer to figures.

active lifestyles 15, 187, 188f, 189f
adolescents, social spaces for 185
agglomeration 23, 25
Aging in Place 185
aging populations 5–6, 6f
agricultural heritage 150, 151f
agriculture, urban 67–9, 68f; "edible landscapes" 55, 55f, 70f
Alaska, SES study in 49–50
Alessa, L. 49
Alexander, C. 114, 115
Alonso, W. 32
amenities, urban: attracting people to towns through 183, 184f; choices between employment and 12; demise of downtown 132; financing of improved 12, 29, 176, 176f, 178; as local activity generators 134; location of 80, 93, 96f; size of city and extent of 29; study in Dutch regions 29
anaerobic digestion 53, 53f
analytical communities 157, 158f
architectural guidelines 69, 135, 150; for renewal and development of core 138f; and urban fit for infill housing 116–18, 117f, 118f
Armstrong Food Initiative 55
art, public 140, 193, 193f, 205

Batista, A. 190–1
Bear Mountain, Canada 174
bed and breakfast (B&B) 170, 170f
Beechworth, Australia 167
big box retail outlets 93, 130, 130f, 132, 174, 199; opposition to 131f
bio-swells 16, 17f, 62

biodiversity conservation 50
Blakely, E.J. 157, 158
Bramley, G. 35
Brand, S. 145, 145f
branding 143, 163, 164, 171, 172f
building: lifecycles 143, 144; standards 10
Burton, E. 31
bus services 72–3, 81–3, 83f, 88f, 187

Canada: average household size 1971-2006 6f; car usage 73; migration patterns in British Columbia 7; population by place of residency 2, 3f; public health 73; shaping of urban system in 5
car ownership 81f
car usage: carbon emissions 8, 9f, 10, 74f; and erosion of social fabric of towns 74; impact on children 73; and links with density 8, 8f, 80, 81f; mixed land uses and lower 38f, 81, 82f; new roads and new 75; planning road networks to reduce 79–80, 80f, 87; in small towns as compared to large cities 86
Carson, R. 48
center, importance of a 127–32
children: mobility of 73; obesity in 187; play activities 187, 188f; spaces for 111, 185, 187; television viewing 187
choosing to live in small towns 4–5
circulation networks 107–8
civic-mindedness 38
climatic considerations in design 56, 120, 121, 125f
Commission on Sustainable Development 163
communication technologies 12f, 13, 25, 143, 157, 183
community identity 50, 111–13, 112f
community, planning a 121–5

commuter transit corridors 78, 78f

commuting to work 10, 46, 73, 75, 86

compact cities 35–6

compactness 29–31, 30f, 31f, 32f, 36

composting 54, 69f

conservationist view of heritage buildings 16, 143, 144f

consumption patterns 36

core areas, strengthening 126–51; in downtown Peace River 199–205; in downtown Westlock 145–51; heritage preservation 143–5; implementing renewal 140–3; importance of a center 127–32; vision for renewal 132–40; Ypres 126, 127f

Cornwall, Canada 133f, 154, 154f

Courseulles-sur-Mer, France 180–1, 180f

"Creative Class" 161, 182

Crime Prevention Through Environmental Design (CPTED) 137f, 139

Crowhurst, S.H. 133, 190

cultural industries 134, 163–5, 183, 202; Kaap Skil museum, Netherlands 167–8, 169f; museums 135, 148, 150, 165, 169f; in Westlock 150

cycling: bike-sharing programs 69, 85f, 86; compact towns and levels of 31; fostering habit of 85–90, 85f, 88f; paths 67, 69, 85f, 98, 98f, 188f, 189f, 205; to school 81, 101, 187; TOD and increase in 77; to work 86

Daniels, T. 153, 157, 158, 162

Davis, J.S. 165

De Koog, Netherlands 167

defender communities 157–8, 158f

definitions of small and mid-sized towns 2

demographics 2–3, 3f; aging populations 5–6, 6f; household size 6f, 7; migration patterns 7, 7f; young and elderly cohorts 6–7, 161–2

Den Burg, Netherlands 45, 46f

density 29, 30f, 31f, 32f; calculations for public transport services 115; and calls for densification 8; car usage and links with 8, 8f, 80, 81f; in designing a new neighborhood 103–7; effect in small town planning 29, 31; and impact on walkability 80, 81f; infill housing 115–16; organic urban forms and high 26, 27f, 30f; social dimensions and 31; and social sustainability 35; in Stony Plain 93, 94f; sustainable urban forms and 36, 37f, 80–1, 82f, 93, 95f; urban typologies and 31, 31f

designing new neighborhoods 102–13; choosing a form 103–7; circulation 107–8; in Iqaluit 119–25; open spaces 109–11; parking 108, 108f; Porvoo 101, 102; unit and community identity 111–13

desperate communities 158, 158f

destroyer communities 158, 158f, 159f

Diagram City 27, 28f

digital communications 12f, 13, 48, 183

district heating 58, 60

downtown, decline of 102, 129–32, 129f, 131f; big box retail outlets and 130, 132, 199; and safety concerns 136, 137f, 139

downtown renewal: heritage preservation 143–5; implementing renewal 140–3; importance of the center 127–32; in Peace River 199–205; in Ponoka 41–4, 42f, 43f, 44f; vision for renewal 132–40; in Westlock 145–51

early settlements 22–3, 22f, 24f; Roman 23, 24f, 56, 58, 59f, 136f

eco-cities 36, 46 *see also* green small towns

eco-tech cities 48

ecological footprints 22, 34–5, 36, 46

economic sustainability 15f, 16, 49

economies of small towns 153–7; categorization of 160–1, 160f; developing tourism and cultural industries 163–71; economic community types 157–8, 158f; economic decline scenario 155–6, 155f; and economic realities 11–13; impact of mobility on 74; in Langford 172–9; relations between environmental practices and cost-saving impacting on 49, 49f; strategies for sustainable economies 157–63; Zhouzhuang 152, 153f

Economy of Cities 22

Edge City 26

"edible landscapes" 55, 55f, 70f

Edwards, M.M. 36

elderly populations 5–6, 6f, 161–2; and social space 185–7, 186f

Elliot Lake Retirement Living, Canada 162

employers: attracting 12, 143, 156, 157, 162, 174; departure of major 155f; reliance on single 154–5, 156, 158, 160, 162

employment generation in Langford 174, 174f

energy management 10, 10f, 56–60

entrepreneurial communities 157, 158f

environmental considerations 7–10, 36, 37, 46–50; energy management 10, 10f, 56–60; in Komoka 64–70; land management 50–5; in Stony Plain

68f, 69–70f; planning in Stony Plain 92–7, 94f, 95f, 96f, 97f; principles of sustainable systems 17–19, 18f

sustainable development: defining 13–14; pillars of 15–16; underlying principles 14f

sustainable economies: building a sustainable economy in Langford 172–9; strategies for 157–63

sustainable urban forms 34–9, 37f, 38f, 93, 95f

taxes: attracting investors with incentives on 12, 143, 156, 157, 162, 174; broadening tax base 93, 114, 130, 148, 156, 160; investing revenue from 141f; in Langford 173, 174, 176, 176f; property 26, 155; residential 12; from town centers 129, 194

television viewing, youth 187

third places 181, 183f, 194–5, 195f

Thünen, Johann Heinrich von 32

TOD (Transit-Oriented Development) 76–8

tourism 163–72; accommodation 170, 170f; cultivation of natural assets 134, 165, 165f, 167; heritage 127, 164, 165f, 168, 169f, 205; key determinants 165f; negative consequences of 165–6; in Peace River 205; steps in process 166, 167f; types 164; in Westlock 150

traffic calming 69, 89–90, 89f

transit corridor types 78, 78f

Transit-Oriented Development (TOD) 76–8

transportation links 42f, 72, 75–9; in Ponoka 41, 42f; in Stony Plain 98, 98f, 99f *see also* mobility; public transport

trees: environmental benefits of 50; lining streets 49, 129, 189; planting 47, 140; planting in Inverurie 103, 105f; urban forests 49, 50, 140

unit and community identity 50, 111–13, 112f

United Nations Food Price Index 55

United States of America: growth of cities 23; population in cities and towns 2, 3f; water consumption 61, 61f

urban containment 36, 103

urban forms 26–9; choosing 103–7, 104f; effect of 29–33; in Ponoka 39–44, 42f, 43f, 44f; sustainable 34–9, 37f, 38f, 80–1, 82f, 93, 95f; in Volterra 20–2, 20f, 21f

urban growth 23–6

urban land market model 32

urban planning typologies 26–8, 27f, 28f

urban sprawl 8, 33, 60, 80; containment 36, 103;

reducing 8, 18, 104, 114; TOD and minimizing of 77

urban typologies 31, 31f

Valkenburg, Netherlands 63

Västra Hamnen, Sweden 62, 62f

vegetation in design of new developments 50–1, 52f

vehicle ownership 81f

ventilation, natural 56

Volterra, Italy 20–2, 20f, 21f

volunteers 6

Vulcan, Canada 168

walking: conditions for 74, 75f, 187; density levels and impact on 80, 187; fostering habit of 85–90, 86f, 87f, 88f, 188f; in Komoka 67, 69; in Langford 174; in Peace River 200, 202, 205; pedestrian paths and malls 71–2, 72f, 86f, 142f, 174; pedestrian paths in Komoka 67; in Stony Plain 93, 96f, 98, 99f

waste management 51–4, 53f, 54f

water: consumption 60–1, 61f; harvesting 62, 62f, 63, 69f; management 60–3

wayfinding 140, 171, 171f

wealth generation: building an economy in Langford 172–9; developing tourism and cultural industries 163–72; economy of small towns 153–7; strategies for sustainable economies 157–63

websites 163, 171

well-being 182–8

Westlock, Canada 145–51; history and context 146–7; proposal 148–51, 149f, 150f, 151f; strengths and weaknesses 148

Whitehorse, Canada 33, 34f

wind: direction 56, 57f, 120, 121; energy 56, 58, 59f, 60

Wisdom of Cities 190

World Commission on Environment and Development (WCED) 13–14, 14f

World Wildlife Fund 34

xeriscapes 63

young cohorts, attracting 6–7, 18, 74, 93, 133, 134, 161, 202

Ypres, Belgium 126, 127f

Zhouzhuang, China 152, 153f

zoning 31, 33, 33f, 34, 83, 114, 162